"*Character Traits in Presidential Elections* is an extraordinary analysis that contributes a new level of understanding to an area much discussed but relatively neglected by social scientists. The personal qualities and character perceptions of presidential candidates are assumed to affect voter decision-making. Precisely how and of what degree of importance compared to other influences has been a murky area for interpretation. This is no longer the case. Holian and Prysby assess how such qualities impact the vote; what shapes and influences the development of such attributes; and the type of voter most likely to perceive individual personalities as determined of the vote. They do it with style and an in-depth familiarity with their subjects that in itself provides a good read. This is an exceptionally sophisticated study, one that fills a major void in our analysis of voting behavior. It should be required reading for all students of elections and the forces that serve to shape the outcomes"
—*William Crotty, Thomas P. O'Neill Chair in Public Life and Professor of Political Science at Northeastern University*

"Everyone knows that candidate character matters in presidential elections but until now political scientists have not shown how, when and why it matters. This book by Charles Prysby and David Holian finally provides answers to these critical questions. It should be must reading for anyone interested in understanding the way American presidents are chosen."
—*Alan I. Abramowitz, Emory University*

Candidate Character Traits in Presidential Elections

Voter perceptions of the personal traits of presidential candidates are widely regarded to be important influences on the vote. Media pundits frequently explain the outcome of presidential elections in terms of the personal appeal of the candidates. Despite the emphasis on presidential character traits in the media, the scholarly investigation in this area is limited.

In this book, David Holian and Charles Prysby set out to examine the effect that trait perceptions have on the vote, how these perceptions are shaped by other attitudes and evaluations, and what types of voters are most likely to cast a ballot on the basis of the character traits of the presidential candidates. Using the American National Election Studies (ANES) surveys, the authors find that traits do have a very substantial effect on the vote, that different candidates have advantages on different traits, and that the opinions expressed by media pundits about how the candidates are viewed by the voters are often simplistic, and sometimes quite mistaken. Character traits are important to voters, but we need a better and more complete understanding of how and why these factors influence voters.

An essential read which provides a clear and original argument to all those interested in furthering their understanding of the importance of candidate character traits for the quality of American elections and democracy.

David B. Holian is Associate Professor of Political Science at the University of North Carolina at Greensboro

Charles L. Prysby is Professor of Political Science at the University of North Carolina at Greensboro

Routledge Research in American Politics and Governance

Candidate Character Traits in Presidential Elections

David B. Holian and Charles L. Prysby

Routledge
Taylor & Francis Group
NEW YORK AND LONDON

First published 2015
by Routledge
711 Third Avenue, New York, NY 10017, USA

and by Routledge
2 Park Square, Milton Park, Abingdon, Oxfordshire OX14 4RN

First issued in paperback 2016

Routledge is an imprint of the Taylor & Francis Group, an informa business

Library of Congress Cataloging-in-Publication Data

Holian, David B., 1967–
  Candidate character traits in presidential elections / David B. Holian and
Charles L. Prysby.
      pages cm. — (Routledge research in American politics and governance ; 18)
  Includes bibliographical references and index.
  1. Presidential candidates—United States—Psychology.   2. Presidential
candidates—United States—Public opinion.   3. Presidents—United States—
Election.   4. Character—Political aspects—United States.   5. Political
psychology—United States.   6. Voting research—United States.   I. Prysby,
Charles L.   II. Title.
  JK521.H65 2014
  324.973001'9—dc23
  2014017013

Typeset in Sabon
by Apex CoVantage, LLC

ISBN 13: 978-1-138-28617-7 (pbk)
ISBN 13: 978-1-138-78269-3 (hbk)

For Heather
            —D.B.H.

Anita, Nicole,
and Michelle
            —C.L.P.

Contents

Figures

Tables

Preface

One of the most interesting sources of variation from one presidential election to the next is the candidates themselves. In the post-war era, the two major political parties have conferred their nominations on a wide range of individuals, including: war heroes and those who went to great lengths to avoid war; sitting and former vice presidents; well-known and little-known governors; senators who barely served in the institution and senators who served with distinction for decades; ideologues and pragmatists; the righteous and the roguish; and, of course, a politically liberal B-movie actor turned corporate spokesman turned conservative, two-term California governor. Many fine biographies have attempted to capture the character of these candidates as they grew from childhood to adulthood and into political careers that led to winning or losing the White House—and, in a few cases, winning *and* losing the White House.

This book is not about the personalities of these men from the perspective of the psychiatrist's couch or the biographer's pen, but their character as judged by American citizens. The landmark study of the electorate, *The American Voter,* published over 50 years ago, made it quite clear that assessments of the candidates as individuals were a crucial component of vote choice. However, little has been written about character perceptions relative to the wealth of research on other factors that influence the vote, such as partisanship, economic conditions, and issue orientations. The one book-length treatment that focused on character traits was published nearly 40 years ago and is long out of print. We offer this in-depth assessment of voter perceptions of candidate character in each presidential election since 1980 as an interesting piece of the larger voting behavior puzzle worthy of greater discussion.

As we began the research for this project, we were struck by two facts. First, the public's perception of candidate character varied a great deal from one election to the next in ways that could not be dismissed simply as reflecting the election results. Second, the interpretations that media commentators advanced regarding how voters perceived and assessed the candidates frequently were not borne out by the public's actual perceptions as reflected in survey data. For example, media pundits often argued that voters rejected a presidential candidate because he was not warm and personally likeable, but our analysis reveals that this was never the case. Furthermore, the pundits sometimes portrayed candidates as weak leaders or untrustworthy individuals when voter assessments indicated otherwise. These kinds of misperceptions tend to be based on flawed narratives that tend to solidify as the pundits generalize from events that occur in the heat of the campaign. Our study, on the other hand, is based on the analysis of over three decades of data drawn from the American National Election Studies (ANES), the best source of data that we have on the actual attitudes and opinions of the American electorate.

We have a number of people we would like to thank for their help along the way. Thanks to the many colleagues, anonymous and otherwise, who provided input that we took to heart and incorporated into the manuscript. We know these suggestions made the arguments presented in these pages stronger, and, of course, any mistakes and oversights that remain are our own. We would also like to thank the people at Routledge who shepherded this project from prospectus to publication. Special thanks are due to Natalja Mortensen, Deborah Kopka, and Amy Freitag for their patience and hard work.

We appreciate the assistance of Benjamin Riesser, a recent graduate of the MPA program in the Department of Political Science at the University of North Carolina at Greensboro, who constructed the graphic images for the book. We also have family members to thank. Michelle Prysby, Charles's daughter, constructed the website where we have placed the many tables of data analysis that would not fit into the book. Special thanks goes to our spouses, Heather Holian and Anita Prysby, who all too often heard us say, "I'll do that later. Right now I have to work on the book."

1 Candidate Character Traits in Presidential Elections

As the 2012 presidential election campaign unfolded, it became clear that the Democratic and Republican candidates held clear and distinct positions on a wide range of policy issues. With the U.S. economy stuck in first gear, Barack Obama and Mitt Romney argued the merits of austerity versus stimulus and of continued tax cuts for everyone versus raising taxes on the wealthy. The two candidates vigorously debated health care policy, with Obama defending his signature legislative achievement, the Affordable Care Act, and Romney promising to repeal "Obamacare" as soon as he occupied the White House. Equally sharp differences over energy and environmental policies divided the candidates. Given the economic issues facing the country, it was not surprising that social issues received less attention in the campaign, but the candidates nevertheless had quite different views on these issues as well. Yet with all of these policy differences between the candidates, many political commentators saw the election as being decided just as much on the basis of the personal characteristics of the candidates. It was not just a question of which direction voters wanted the ship of state to sail; it was also a question of whom the voters wanted as the captain of the ship. Voters, many commentators argued, were inclined to vote for the candidate whom they most liked.

For President Obama, pundits considered whether his personal likability, captured in the president's persistently strong favorable ratings, would be enough to overcome the weak economy. According to *New York Times* columnist David Brooks, Obama's leadership style, which Brooks described as "hypercompetitive, restrained, not given to self-doubt, rarely self-indulgent," was keeping him competitive for a second term despite circumstances that normally make leaders look weak, thus sealing their electoral fates.[1] If Obama's personal strengths were undermined by the weak economy, the media described the challenger, former Massachusetts governor Romney, as the president's mirror image: a candidate whose personal liabilities diminished his party's golden opportunity to defeat the incumbent president. Another *Times* columnist, Maureen Dowd, wrote that a key distinction between the candidates, "one that will probably decide this presidential race, is this: Barack Obama is able to convey an impression of likability to voters." Dowd argued that the Obama versus Romney election matched two introverts, but that a "graceful introvert beats an awkward one every time."[2]

Media pundits identified several problems with Romney's character, at least as it was perceived by the voters. Timothy Egan wrote that focus groups perceived Romney as "a tin man, a shell, an empty suit, vacuous . . ."[3] Dowd saw Romney as having "meager social and political agility" and being "banally handsome with an empty look."[4] Some commentators used the term "robot" or "android" to describe Romney. Besides lacking in warmth and likability, Romney also was widely portrayed as unable to understand or empathize with the problems of ordinary people. Two *Washington Post* journalists wrote that "Romney must—MUST—close the empathy gap to win this fall."[5] Moreover, some pundits thought that Romney did not seem to be a strong leader to many voters. In August 2012, *Newsweek* reprised its controversial 1987 cover story about then Vice President George H. W. Bush titled "The Wimp Factor," only this time Romney was the subject. The article claimed that in the pantheon of Republican presidential tough guys, Romney fell well short of the likes of Reagan, George W. Bush, and even the latter's once impugned father who, "looks like Dirty Harry Callahan compared to Romney, who spent his war (Vietnam) in—ready?—Paris. Where he learned . . . *French*" (emphasis in original).[6]

While the media consensus was that Obama was ahead of Romney on character traits, the president was not without his faults, according to several columnists. Dowd described both candidates as "cold, deliberative fish, self-regarding elitists, with . . . trouble connecting at times."[7] Mark Shields felt that neither candidate possessed any humility or humor, in contrast to many other successful presidential candidates, such as Reagan or the younger Bush.[8] Obama's poor performance in the first presidential debate led some pundits to conclude that he did not seem to be a strong leader, something that could cost him dearly in the election.[9] But as election day approached and it became clear that Obama would triumph, the prevailing view in the media was that voters found Obama more likable than Romney. In particular, pundits argued that Romney failed to define himself early in the campaign, thereby allowing Democrats to create an unflattering caricature of an out-of-touch plutocrat and rapacious capitalist. A lengthy post-election analysis in the *Boston Globe* concluded that one of the Romney campaign team's gravest errors was the "failure, until too late in the campaign, to sell voters on the candidate's personal qualities and leadership gifts."[10]

Media accounts of presidential elections routinely emphasize the role of the likability and perceived character of the presidential candidates. Voters react to the candidates as people, evaluating their character traits, and thus making the presidential vote a very personal one. They embrace candidates they see as honest and competent leaders whom they can relate to personally, and they reject candidates they see as untrustworthy, as uninspiring, or as lacking in warmth. Given this perspective, it is not surprising that both media interpretations of campaigns as they are happening and media explanations of election results often stress how well the candidates appeal to voters on a personal level. In the eyes of many pundits, defeats in presidential elections are frequently a result of the personal failings of the losing candidates, while victories reflect how well the winning candidates connected with the voters.

As in 2012, the 2008 campaign focused a great deal on the character of the major party nominees, Obama and John McCain. The media and the public paid particular attention to the likelihood that the candidates would provide strong leadership in troubled times, along with the degree to which they could relate, in both personal and policy terms, to regular folks, represented by the surprising and somewhat amusing addition of "Joe the Plumber" to the campaign trail.[11] Furthermore, there were myriad compelling contrasts between the life experiences and perceived personal traits of the two candidates, even setting aside the fact that Obama was the first African American presidential candidate nominated by a major political party. No presidential campaign in the nation's history has featured a larger gap in the ages of the two candidates. Moreover, while Obama and McCain spent significant and formative parts of their lives outside the United States, they did so facing dramatically different circumstances: the former as a child in Indonesia, the latter as a prisoner of war in Vietnam. The differences in their personal narratives naturally led voters to see differences in the character traits of the candidates. By the end of the campaign, and depending on one's point of view, Obama was either calm or distant, visionary or naive, thoughtful or elitist. McCain, on the other hand, was either decisive or impulsive, experienced or old, a gutsy maverick or an all-too-typical insider.

Journalists often focused on small and sometimes trivial incidents to illustrate prevailing views of each candidate's character. Since Obama's lack of substantial political experience was a major theme in the coverage of the campaign, minor statements by the Democratic candidate that might indicate that he was not ready to assume the presidency were highlighted in the media. Reporters also ridiculed Obama's inept attempt at bowling, implying that he was a prissy elitist, which also fit a prevailing narrative.[12] Obama's failure early in the campaign to wear a flag pin on his suit lapel led to questions about his patriotism, while McCain's failure to do so did not produce similar speculation.[13] The difference, of course, was that McCain had a well-deserved reputation for patriotism, whereas Obama had no military service, a Kenyan father, and lived in Indonesia for part of his childhood. Many of McCain's actions and statements did receive sharp scrutiny. For example, when McCain was unable to state how many houses he owned, many journalists latched onto that failure as an indicator of his inability to understand the economic problems of the average citizen.[14]

The focus on candidate character traits was not limited to the musings of journalists. The presidential campaigns also advanced character-based storylines. Republicans raised questions about Obama's lack of experience and leadership skills, traits that many in the press and political circles agreed were McCain strengths. The McCain campaign even tried to turn the large and enthusiastic crowds drawn to Obama into a negative by arguing that Obama's appeal was that of a celebrity without substance. On the other hand, the Obama campaign deftly used the deepening economic crisis to portray McCain's "suspension" of his campaign and threat to skip the first debate as ill-considered and erratic, the latter a word that also served as a none-too-subtle reminder of McCain's advancing age.

The 2008 and 2012 presidential campaigns were not unusual in their emphasis on the personal traits of the candidates. The 2004 campaign was much the same. A common theme in the media coverage of the election was that President George Bush had a shallow understanding of policy issues. He was firm in his positions, making him decisive, but he arrived at his positions without a careful consideration of various alternatives. The Democratic candidate, John Kerry, was repeatedly characterized as a flip-flopper by the Republican campaign, an accusation that was frequently picked up in media coverage of the election. Moreover, Kerry was frequently described by commentators as too cold and too elitist, someone who could not connect with the common man, while Bush, on the other hand, was seen as a warm individual, someone to whom the ordinary person could relate.[15] Sometimes journalists latched onto small incidents to illustrate these points. For example, commentators lampooned Kerry when he improperly ordered a Philly cheese steak, choosing Swiss cheese instead of Cheez Whiz, and then compounded his error by nibbling daintily at his lunch, so as not to jeopardize his expensive shirt and tie.[16]

As in other election years, the discussions in the media in 2004 were reinforced by campaigns that were quite willing to focus on the personal traits of the candidates, either emphasizing the positive personal traits of their candidate or attacking the opposing candidate for character deficiencies. For example, when Kerry windsurfed off Nantucket Island during a brief respite from the campaign trail, the Bush campaign produced a memorable advertisement that turned Kerry's vacation exercise into a metaphor for both indecisiveness and all-too-highbrow recreational pursuits.[17] Recognizing that the voters had doubts about Bush's competence, Democrats attempted to exploit those concerns with an ad that showed the president responding to a press conference question about any mistakes that he had made while in office; in the ad, Bush is shown stating repeatedly that he cannot think of any mistakes, while messages about the failure of the war in Iraq flash across the screen.[18]

The character traits of the presidential candidates may have played an even greater role in the 2000 election, at least in popular accounts. A late September *New York Times Magazine* cover story went so far as to describe that year's election as boiling down to "The Stiff Guy vs. the Dumb Guy."[19] The "dumb guy," Republican candidate George W. Bush, was characterized by many commentators as amiable but uniformed.[20] Some questioned his qualifications to be president in spite of his election and reelection as governor of the nation's second-largest state. During both the primary and general elections, Bush frequently seemed to have a shallow understanding of national and foreign affairs, and he was prone to verbal errors in his public speaking—for example, referring to Greeks as "Grecians" and describing hidden messages in advertisements as "subliminable."[21] The "stiff guy," Democratic candidate Al Gore, was described as extremely knowledgeable but passionless and aloof, similar to the characterization of Kerry four years later, as well as Dukakis in 1988.[22] Pundits frequently labeled him a "policy wonk" who lacked personal warmth and charm. During the debates, he displayed his mastery of the details of public policy. On the other hand, this knowledge of governmental affairs, especially as it was displayed in the first debate, during which Gore, impatient with his opponent's answers, sighed theatrically and quite audibly, led many to characterize Gore as pedantic and condescending.[23] Additionally, Gore was portrayed as someone who would exaggerate or distort the truth to make himself look good. An example of this supposed tendency was the charge that Gore said that he invented the Internet, a claim that itself was a misrepresentation of what he really said, but one that was repeated so often that it became widely accepted as fact.

During the general election campaign, misstatements by Gore or Bush that fit the above stereotypes were highlighted by reporters. Small exaggerations or distortions of the facts by Gore were scrutinized and publicized. For example, in one debate, Gore stated that as vice president he toured fire-ravaged areas of Texas with the director of the Federal Emergency Management Agency, when in fact he was accompanied by the regional director of FEMA—a small inaccuracy that was irrelevant to the point that Gore was making, but an example seized on by the media to illustrate Gore's proclivity to distort the truth.[24] Similarly, small errors that might illustrate Bush's lack of information received considerable attention. An examination of the treatment of the candidates by television comedians, such as Jon Stewart of the *Daily Show,* emphasized how much Bush was the subject of jokes about his intelligence, knowledge, or verbal slips.[25] Media coverage of the election consistently framed the contest as one between "the gregarious chairman of the Inter-Fraternity Council" and the "earnest leader of the Science Club."[26]

Our research leads us to conclude that the media pundits are correct in concluding that perceptions of the personal traits of the candidates play an important role in presidential elections. However, pundits frequently err in two fundamental ways in their view of how these trait perceptions influence voting. First, they often emphasize traits that really are not very important to voters. Many commentators claim that voters care a great deal about the personal warmth and congeniality, or lack thereof, of the men and women who compete for elective office. Voters, this narrative suggests, want a candidate they would feel comfortable sharing a beer with or inviting over for dinner. Our research casts doubt on this view. When surveyed about what they like or dislike about presidential candidates, voters rarely mention anything about warmth, congeniality, friendliness, or similar personality traits. Instead, voters volunteer qualities such as leadership ability, experience, and honesty—all of which seem more relevant to being a good president than an enjoyable drinking companion.

A second problem is that popular interpretations of specific elections often erroneously conclude that a particular candidate has a significant advantage on personal characteristics, which often leads to incorrectly attributing the failure of a presidential campaign largely to a candidate's inability to connect with voters on a personal level. While media personalities made much of Kerry's failings in this regard, including his supposed lack of personal warmth, our analysis in this study suggests something quite different. Voters in 2004 perceived Bush to be superior to Kerry when it came to leadership and decisiveness, but Kerry was seen as more intelligent, knowledgeable, and empathetic. Overall, voter assessments of the candidates' character balanced out, and Kerry scored as well as Bush in terms of voter perceptions of the candidates' personal traits.[27] Similarly, many interpretations of the 2000 election concluded that Gore suffered because of widespread perceptions that he would routinely stretch the truth for political advantage. Yet our data show that Gore received fairly positive marks from voters on honesty, falling only somewhat short of Bush on this measure of voter perceptions of integrity.[28]

In this study, we attempt to explain how perceptions of the character traits of the presidential candidates influence voting behavior. Our findings suggest that some of the popular conceptions of this relationship are misleading or even incorrect, largely because many popular interpretations are based on anecdotal evidence and casual empiricism. Our research is based on a comprehensive analysis of three decades worth of the American National Election Study survey data: from 1980, when the ANES first began to ask specific questions about character traits, to 2012, the most recent election for which these data are available. But before looking at these data, we first consider some general questions about why character traits should play a substantial role in voting behavior.

THE QUESTION OF CHARACTER TRAITS IN PRESIDENTIAL ELECTIONS

The importance attached to the character of a potential president is not a recent phenomenon or even a creation of the television age. Concerns about the ambition and capability of those who run for president are as old as the republic. Some combination of mythologizing and demonizing presidential candidates on a personal level has been with us since accounts of Washington's cherry tree, Thomas Jefferson's sex life, and Andrew Jackson's battlefield exploits. However, the importance of character traits may have increased as a result of the interaction between executive power, which has grown substantially and become more centralized, and information technology, which has created a far more intimate relationship between candidates and voters.

The nature of press coverage of the modern presidential campaign, which too often requires content even in the absence of campaign-trail substance, makes character-based discussions more prevalent, but often less meaningful. Political theater, usually at the expense of policy and ideology, has become a significant part of presidential campaigns, which generate tens of thousands of column inches of newsprint and countless hours of reporting and discussion—often heated, sometimes inflammatory—on network news, cable television, talk radio, and, more recently, politically oriented blogs. The daily interaction among reporters, pundits, and campaign spokespersons produces a variety of themes over the course of any campaign. Campaign discourse can range from the consequential (Was the Iraq War a vital part of or a distraction from the War on Terror?), to the routine (Was the incumbent a good or bad manager of the economy?), to the ludicrous (What do Kerry's windsurfing or Obama's inept bowling tell us about their ability to be president?). Given the amount of hours devoted to campaign coverage across the political media, relative to the minutes set aside for in-depth analyses of the potential consequences of opposing policy proposals, it is not surprising to find talking heads immersed in discussions that are hardly central to the health or survival of the republic. As presidential campaigns have moved from the front porch to the train station to the airport tarmac to YouTube—from party-centered undertakings to candidate-centered events—concerns about and interest in the personal qualities of the candidates have become more important to media coverage and campaign rhetoric.

Of course, questions of character have been crucial in presidential elections before the emergence of television. The Framers of the U.S. Constitution were concerned with the interaction between individual character and power on their journey from the diffuse, highly decentralized Articles of Confederation to the more centralized Constitution and its single and independent executive. The Framers debated the wisdom of vesting executive authority in one person, given their general distrust of human nature and the resulting fear that centralized power and personal ambition would ultimately lead to tyranny. The colonial experience led the Framers to approach executive power cautiously, given the fallibility of the individuals who—after Washington, at least—would hold the office.[29] Ultimately, Alexander Hamilton's arguments in the Federalist Papers concerning the need for energy in the executive won the day in the form of ratification of the Constitutional Convention's work. For Hamilton, sufficient energy would be achieved by vesting power in one president, not a council, and providing that person with the possibility of indefinite reelection, and sufficient powers to withstand the inevitable attempts at encroachment by ambitious politicians in the Congress and the states.[30] While the Framers' vision of how this energetic executive would interact with the public was far afield from the modern experience of the president as popular leader, the competent, independent executive created by Article II has proven to be a sufficient foundation for the massively expanded federal government symbolized by a single president, with all his attendant character strengths and weaknesses.[31] As Jeffrey Tulis argues, the connotation of the term "popular leader" has changed from the Framers' understanding that such persons were potentially dangerous demagogues to our contemporary interpretation that emphasizes a leader who will provide robust, rhetorical leadership from a national perspective.

The modern, direct relationship between the president and the public, represented by the relative ease and frequency with which the president enters the nation's living rooms, has also served to place an increasing emphasis on character. Voters can infer character traits from direct observation of debate performances, campaign advertisements, town hall question-and-answer sessions, appearances on the Sunday interview shows, and the increasingly obligatory appearance on one of the late-night talk shows. Moreover, as we have already contended, television and radio personalities, as well as opposing campaigns, are happy to use photo opportunities gone awry, such as Michael Dukakis's tank ride or McCain's ill-conceived "green-screen" speech, to reinforce campaign themes, conventional wisdom, or both.[32]

Furthermore, the post-war emergence of the national security presidency has focused attention, both media and scholarly, on character. Political scientists, presidential historians, and members of the press have traveled a road from advocating for robust presidential power, best represented by Richard Neustadt's Franklin Roosevelt-like president, who skillfully wields persuasive power in the service of the public good, to raising doubts about powers that have become increasingly disconnected from sufficient checks and accountability.[33] This pessimistic view of executive power is represented by Arthur Schlesinger's imperial president, and has become increasingly prevalent today in an age of preemptive war and warrantless surveillance.[34] On the one hand, ambitious presidents have sought to centralize authority in the White House, a perfectly predictable turn of events. On the other hand, Congress, the press, and the public have either been complicit in this shift or slow to understand the consequences, which have included presidents acting outside the Constitution, with tragic results at times. Two such disasters, Vietnam and Watergate, briefly encouraged Congress to try once again to share national security responsibilities with the president, but a new era of vigorous consultation and oversight proved fleeting, as legislators found that the path of least resistance to reelection was to enable a president's foreign adventures, but reserve the right to hold the president responsible when and if things went wrong.[35] The Framers probably did not foresee that Congress would fail to meet executive overreach with equal amounts of ambition and institutional loyalty. This pessimistic take on presidential powers suggests to some analysts that the American political system has tilted toward rule by presidential fiat, especially in the realms of foreign and defense policy. Regardless of whether one considers the evolution of presidential power to be desirable or not, the disruption in the Framers' careful checks-and-balances system has made the character traits of people who would wield presidential power all the more important.

Presidential scholars have tried to tease out how individual character traits lead to success, distinct from the institutional and environmental constraints that all presidents face. James David Barber's controversial yet influential book on presidential character suggests that understanding two essential motivations of potential presidents can help the public select the candidate who is more likely to succeed in office.[36] Barber argues that voters should assess the amount of energy a political leader would bring to the presidency and the degree to which a candidate experiences political life as joyful, as opposed to something to be endured. Such insights are windows into the candidate's essential character, which develops in childhood, reveals itself over the course of a political career, and accompanies the victorious candidate to the White House. Human beings, presidents included, do not change their essential natures when starting a new job. Therefore, candidates who have exhibited low self-esteem are most likely, once in office, to use the presidency to overcome perceived personal shortcomings and abuse power. Optimistic and energetic candidates, who enjoy the exercise of power, are most likely to devote themselves to the public interest and provide strong, constructive leadership. While Barber's method for assessing presidential character, as well as other attempts in his wake, has endured justified criticism, this type of analysis has succeeded in focusing attention on the importance of the personal strengths and weaknesses of whoever wins the White House.

While political scientists have collectively focused more attention on policy issues, economic conditions, and presidential approval as determinants of election outcomes, there is general agreement in the voting behavior literature that perceptions of the personal qualities of the candidates are important short-term forces that influence voting in presidential elections. The authors of the *American Voter* found that voters in the 1952 and 1956 presidential elections provided many positive and negative comments about the personal qualities of the presidential candidates in those elections.[37] Eisenhower's victories in these years were in large part a result of his personal appeal, an appeal that was strong enough to overcome the substantial Democratic advantage in party identification.[38] Other models of voting behavior have similarly viewed perceptions of candidate personal traits as important short-term forces, along with issue orientations and retrospective evaluations of the performance of the incumbent administration.[39] These short-term forces are strongly influenced by party identification, ideology, and general policy dispositions, which are farther up the funnel of causality. While political scientists may disagree with media pundits about what candidate traits are important, how candidates are perceived in personal terms, and how these perceptions influence voting, most agree with the general proposition that perceptions of candidate traits play a significant role in the vote decision, at least as immediate influences on the vote.[40] It is not surprising that the limited amount of research into this topic has found that trait perceptions exert strong effects on voters. There are good reasons for voters to evaluate candidates based on voter perceptions of character traits, a topic that we now consider.

REASONS FOR VOTERS TO JUDGE CHARACTER TRAITS

Why should voters decide between presidential candidates on the basis of character traits? They could base their vote on how the presidential candidates stand on public policy issues or on the performance of the incumbent administration. In fact, we know that policy issues and performance assessments are important influences on the vote; numerous studies have established that fact.[41] However, there are good reasons to expect voters to go beyond policy issues and performance and to also rely on their perceptions of the character traits of the candidates in deciding for whom to vote. There are three reasons why this should be so: first, it is easy for voters to use this information; second, voters are encouraged to do so; and third, it is rational for voters to do so.

Voters Find It Easy to Use Character Traits

Voters do not need a great deal of information about government and politics, about the presidential election, or about the candidates in order to form images of the personal traits of presidential candidates. Making judgments about the character traits of a candidate can be done with limited information and effort. Individuals in their daily lives routinely make personal judgments about others, such as coworkers or neighbors. These judgments often are made on the basis of limited information. It seems likely that voters can just as easily make similar assessments of presidential candidates.[42] Even a small amount of personal information about candidates might allow voters to make judgments about future job performance in a reasonably rational way.[43] Some voters may use a single televised presidential debate as an information shortcut that leads to greater confidence in one candidate's leadership abilities or another's integrity. The very first televised presidential debates, between John F. Kennedy and Richard Nixon in 1960, resulted in many voters seeing Kennedy in a more positive light. The sole debate between Jimmy Carter and Ronald Reagan in 1980, held less than a week before election day, appeared to dispel some of the doubts that voters had about Reagan, whose affable nature and "There you go again" parrying of Carter's attacks contributed to the late surge toward his candidacy and comfortable victory. Many analysts attributed Gore's loss to Bush in 2000 as due in part to Gore's inability to project a positive personal image in the debates, especially the first one, during which the vice president was criticized for showing his exasperation with some of his opponent's answers. Similarly, voters may form perceptions of the personal traits of the candidates from limited news coverage or from televised political advertisements. Many voters seem willing to judge a candidate to be trustworthy (or untrustworthy), decisive (or indecisive), or compassionate (or unconcerned) on the basis of limited information.

Of course, perceptions of the character traits of presidential candidates that are based on limited information may be incorrect, or at least exaggerated or oversimplified. Many voters in 1992 concluded that President Bush did not care much about the plight of the average person. Did that truly reflect Bush's feelings, or did he simply not display his concern very well to the public? Senator Kerry was seen by many voters as indecisive in 2004, but that judgment was ostensibly based largely on a couple of votes concerning the war in Iraq and the Bush campaign's strategy of focusing relentlessly on these supposed missteps. Was Kerry truly a "flip-flopper," or were voters inferring too much from too few actions on a complicated issue? These questions are not easily answered, as it is very difficult to determine what candidates truly think. However, the important fact is that voters form such perceptions and act on the basis of these perceptions. In this sense, the perceptions are reality.

The ease of assessing the character traits of presidential candidates may be contrasted with the difficulty of voting on the basis of public policy issues. To cast a ballot on this basis, the voter must be familiar with the issue, have some minimal intensity of feeling about it, perceive where the candidates stand on it, and see one candidate as closer to his or her position. Voters often fail to meet these conditions on many issues. Some issues are complex, so voters may be uncertain about where they stand. The controversies over the government's attempt to deal with the acute crisis in the nation's financial institutions that erupted in late 2008 probably exemplify such a set of issues. Recent battles over health care reform may also fall into this category. For other issues, voters may have strong opinions but fail to perceive clear differences between the candidates. This may result from voters not paying enough attention to what the candidates have said about the issue or from the candidates failing to address the issue with clear positions. Sometimes this is true even for highly salient issues. In the 1968 presidential election, for example, there was considerable ambiguity in public perceptions of where the two major-party candidates, Hubert Humphrey and Richard Nixon, stood on the central issue of the day: the Vietnam War.[44]

In sum, many voters fail to meet the criteria for issue voting. One analysis of the 2004 election found that less than one-half of the voters met these conditions in areas as basic as whether government services and spending should be increased or decreased, whether defense spending should be increased or decreased, or whether the government should guarantee a job and good standard of living to everyone.[45] The voters who fail to meet these conditions tend to be the ones who are less educated, who are less aware of politics, and who are less attentive to the presidential election campaign. Even these voters, however, should be able to form perceptions of the personal traits of the presidential candidates, should they desire to do so.

Of course, there are issues on which voters meet the conditions for issue voting. "Easy issues" are straightforward, highly salient, and manifest a high level of partisan disagreement.[46] Even voters who are not particularly attentive to politics will be able to cast a ballot on the basis of easy issues, if they choose to do so. Moreover, while a voter may fail to meet the criteria for issue voting on a range of public policy issues, that may not be the case for a select few issues that the voter is particularly concerned about. Farmers, for example, may be well informed about government farm policy and knowledgeable about candidate positions on agricultural issues. Even these voters, ones who are able to cast a ballot on the basis of issues, also may vote partly on the basis of candidate character. In fact, judgments made on these two different sets of criteria are likely to be complementary, not contradictory, as we shall see.

Although it is easy for voters to form perceptions of the personal traits of presidential candidates, this does not mean that these assessments necessarily are made on the basis of limited information. Perceptions of candidate character traits can be based on careful and sophisticated assessments that are arrived at only after weighing considerable information. Some voters who felt in 1996 that Clinton lacked integrity may have come to that judgment only after absorbing an abundance of relevant information. Similarly, some of the voters in 2004 who thought that Bush was not very knowledgeable about governmental affairs may not have been making a snap judgment, but a reasoned inference based on substantial evidence. The important point is that assessments of the character traits of presidential candidates can be based on limited information, making it easy for less attentive voters to form such perceptions, but more attentive voters also can assess the character traits of the candidates.

Voters Are Encouraged to Rely on Character Traits

Presidential candidates contribute to the importance of personal traits by stressing such characteristics in their campaigns. They frequently emphasize their desirable attributes and highlight the shortcomings of their opponents, a campaign strategy that probably results from an assumption that such an approach is more effective than appealing to voters on policy issues. For example, when Bush argued in 2004 that he was a strong leader and that Kerry was not, almost any voter who accepted that claim would be pulled at least somewhat toward Bush, as nearly all voters prefer a strong leader to a weak one. However, when Bush argued that he was protecting the sanctity of life with his positions on abortion and stem cell research, not every voter who understood Bush's positions on these issues would have been drawn closer to him; some may have become less likely to vote for him upon hearing his views. The more closely divided public opinion is on an issue, the less that a candidate stands to gain by clarifying his policy stance or by outlining the difference between his or her position and that of his or her opponent. Since personal images of the candidates can be based on limited information, as we discussed above, candidates may feel that they can more easily create positive images of themselves, or negative images of their opponents, than they can win votes through issue appeals. For these reasons, presidential candidates may prefer to speak about character rather than policy issues in their campaign messages. When they do talk about issues, candidates often do so by stressing general goals that are broadly shared rather than by outlining specific policy measures. The rise of candidate-centered elections may have contributed to such campaign behavior.[47]

Media coverage of the presidential candidates, including the kind of coverage we have discussed above, also contributes to voter reliance on the character traits of candidates. Many studies have commented on the shallow and disjointed discussion of policy issues and excessive emphasis on the "horse race" that characterize media coverage of election campaigns. The media's focus on individual personalities rather than on questions of public policy may reflect, in part, what the candidates highlight in their campaigns. While this is no doubt the case, campaigns have an incentive to portray elections in personal terms because of the contemporary media's tendency to emphasize conflict and drama, rather than the dry material of policy debates. Several scholars have noted the increase over time of media coverage that treats the campaign as a game played by opposing candidates seeking short-term strategic advantage.[48] The increasing reliance of voters on television for campaign information, relative to newspapers, may be particularly significant as television appears to emphasize the personal dimension of candidates more so than do the print media.[49] Television can, moreover, involve viewers emotionally in ways that are unavailable to other media.[50] Furthermore, to the extent that television features campaign news about important public policy concerns, such coverage is likely to be episodic in form rather than thematic, and, therefore, lacking in context and perspective.[51] Whereas thematic coverage would present elections as contests between competing ideological and partisan visions of the direction of public policy, the media are more likely to prime the public to view campaigns as contests among strategic and manipulative individuals, thus increasing the salience of individual character traits. Recent presidential campaigns provide many illustrations of such coverage. In 2004, for example, the national media devoted considerable attention to the truthfulness of the candidates' accounts of their behavior more than three decades before the election, during the Vietnam War. In 2008, the media devoted substantial attention to what Obama's previous associations with controversial figures said about the Democratic candidate's character. The media covered these connections with (in the case of William Ayres) and without (in the case of the Rev. Jeremiah Wright) the urging of the McCain campaign. Similar in-depth attention was not devoted to examining the relative merits of, for example, the health care plans of these candidates, an examination that would have been informative and valuable, but dull.

The use of personal traits to assess presidential candidates may be encouraged by the fact that presidents are commonly portrayed in personal terms by historians and biographers. Recent presidents such as Reagan, Nixon, Kennedy, and Clinton are probably remembered as much in personal terms as for their policy accomplishments. Popular historical portraits of presidents frequently attempt to connect formative life experiences to the paramount personal and political qualities exhibited by those who assume the presidency. Doris Kearns Goodwin links the patrician-born Franklin Roosevelt's deepening empathy for the plight of the common man to his struggle with polio.[52] H. W. Brands attributes Theodore Roosevelt's relentless perfectionism and hard-charging leadership style to his drive to live up to his father's example, frozen in the 19-year old Teddy's memory when the elder Roosevelt died.[53] Robert Dallek connects Richard Nixon's lack of self-confidence to a harsh father and an austere and distant mother.[54] Biographers of Lyndon Johnson and Bill Clinton link aspects of the former's notorious "treatment" and the latter's famous empathy to childhoods spent mediating between contentious parents.[55] If assessments of past presidents by historians seem to highlight the personal qualities of the individuals, voters may naturally feel that future presidents should be evaluated in large part by their personal traits.

It Is Rational for Voters to Make Character Judgments

Some analysts view voting on the basis of candidate character traits as a less-informed vote, one that is based on unsubstantiated personal judgments about the candidates. Those who vote largely on this basis may be criticized for being simple-minded voters who fail to fulfill their responsibilities as democratic citizens. In contrast, voting on the basis of policy issues is frequently viewed as a more rational way to behave, one that should be encouraged in a democracy such as ours. In fact, when candidates fail to address policy issues during the campaign, they are often attacked by journalists for ignoring what should be the central questions in the election. While there are good reasons to want to have policy issues fully addressed during a presidential election campaign, it also is quite rational for voters to make judgments based in part on their assessments of the character traits of the candidates.

First of all, the issues that are discussed during the election campaign may not turn out to be the most important issues during a president's term. Foreign policy and national security issues did not receive much attention during the 2000 presidential campaign. Less than a year into Bush's presidency, the September 11 terrorist attacks drastically changed the issue agenda. While President Bush's decision to order the invasion of Afghanistan had widespread support, other national security decisions did not. The decision to send troops to invade Iraq, a country that was not involved in the terrorist attacks, was more controversial, especially because it rested in part on a foreign policy doctrine of preemptive action. Decisions about where to detain and how to treat alleged terrorists who had been captured in Afghanistan and elsewhere sparked much discussion and disagreement, especially regarding what interrogation techniques could be used on such individuals. Contentious discussions also centered on what domestic and foreign surveillance techniques were both desirable and constitutionally permissible in this new war on terrorism. None of these divisive issues received discussion during the 2000 campaign, for the simple reason that no one anticipated that they would be issues in 2001 and beyond.

Even when new issues do not emerge, circumstances change, making old issues into quite different ones. Economic issues in particular can change a great deal. Some presidents, such as Reagan, enter office during an economic recession, but later find themselves in a period of economic growth. Others, such as the two Bushes, experience the opposite pattern. The economic policies that these presidents proposed during their election campaigns may be inappropriate two or three years later. Should a president who campaigned on not raising taxes adhere to that pledge, even if changed economic circumstances justify such action? The very people who voted for the candidate because of his economic proposals may prefer different policies two or three years later.

Because the issues that are discussed during the election campaign will be an imperfect guide to the issues and circumstances that a president will face over the course of his term in office, it is rational for voters to rely on factors that provide some indication for how the president would behave in changed circumstances. Voters legitimately should be interested in how the president makes decisions. Is he deliberative or prone to snap judgments? Does he make decisions on pragmatic grounds or on strong ideological principles? Is he rigid or willing to adjust to changed circumstances? Does he understand public policy well enough to deal with unforeseen developments? Will he marshal a wide range of evidence or rely on a small, core group of advisors when making decisions? Will he listen to expert opinion or rely on his own instincts? It clearly is rational for voters to assess presidential candidates in terms of their experience, decision-making style, knowledge, and intelligence. While issues can emerge, fade, or evolve, a person's character is fixed long before a successful presidential election campaign.

Presidents also must accomplish things to be effective. A president who proposes policies that voters prefer, but is unable to command or cajole their passage, will be a less successful president. A president who does not effectively control and manage his administration will also be less successful. Thus, voters are right to be interested in a presidential candidate's ability to accomplish things. Is the candidate someone who will be able to forge a coalition and achieve the necessary consensus, both in Congress and in the nation, to enact his agenda? Is the candidate someone who will be a good manager of government, someone who will ensure that policies are implemented effectively? Is the candidate someone who is strong enough to resolve the various personnel and policy conflicts that mark every administration? Can the candidate be trusted to run an honest and ethical administration? There are sound reasons for voters to be concerned with the leadership, managerial ability, competence, and integrity of those who would be president.

THE FOCUS OF THE BOOK

How voter perceptions of candidate character traits influence the outcomes of presidential elections is an interesting and relevant question. Unfortunately, it is not one that has been studied in great detail. The scholarly literature on this topic is quite small compared to the amount of work on other factors that influence voting behavior. There is an enormous literature, including many books, dealing with the role of public policy issues in elections. There is an extensive list of studies of how economic conditions affect the outcome of national elections. When it comes to the study of character traits in presidential elections, no books and only a modest number of articles have been published in the past 30 years.[56] The result is that we do not have a comprehensive understanding of this topic. While the articles that have been published have contributed to our knowledge, they are limited in their focus, as would be expected from journal articles. Many examine data from only one election. Many focus on just one aspect of the broader topic. The result is that these articles do not add up to a full picture of how character traits influence voting behavior. This study aims to correct that situation. In this book, we attempt to examine a wide range of questions, and we do so using data from the 1980 presidential election to the present. The key questions that we attempt to answer in this book are as follows:

(1) *Which character traits of presidential candidates are important to voters and which are not?* We discuss the different traits that have been suggested as relevant and examine the evidence for the impact of each of these traits on the vote.

(2) *How are voter perceptions of candidate character traits best measured?* We examine two different methods for measuring these perceptions, one using closed survey items and the other using open-ended questions, comparing the strengths and weaknesses of each approach.

(3) *How much do perceptions of candidate character traits influence the vote for president?* In answering this question, we are particularly

concerned with determining the extent to which changes in trait perceptions produce changes in the vote.

(4) *What factors influence the perceptions of candidate character traits?* In every presidential election there is considerable variation in how voters perceive the candidates. We attempt to identify the attitudes and orientations of voters that affect how they see the candidates, and we discuss differences across election years that affect perceptions of the candidates.

(5) *How does media consumption affect voting on the basis of candidate character traits?* A common theme in the literature is that television has personalized politics. We investigate whether voters who rely more on television rather than newspapers for their election news are more likely to emphasize candidate character. For the most recent election, we examine the effect of the Internet on the relationship between trait perceptions and the vote.

As we shall see, the answers to each of these questions are interrelated. By covering all of them in this study, we believe that we provide a comprehensive understanding of the role that perceptions of candidate character traits have in contemporary presidential elections.

NOTES

1. David Brooks, "The ESPN Man," *New York Times,* May 15, 2012, national edition.
2. Maureen Dowd, "Likability Index," *New York Times,* August 12, 2012, national edition, Sunday Review.
3. Timothy Eagan, "Romney the Unknowable," *New York Times,* August 16, 2010, national edition.
4. Maureen Dowd, "Odyssey of a Statue Candidate," *New York Times,* August 2, 2012, national edition.
5. Chris Cilliza and Aaron Blake, "Barack Obama's Empathy Edge," posted to "The Fix," *Washington Post,* April 10, 2012, http://www.washingtonpost.com/blogs/th-fix/barack-obama's-empathy-edge.html (accessed August 1, 2013).
6. Michael Tomasky, "A Mouse In the White House?" *Newsweek,* August 6, 2012, 24.
7. Maureen Dowd, "Pampered Princes Fling Gorilla Dust," *New York Times,* October 21, 2012, national edition, Sunday review.
8. Mark Shields, "Campaign 2012 Deficits—Humility and Humor," Creators Syndicate, October 18, 2012. Available at www.creators.com/liberal/campaign-2012-deficits-humility-and-humor.html (accessed August 1, 2013).
9. Mark Shields, "Discovering Columbus 2012," Creators Syndicate, October 11, 2012. Available at www.creators.com/liberal/mark-shields/discovering-columbus-2012.html (accessed August 1, 2013).
10. Michael Kranish, "Mitt Romney Was Hesitant to Reveal Himself," *Boston Globe,* December 23, 2012.
11. From the file labeled "only in America" comes Samuel Joseph Wurzelbacher, better known to the nation as "Joe the Plumber." Wurzelbacher launched his

career as a conservative commentator and, more recently, a 2012 Republican candidate for the House of Representatives as the result of a 2008 campaign encounter with then Senator Obama. The two engaged in a brief, videotaped discussion about how Obama's tax proposals would affect Wurzelbacher's plans to own a plumbing business. During the third and final 2008 presidential debate, McCain seized on the exchange to charge that the Democrat's tax plan would overburden small business owners in order to "spread the wealth around," a phrase used by Obama during his fateful conversation with Joe. By the time the third debate ended, McCain and Obama referenced "Joe the Plumber" or "Joe" 25 times, 20 of which were by McCain. During the same debate, by contrast, another reasonably important Joe, Obama's running mate, Joe Biden was mentioned six times.

12. Obama managed to score a meager 37 over seven frames of bowling at a campaign stop in Altoona, Pennsylvania, in advance of that state's Democratic primary. On the March 31, 2008, edition of MSNBC's *Morning Joe* program, the host, former Republican House member Joe Scarborough, criticized Obama's dainty release, adding that "Americans want their president, if it's a man, to be a real man." Former Democratic House member Harold Ford, Jr., tried to come to Obama's defense later in the same show by awkwardly suggesting that Obama's inability to bowl showed his "human" side. Scarborough replied that, if anything, the Altoona campaign stop highlighted Obama's "prissy" side.

13. The flag pin question is discussed by Michael Dobbs, "The Great Flag Pin Debate," posted to Glenn Kessler's "The Fact Checker," *Washington Post,* June 17, 2008, http://www.washingtonpost.com/fact-checker/2008/06/the_great_flag_pin_debate.html (accessed November 18, 2013).

14. When asked by reporters in August 2008 about the number of homes that he owned, McCain said that he did not know and that he would have his staff get back to the reporters with a specific number. The incident is discussed in Patrick Healy and Katharine Q. Seelye, "2 Rivals Quest: Common Touch," *New York Times,* August 22, 2008.

15. Patricia Conley, "The Presidential Race of 2004: Strategy, Outcome, and Mandate," in *A Defining Moment: The Presidential Election of 2004,* ed. William J. Crotty (Armonk, NY: M. E. Sharpe, 2005), 108–135; Wilson Carey McWilliams, "The Meaning of the Election: Ownership and Citizenship in American Life," in *The Elections of 2004,* ed. Michael Nelson (Washington, DC: CQ Press, 2005), 187–213.

16. Dana Milbank of the *Washington Post* went so far as to cite Kerry's cheesesteak gaffe as the potential beginning of the end of his campaign for the Democratic presidential nomination. In the August 13, 2004, edition of the paper, Milbank wrote, "If Sen. John F. Kerry's presidential aspirations melt like a dollop of Cheez Whiz in the sun, the trouble may well be traced to an incident in South Philadelphia on Monday."

17. The ad can be found on the Museum of the Moving Image's website, *The Living Room Candidate.* The web address for a selection of 2004 ads produced by both major party campaigns, including "Windsurfing," is http://www.livingroomcandidate.org/commercials/2004.

18. The ad can be found at http://www.livingroomcandidate.org/commercials/2004.

19. Marshall Sella, "The Stiff Guy vs. the Dumb Guy," *New York Times,* September 24, 2000, Sunday Magazine section. The larger purpose of the article was to discuss the increasing relevance to the campaign, particularly among young voters, of late-night comedy programs such as *The Daily Show* and *Late Night with David Letterman.*

20. James W. Caeser and Andrew E. Busch, *The Perfect Tie: The True Story of the 2000 Presidential Election* (Lanham, MD: Rowman and Littlefield, 2001), 33.
21. Marjorie Randon Hershey, "The Campaign and the Media," in *The Elections of 2000*, ed. Michael Nelson (Washington, DC: CQ Press, 2001), 58; Paul J. Quirk and Sean C. Matheson, "The Election and the Prospects for Leadership," in *The Elections of 2000*, ed. Michael Nelson (Washington, DC: CQ Press), 170.
22. Wilson Carey McWilliams, "The Meaning of the Election," in *The Election of 2000*, ed. Gerald M. Pomper (New York: Chatham House, 2001), 180.
23. Ceasar and Busch, *The Perfect Tie*, 150; Hershey, "The Campaign and the Media," 62.
24. Hershey, "The Campaign and the Media," 62.
25. Marshall Sella, "The Stiff Guy vs. the Dumb Guy."
26. Hershey, "The Campaign and the Media," 70.
27. Charles Prysby, "Perceptions of Candidate Character Traits and the Presidential Vote in 2004," *PS: Political Science and Politics* 41 (2008): 115–122.
28. On the other integrity measure, whether "he is moral," the public held Gore in slightly higher regard.
29. Michael Nelson, "The Psychological Presidency," in *The Presidency and the Political System*, 10th ed., ed. Michael Nelson (Washington, DC: CQ Press, 2006), 167–190.
30. Hamilton's arguments for a competent and energetic executive are introduced in *The Federalist Papers* No. 70 and defended in No. 71 through No. 77.
31. Jeffrey K. Tulis, *The Rhetorical Presidency* (Princeton, NJ: Princeton University Press, 1987), 26–27.
32. To bolster his commander-in-chief credentials, the 1988 Democratic nominee took a ride in an M1 tank as cameras rolled. The ill-advised photo opportunity did not burnish Dukakis's reputation for strong leadership. In fact, the Bush campaign turned the video of Dukakis waving from the tank's turret into a commercial to claim that, despite the visual, Dukakis was no friend of weapons systems. The ad can be viewed at http://www.livingroomcandidate.org/commercials/1988/ tank–ride.
   On June 3, 2008, Obama claimed enough pledged delegates to become the Democratic Party's presumptive nominee. The Republican campaign attempted to share the spotlight with Obama on his big night by having McCain give a speech of his own. The resulting address provided immediate fodder for pundits who contrasted McCain's stilted speech in front of about 600 supporters in New Orleans to Obama's soaring rhetoric before a raucous crowd of 17,000 in St. Paul. To see what the pundits saw that evening, here are links to Obama's (http://www.youtube.com/watch?v=dtL–1V3OZ0c&feature=fvw) and McCain's (http://www.youtube.com/watch?v=A7RuX4pQPLY) speeches. During a discussion on CNN in the immediate aftermath of McCain's speech, Alex Castellanos, a Republican strategist, said, "Well, last I checked, this was not a speech making contest. Thank God." McCain gave his speech in front of a large, green background, which prompted comedian and faux conservative talk show host Stephen Colbert to issue a "green-screen challenge" to his audience. Colbert charged his viewers with making McCain more exciting by using the green backdrop as inspiration for adding special effects to the speech. The authors' favorite entries in Colbert's contest can be found at http://www.youtube.com/watch?v=9rOF–j1L0vE and http://www.youtube.com/watch?v=8G9jA–FGGd8&feature=related.

33. Richard E. Neustadt, *Presidential Power and the Modern Presidents: The Politics of Leadership from Roosevelt to Reagan* (New York: Free Press, 1991).
34. Arthur M. Schlesinger, *The Imperial Presidency* (Boston: Houghton Mifflin, 1973).
35. Andrew Rudalevige, *The New Imperial Presidency* (Ann Arbor: University of Michigan Press, 2006), 276.
36. James David Barber, *The Presidential Character* (Englewood Cliffs, NJ: Prentice-Hall, 1972).
37. Angus Campbell, Philip E. Converse, Warren E. Miller, and Donald E. Stokes, *The American Voter* (New York: John Wiley, 1960), 54–58.
38. A November 1952 Gallup Poll found that 53 percent of Americans considered themselves or leaned toward Democrats, while 41 percent considered themselves or leaned toward Republicans. Despite this advantage in party identification, Stevenson lost to Eisenhower in the national popular vote 55 percent to 44 percent. A November 1956 Gallup Poll showed that Democrats enjoyed a 51 percent to 41 percent party identification advantage, yet Stevenson lost to Eisenhower again, this time by 57 percent to 42 percent.
39. Gregory B. Markus and Philip E. Converse, "A Dynamic Simultaneous Equation Model of Electoral Choice," *American Political Science Review* 73 (1979): 1055–1070; Warren E. Miller and J. Merrill Shanks, *The New American Voter* (Cambridge: Harvard University Press, 1996); Benjamin I. Page and Calvin C. Jones, "Reciprocal Effects of Policy Preferences, Party Loyalties, and the Vote," *American Political Science Review* 73 (1979): 1071–1089.
40. Larry M. Bartels, "The Impact of Candidate Traits in American Presidential Elections," in *Leaders' Personalities and the Outcomes of Democratic Elections,* ed. Anthony King (Oxford: Oxford University Press, 2002), 44–69; Carolyn L. Funk, "Bringing the Candidate into Models of Candidate Evaluation," *Journal of Politics* 61 (1999): 700–720; Paul Goren, "Character Weakness, Partisan Bias, and Presidential Evaluation," *American Journal of Political Science* 46 (2002): 627–641; Danny Hayes, "Candidate Qualities through a Partisan Lens: A Theory of Trait Ownership," *American Journal of Political Science* 49 (2005): 908–923; Arthur H. Miller, Martin P. Wattenberg, and Oksana Malanchuk, "Schematic Assessments of Presidential Candidates," *American Political Science Review* 80 (1986): 521–540.
41. Paul R. Abramson, John H. Aldrich, and David W. Rohde, *Change and Continuity in the 2008 and 2010 Elections* (Washington, DC: CQ Press, 2012); Michael S. Lewis-Beck, William G. Jacoby, Helmut Norpoth, and Herbert F. Weisberg, *The American Voter Revisited* (Ann Arbor: University of Michigan Press, 2008); Miller and Shanks, *The New American Voter.*
42. Carolyn L. Funk, "Understanding Trait Inferences in Candidate Images," in *Research in Micropolitics: Rethinking Rationality,* vol. 5, ed. Michael X. Delli Carpini, Leonie Huddy, and Robert Y. Shapiro (Greenwich, CT: JAI, 1996), 97–123; Wendy Rahn, John H. Aldrich, Eugene Borgida, and John L. Sullivan, "A Social-Cognitive Model of Candidate Appraisal," in *Information and Democratic Processes,* ed. John A. Ferejohn and James H. Kuklinski (Urbana: University of Illinois Press, 1990), 136–159.
43. Samuel L. Popkin, *The Reasoning Voter: Communication and Persuasion in Presidential Campaigns* (Chicago: University of Chicago Press, 1991).
44. Benjamin I. Page and Richard A. Brody, "Policy Voting and the Electoral Process: The Vietnam War Issue," *American Political Science Review* 66 (1972): 979–995.
45. Lewis-Beck et al., *The American Voter Revisited,* 181.

46. Edward G. Carmines and James A. Stimson, "The Two Faces of Issue Voting," *American Political Science Review* 74 (1980): 78–91.
47. Martin P. Wattenberg, *The Rise of Candidate-Centered Politics* (Cambridge, MA: Harvard University Press, 1991).
48. Joseph Cappella and Kathleen Hall Jamieson, *Spiral of Cynicism: The Press and the Public Good* (New York: Oxford University Press, 1997); Thomas E. Patterson, *Out of Order* (New York: Alfred A. Knopf, 1993).
49. Scott Keeter, "The Illusion of Intimacy: Television and the Role of Candidate Personal Qualities in Voter Choice," *Public Opinion Quarterly* 51 (1987): 344–358.
50. Diana C. Mutz, "Effects of 'In–Your–Face' Television Discourse on Perceptions of a Legitimate Opposition," *American Political Science Review* 101 (2007): 621–635.
51. Shanto Iyengar, *Is Anyone Responsible? How Television Frames Political Issues* (Chicago: University of Chicago Press, 1991).
52. Doris Kearns Goodwin, *No Ordinary Time* (New York: Simon & Schuster, 1994), 16.
53. H. W. Brands, *TR: The Last Romantic,* (New York: Basic Books, 1997), 83.
54. Robert Dallek, *Nixon and Kissinger* (New York: HarperCollins Publishers, 2007), 6.
55. Doris Kearns, *Lyndon Johnson and the American Dream* (New York: Harper & Row, 1976); David Maraniss, *First in His Class: A Biography of Bill Clinton* (New York: Simon & Schuster, 1996).
56. The political science journal articles that have analyzed the effect of character trait perceptions on voting behavior in presidential elections include: Bishin, Stevens, and Wilson 2006; Campbell 1983; Doherty and Gimple 1997; Funk 1999; Gant 1983; Glasgow and Alvarez 2000; Glass 1985; Goren 2002, 2007; Hayes 2005, 2009; Holian and Prysby 2012; Jacobs and Shapiro 1994; Keeter 1987; Kenney and Rice 1988; Kilburn 2005; Kinder et al. 1980; Markus 1982; McCann 1990; Miller, Wattenberg, and Malanchuk 1986; Pierce 1993; Prysby 2008; Sullivan et al. 1990. Some journal articles have investigated the effects of trait perceptions on other aspects of political behavior, such as voting in congressional elections or approval of presidential performance: Conover 1981; Funk 1996 ("The Impact of Scandal on Candidate Evaluations"), 1997; Greene 2001; Lodge, McGraw, and Stroh 1989; McGraw et al. 1996; Rahn, Krosnick, and Dimock 1994; Rapoport, Metcalf, and Hartman 1989; Sullivan et al. 1990. Also, there have been a few articles in edited books that have dealt with candidate character traits: Bartels 2002; Funk 1996 ("Understanding Trait Inferences"); Hellweg 1995; Kaid and Chanslor 1995; Kinder 1986; Lau 1986; Lodge and Stroh 1993; Rahn et al. 1990. The only book published on this topic was written almost 40 years ago: Nimmo and Savage 1976. Full citations for these publications are in the bibliography.

2 Conceptualizing and Measuring Candidate Character Traits

Candidate character traits are relatively stable aspects of a candidate's personality or character. They are psychological or mental qualities or highly related behavioral dispositions, not physical or demographic characteristics, such as race, gender, or age. Furthermore, character traits are assumed to be fairly stable, at least in the short run. When voters say that an individual is honest or intelligent, for example, they presumably are stating how the individual will behave in the foreseeable future, not that the individual is honest or intelligent for the moment. What we need to know is which character or personal traits are important to voters, especially for presidential elections. Which traits are voters primarily concerned with when they decide which candidate to vote for? To answer this question, we need a conceptual framework for analyzing candidate character traits.

CONCEPTUALIZING CHARACTER TRAITS

The list of candidate character traits that might be important to voters is long. Scholars and pundits have suggested that voters desire a candidate who is: honest, sincere, trustworthy, moral, decent, inspiring, intelligent, knowledgeable, open-minded, stable, resolute, courageous, bold, a strong leader, respectable, energetic, believable, responsible, just, fair, admirable, extroverted, cheerful, kind, compassionate, good-natured, experienced, competent, poised, dignified, decisive, determined, forthright, altruistic, warm, humble, concerned about ordinary people, in touch with the problems that confront ordinary people, and good at communication; voters do not want a president who is naive, prejudiced, reckless, impulsive, indecisive, power hungry, boring, irritable, or moody. It is difficult to examine all of these possible traits, so it is theoretically useful to distill this long list down to a small number of basic characteristics or trait dimensions. Several scholars have done exactly that, and we build on their work.

One very influential attempt to conceptualize candidate character traits is Donald Kinder's 1986 study, which analyzed a large number of character traits and found that they could be reduced to four basic trait dimensions: leadership, competence, integrity, and empathy.[1] These four dimensions of candidate character traits have been accepted as the appropriate conceptualization by a number of other researchers.[2] There are divergent views, however. In some cases, the divergence is simply a case of combining two dimensions. For example, Carolyn Funk started with the above four dimensions—leadership, competence, integrity, and empathy—but found that leadership and competence are best combined into one dimension.[3] Another study used only two dimensions, competence and integrity, but the competence dimension included leadership items and the integrity dimension included empathy items.[4] Kinder also found that leadership and competence are highly correlated, as are integrity and empathy, so reducing the four dimensions down to two or three is not inconsistent with Kinder's framework.

Other scholars have employed somewhat different conceptualizations. Some agree that leadership, competence, and integrity are important trait characteristics, but they drop empathy as a relevant trait dimension. For example, Gregory Markus defined two trait dimensions, competence and integrity, with leadership encompassed by competence; his conceptualization ignores empathy.[5] Pamela Conover also found that leadership, competence, and integrity are sufficient.[6] Other scholars include some aspect of personal appeal to the list. One study classified personal traits into four groups: competence, reliability (which is similar to leadership), integrity, and charisma; this analysis considers charisma as important, something others do not, and it leaves out empathy.[7] Another study arrayed trait assessments along the dimensions of competence, character, and personal attraction; the character dimension combines leadership and integrity, and the personal attraction dimension measures warmth among other factors.[8] Still another study used four trait dimensions: leadership, competence, trustworthiness, and personality, with the latter referring to how interesting and appealing the candidate is, a concept that seems similar to warmth.[9]

In sum, almost all researchers see leadership, competence, and integrity as important traits, although some reduce these to two dimensions (most commonly by combining leadership and competence). Empathy is viewed as important by some researchers, sometimes as a separate dimension and sometimes as part of integrity, but others do not regard it as significant. A few researchers include warmth or personal appeal as a relevant trait, but most do not think that general warmth is particularly relevant.

Given that the personal traits of presidential candidates that are most often identified as relevant include leadership, competence, integrity, and empathy, even if some of these dimensions might be highly related, we begin our analysis with this conceptualization and attempt to define these four trait categories. As we will see later, our analysis shows that these four dimensions are an appropriate conceptualization of character traits. In particular, we find empathy to be just as important as the more commonly identified dimensions of leadership, competence, and integrity despite the fact that empathy is dismissed as unimportant by some researchers. We also examine warmth and some related traits, since the popular media often see them as important. However, we find little evidence that general warmth is a significant trait dimension for most voters.

Leadership

Leadership is considered to be an important candidate character trait by almost all scholars, but the definition of this concept is often vague. We see leadership as embodying several related attributes. Most of all, a strong leader is someone who will act, someone who is not reluctant to make decisions, especially in crisis situations. Past presidents have often been judged as great because of the actions that they took in crisis situations, foreign or domestic. Abraham Lincoln's greatness reflects his handling of the Civil War. Franklin D. Roosevelt's reputation derives from his actions to combat the Great Depression and to achieve victory in World War II. Moreover, a strong leader is someone who is in control and who accomplishes things, even when the nation does not face a crisis. For a president, this often means forging a coalition and creating a consensus that allows for policy goals to be realized. Lyndon Johnson, for example, was able to enact a number of major pieces of legislation, including landmark civil rights and social welfare bills. Presidents who are unable to accomplish much, at least in the eyes of the public, are almost always regarded as weak leaders. Among recent presidents, Jimmy Carter stands out as one who was regarded as such by the end of his first term, given that he failed to harness the substantial congressional majorities of his own Democratic Party. His successes in domestic and foreign policy were outweighed by his failures, including a deteriorating economy, sharply higher energy costs, American embassy workers held as hostages in Iran, and the Soviet invasion of Afghanistan—all of which contributed to his reelection defeat in 1980.

A strong leader also is one who commands respect, one whom others will follow. This suggests that being inspiring to citizens is part of being a strong leader. For presidents, this involves being able to present a vision of society that the nation should strive to achieve. Thus, a president should not simply respond to what voters want; he or she should help society define its goals and aspirations. Ronald Reagan was widely credited with shifting the nation's political orientation in a more conservative direction, and his success in advancing a conservative agenda contributed to his being viewed as a strong leader. This suggests that being an effective communicator is part of being a strong leader. President Reagan, for example, was nicknamed the "Great Communicator," but his successor, George H. W. Bush, was frequently criticized for his inability to effectively express his goals and ideals to the public.

Being in control, willing to act, and able to define goals indicates that decisiveness is an attribute of a strong leader. A president should be capable of making up his or her mind about matters, rather than being too easily swayed or influenced by others. While a strong leader is resolute, decisiveness in the extreme becomes stubbornness, so some degree of flexibility seems important as well. President George W. Bush was judged by many as being too willing to make a decision without careful consideration of the alternatives and too unwilling to change his mind after the fact, even in the face of mounting evidence of failure. President Barack Obama's leadership style has emerged as the converse of his immediate predecessor's. Some veterans of the Bush administration criticized President Obama's long and detailed interagency review of Afghanistan policy as overly cautious and, ultimately, a signal of weakness and lack of fortitude. On the other hand, the Obama administration and its allies framed the process as necessary deliberation given the stakes: whether or not to send more young Americans into harm's way. In further contrast to President Bush's leadership style, President Bill Clinton showed flexibility in proposing policies and accepting compromises on less sweeping legislation after the defeat of his more ambitious health care legislation.

In some cases, having the courage to support the correct policy even when it is not politically popular can be regarded as a mark of a strong leader. During the 2008 presidential campaign, Senator John McCain pointed to his support for a troop surge in Iraq in 2007, a time at which public sentiment was leaning the other way, as an indication of his willingness to push for policies that he thought were best, regardless of what the public opinion polls said. In other situations, however, supporting an unpopular policy has not resulted in the candidate being viewed as decisive or courageous. In the 1984 presidential election, the Democratic candidate, Walter Mondale, argued that federal taxes needed to be raised in order to reduce the large budget deficits that had emerged during Reagan's first term. While some voters may have applauded Mondale's courage and honesty, most preferred Reagan's optimistic view, which was that taxes did not need to be raised because the country would simply outgrow the deficits. Six years later, higher-than-projected budget deficits led President Bush to set aside his "read my lips: no new taxes" campaign pledge in order to avoid steep, across-the-board spending cuts mandated by the 1985 Gramm-Rudman-Hollings Balanced Budget Act. Bush's decision was necessary to reach a compromise with congressional Democrats and avoid spending cuts painful to both parties' constituencies. Politically, however, the decision proved harmful to the president's standing, particularly within his own party. Moreover, he received little credit for courageously putting policy ahead of politics.

Competence

Competence refers to a set of qualities that make it likely that the individual can handle the job. Intelligence, knowledge, and experience are frequently mentioned as components of competence. It seems incontrovertible that an individual who is inexperienced, uninformed, and not very smart would most likely be an incompetent president. Clearly, some presidential candidates have failed to win their party's nomination because of questions about their competence. Several candidates who were able to excite a particular constituency and achieve some success in presidential primary elections found that their lack of experience led other voters to question whether they were capable of handling the job of being president. Recent examples of such candidates include Democrats John Edwards and Howard Dean in 2004, Republican Steve Forbes in 1996, and any number of Republican challengers to Mitt Romney in 2012, including Rick Perry, Herman Cain, and Michelle Bachmann. Those who have won the nomination despite limited political experience, such as Barack Obama, found it essential to demonstrate that they had the knowledge to handle the job. Televised presidential debates have helped several relatively inexperienced presidential candidates do this. John Kennedy's debate performances against the sitting vice president, Richard Nixon; Carter's success in his debates with the incumbent president, Gerald Ford; Reagan's performance against Carter four years later; and Obama's showing against the far more experienced Senator McCain helped these candidates convince voters that they were capable of handling the presidency.

Questions of competence also extend to vice-presidential candidates, whose most prominent responsibility, if elected, is to succeed to the presidency on short notice and under the most trying of circumstances. Sarah Palin's inability to demonstrate sufficient understanding of major policy issues in her media interviews during the 2008 campaign hurt the Republican ticket, even though her running mate, Senator McCain, had a lengthy record of government experience. Similarly, Spiro Agnew and Dan Quayle, each plucked from relative obscurity to join their party's ticket in 1968 and 1988, respectively, were widely portrayed as having only a very shallow understanding of public policy issues and world affairs, although this did not prevent Republican victories in the general election in those years. In 2000, on the other hand, when Bush selected Richard Cheney as his running mate, Cheney's legislative experience as a former member of Congress, intimate understanding of the executive branch as Chief of Staff to President Ford, and knowledge of defense policy and foreign affairs from previous service as Secretary of Defense to the first President Bush, strengthened the ticket and helped to diminish concerns about George W. Bush's limited experience in national politics. Similar considerations were behind Obama's choice of Joseph Biden, who had 36 years of service in the U.S. Senate, including 12 as chairman or ranking member of the Foreign Affairs Committee, the jurisdiction of which encompassed Obama's most notable liability as a candidate for president.

Other traits that might be captured by competence are being stable, dependable, and responsible. All of these aspects of competence are qualities that are widely seen as desirable. Nevertheless, candidates do not always appear to benefit from being ranked highly on some aspects of competence. While it is hard to imagine any voter complaining that a candidate is too competent, it seems that sometimes being seen as too intelligent or too experienced has hurt a candidate. It may be that the problem in such cases is an inability to relate to the voters. Al Gore was perceived by some voters in 2000 as someone who acted "like he knows it all." In 1992, President Bush was seen by some as a person who had been in Washington so long that he had lost touch with the problems of ordinary citizens. Some candidates, such as Reagan in 1980, have touted their lack of federal government experience as a virtue, presenting themselves as "outsiders" who were not part of the "mess" in Washington. The fact that several governors with no federal government service have been elected president in recent decades (e.g., Carter, Reagan, Clinton, and George W. Bush) demonstrates that while voters probably want someone who has political experience, it need not be experience in Washington. It also may be that once candidates exceed a certain threshold on competence, they benefit little from even more favorable perceptions.

Competence and leadership appear to be highly related traits. It is hard to imagine how someone could be regarded as a strong leader but also incompetent. It is not just that these are two empirically related traits. There is considerable conceptual overlap between leadership and competence. A president who does not seem to exercise sufficient control over his administration may be seen as a weak leader, but we could also regard this as a lack of competence, in the sense that the president is not a capable manager of government. A competent president should be open to facts and opinions, and should carefully weigh these facts and opinions in making a decision. However, making rash and ill-advised decisions also suggests a lack of leadership skills.

While competence and leadership are intertwined, we think that they can be conceptually distinguished, even if a gray area separates the two. We define competence in terms of intelligence, knowledge, experience, good judgment, and stability. A competent president is able to make sound decisions and to manage the government effectively. Leadership refers to the ability to take decisive actions, to get things done, and to inspire and lead the nation. Thus, a president might be regarded as very competent, in the sense of being a good manager of government, but not a strong leader, in the sense of being inspiring and decisive. President Ford probably illustrates this combination as well as any recent president. Robert Dole and the Democratic nominees from Mondale to Kerry who went on to lose the general election also were seen by many voters as experienced and knowledgeable, yet uninspiring. It also is possible for a presidential candidate to be seen as a strong leader, but not particularly knowledgeable about government affairs. That was precisely the assessment that many voters had of Bush in 2000 and 2004, although it did not prevent him from winning both elections. As president, Reagan was considered a strong leader, but one who lacked management skills, which is another aspect of competence.

Integrity

Integrity is widely regarded as a highly desirable character trait. One aspect of integrity refers to how truthful an individual is. Thus, voters prefer a candidate who does not misrepresent facts, who does not bend the truth, and who is not deceptive in his or her statements. Candidates who are perceived as deficient in this area generally suffer; those who can portray themselves positively tend to gain. Gore in 2000, for example, was not helped by perceptions that he exaggerated, made false claims, and stretched the truth for his political benefit. In 1976, the first presidential election after the Watergate scandals, Carter emphasized that he would bring honesty to the White House; voter confidence that he would do so undoubtedly contributed to his narrow election victory. Related to honesty are sincerity and authenticity. Sincere candidates are clear and frank about their beliefs. Being authentic usually is not carefully defined by media pundits, who often cite this characteristic as important to voters, but the pundits seem to mean being believable and sincere, rather than phony; candidates are not authentic if they pretend to be something other than who they really are. In this sense, authenticity seems to be part of sincerity, and therefore integrity. Republican presidential nominee Mitt Romney was criticized throughout his party's primary elections, as well as by the Obama campaign, as an insincere and inauthentic candidate who was all too willing to tell voters what they wanted to hear. Being trustworthy is very similar to being honest, sincere, and authentic, but it also implies that the voters have faith that the individual will behave in an honest and ethical manner once in office.

Integrity also encompasses personal morality. Voters may expect the president to be a principled individual who sets a good moral example for the nation, although there is some disagreement about how important perceptions of personal morality really are to the electorate. Bush emphasized this in 2000, in talking about his intention to restore honor and dignity to the White House, no doubt hoping that voter unhappiness with Clinton's personal behavior would work to his benefit. Another aspect of integrity might be fairness; most voters expect presidents to be just and unprejudiced in their actions.

Integrity is logically quite different from either leadership or competence. It is easy to see how a candidate could be perceived of as honest, sincere, and moral, yet at the same time be seen as not very competent or much of a leader. This was a popular view of Carter near the end of his term in office. The converse—a competent, strong leader who lacks integrity—is equally plausible. Even before the notorious Watergate scandals, Nixon was assailed by critics for a lack of honesty, described by his nickname, "Tricky Dicky." Few called him incompetent, however. Clinton was viewed as similarly intelligent and knowledgeable, but also lacking in terms of personal morality. For these deficiencies, Clinton was dubbed "Slick Willie."

Empathy

Empathy is a slightly more elusive trait than leadership, competence, or integrity. Empathy can be defined specifically to mean the recognition of another person's emotions, to feel what another person feels. When political commentators referred to Clinton's ability to "feel your pain," they were identifying his empathy. In a broader sense, empathy means having compassion or concern for other people, especially most people, average people, or "ordinary" people. Thus, a candidate who is perceived as caring about people would be considered empathetic. Empathy also may be conceptualized as involving understanding as well as concern. Concern suggests a desire to help. Understanding implies comprehension of the situation. Voters who feel that a presidential candidate understands their problems (or the problems of ordinary or average Americans) are likely to see that candidate as being empathetic. A candidate who is perceived as "out of touch" most likely will be regarded as lacking empathy. Being sympathetic to the concerns of average citizens is another way of expressing empathy, as this encompasses concern, compassion, and understanding. In sum, we can regard empathy as comprising compassion, concern, understanding, sympathy, and a general ability to feel what others feel, to walk in others' shoes.

Why should voters care if the president is compassionate or concerned? It seems obvious why voters would desire a president who is trustworthy, competent, and a good leader. It is less clear why empathy should be important to voters. One possible answer is that voters see an empathetic president as one who will pursue policies that benefit the average American, or one who wakes up every morning thinking about the problems average Americans face, to paraphrase Clinton's often repeated articulation of this trait. Voters may believe that a president who understands the concerns and needs of ordinary citizens will be more likely to work on their behalf, as opposed to supporting policies that benefit groups who are already powerful and well-off. If this is the case, then voter perceptions of empathy are more connected to possible government policies than is true for other traits, such as competence or integrity. When voters speak of empathy in a presidential candidate, they probably are not concerned simply with a purely personal sense of sympathy or compassion—a person who is distraught if a coworker suffers misfortune or who feels sorrow if a disaster strikes some town, for example. Rather, they want a president who will understand the concerns of ordinary citizens and who will be supportive of government policies and actions to alleviate the problems faced by those in need. As we shall see later, empirical evidence supports this interpretation.

Warmth, Likability, and a Common Touch

Political commentators frequently identify warmth or likability as a critical trait for presidential candidates. A popular conception is that voters are drawn to candidates who are personally appealing. Media pundits frequently comment that voters like a candidate because he or she is someone whom the voters feel comfortable with or feel would be fun to be with—a person with whom you would like to share a beer or have dinner. For example, by the spring of 2012, pundits had already begun discussing the potential importance of likability to the presidential campaign. *Washington Post* columnist Kathleen Parker opined that a key strategy of the Obama campaign was to focus on personalities in order to make it easier for voters to overlook the president's policy shortcomings "simply because they like him."[10] In 2000 and 2004, Bush was widely portrayed as being a more likeable person than either of his opponents, Gore or Kerry, who were frequently described as cold, aloof, and as we will discuss in more detail below, elitist. Similarly, in 1996, Clinton was widely regarded as warmer than his opponent, Bob Dole, who was known for his dour disposition. Reagan was widely regarded as someone whom many voters liked personally, even if they disagreed with his policies. While many political analysts regard warmth as important, most political scientists do not consider it to be a significant trait, although a few do, as we noted above.

Another personal trait that seems to be related to warmth is what some commentators refer to as elitism. Pundits frequently claim that candidates who are seen as elitist (usually liberal Democrats) suffer at the polls because ordinary voters feel that they are unable to relate to such candidates. Unfortunately, the concept of elitism is often poorly defined by commentators. Having liberal social or cultural values sometimes seems to make a candidate an elitist, presumably because "ordinary" Americans are unable to understand how someone could favor such things as gay marriage, limitations on religion in public schools, or restrictions on gun ownership. Other commentators seem to focus on non-political lifestyle characteristics, including what kind of food a candidate eats or what kind of recreational activities he or she engages in. For example, Kerry was lampooned in 2004 for the way in which he ordered and ate a sandwich in Philadelphia, and Obama was ridiculed for his poor bowling skills during the 2008 campaign, as we discussed in Chapter 1. On the other hand, Bush received favorable press for attending a NASCAR race in 2000, and Clinton supposedly benefitted from playing his saxophone on a late night television show in 1992, as these appearances demonstrated that the candidates enjoyed activities to which ordinary Americans could easily relate. Similarly, Obama may have compensated for his inept bowling by some well-publicized efforts on the basketball court, including participating in a practice session with the University of North Carolina men's basketball team. The notion that candidates need a common touch in order to appeal to many voters is widespread in the popular media.

A concept that is related to warmth and elitism is authenticity. As we discussed earlier, authenticity can mean integrity; an authentic candidate is straightforward and honest about where he or she stands, not a phony person who says what voters want to hear or who tries to mislead them.

However, authenticity can also mean something else, as pundits sometimes use elitism and authenticity as antonyms. That is, an authentic candidate is someone whom most voters can relate to, in the sense of being "down to earth" or a "regular person," not an elitist. This meaning of authenticity overlaps considerably with warmth. Authentic candidates are the kind of people that a voter would enjoy being with. Thus, authenticity sometimes is used to refer to aspects of integrity, other times to refer to aspects of elitism, and sometimes it is unclear exactly what the term means.

In sum, when commentators view a candidate as likable, they usually seem to be referring to the candidate's warmth, authenticity, or lack of elitism. Typically, this means that the candidate is pleasant, friendly, down to earth, and has a common touch. However, sometimes the view is that a candidate is likable because he or she understands the problems of the ordinary citizen, which we consider to be empathy, a trait that we identify as important and discuss above. Moreover, authenticity can also refer to integrity, another trait that we consider to be important. Finally, we should realize that when voters state that they like or have a favorable opinion of a candidate, this does not necessarily mean that they find the candidate likable, in the sense of being warm. Voters could like the candidate because they see the individual as being empathetic, trustworthy, inspiring, or competent. Unfortunately, discussions of candidate likability in the popular media are too often vague about exactly what this means or why voters find a candidate to be likeable.

MEASURING PERCEPTIONS OF
CANDIDATE CHARACTER TRAITS

The most direct method for measuring voter perceptions of the character traits of presidential candidates is to ask voters to rate candidates on specific traits. The American National Election Study surveys, which are the best survey data on voting behavior available and are the data that we rely on in this study, have asked such questions in every presidential election starting in 1980. The same format has been used in each survey. Respondents are asked how well a phrase, such as "he would provide strong leadership" or "he is honest," characterizes each candidate. In most years, survey respondents were asked about seven different traits, but in some years more questions were asked. Because the ANES surveys also contain a rich set of items on government performance, policy issues, ideological orientations, and party identification, these data allow us to examine the effect of trait perceptions on the vote while also considering the impact of other attitudes and orientations. To illustrate these trait items, we present responses to these questions from the 1992 ANES survey in Table 2.1. This is a particularly good year to use as an example because respondents were asked to rate Bush and Clinton on nine different character traits, more than in most years.[11] Moreover, each of the four trait dimensions—leadership, competence, integrity, and empathy—is represented by at least two questions.

Table 2.1 Perceptions of the Character Traits of the Presidential Candidates, 1992

Character trait	Percent who said that the trait characterizes Bush					Percent who said that the trait characterizes Clinton				
	Extremely well	Quite well	Not too well	Not well at all	Total	Extremely well	Quite well	Not too well	Not well at all	Total
Strong leadership	13.0	42.2	35.9	8.8	100	13.0	51.5	28.6	6.9	100
Gets things done	7.3	35.3	45.9	11.5	100	11.4	60.3	22.8	5.6	100
Inspiring	7.5	32.0	44.6	15.9	100	13.7	47.9	29.8	8.7	100
Knowledgeable	22.4	60.9	14.4	2.2	100	21.1	63.1	13.2	2.6	100
Intelligent	26.0	57.2	13.4	3.5	100	25.4	64.3	9.3	1.0	100
Honest	18.1	43.8	27.4	10.8	100	8.4	45.8	33.7	12.1	100
Moral	28.5	53.5	13.7	4.3	100	5.4	41.6	39.1	13.9	100
Cares about people	8.9	28.7	35.7	26.7	100	17.3	50.7	23.8	8.1	100
Compassionate	14.9	43.2	33.5	8.4	100	16.3	65.5	15.9	2.2	100

Note: See the text for the exact wording of the character trait items.
Source: American National Election Study 1992 election survey. Only major-party voters are included in the analysis.

Each ANES trait item asked the respondent whether a certain personal trait characterized a candidate extremely well, quite well, not too well, or not well at all; this same response set has been used in other years as well. Although most researchers have treated this set of possible responses as a four-point scale, we question that approach. The difference between saying that a trait characterizes an individual "extremely well" versus "quite well" seems theoretically small. Many people might use the two terms almost interchangeably. Furthermore, while "not too well" is not as negative as "not well at all," the two terms seem close to each other, and both seem far from "quite well" or "extremely well." Theoretically, the distance between the second and the third categories seems much greater than the distance between the first and second categories or between the third and fourth categories.[12] For these reasons, we score the responses to each trait item from + 2 to –2, where +2 is the most favorable, +1 the next most favorable, and the two unfavorable responses receive scores of –1 and –2, respectively. This method expands the distance between "quite well" and "not very well" to two points.[13] Using this scoring system, we can calculate mean scores for each item. These are presented in Table 2.2. With this scoring system, positive mean scores indicate a surplus of favorable responses, while negative scores indicate the opposite

We use the ANES trait items for most of the analysis in this book. Sometimes we combine the trait items into an overall index that captures the net advantage that one candidate has over the other on the full set of traits, while at other times we focus on specific trait dimensions. Relying on the scoring system described above, we calculate mean scores for our trait measures, generate correlations between trait items, examine the relationship

Table 2.2   Mean Scores for Trait Perceptions of Bush and Clinton, 1992

	Bush	Clinton
Strong leadership	.15	.26
Gets things done	–.19	.35
Inspiring	–.29	.22
Knowledgeable	.86	.66
Intelligent	.88	.77
Honest	.30	.08
Moral	.86	–.06
Cares about people	–.42	.34
Compassionate	.26	.59

Note: See the text for the exact wording of the character trait items and for the details of the calculation of mean scores.
Source: American National Election Study 1992 election survey. Only major-party voters are included in the analysis.

between perceptions of candidate character traits and the vote, and analyze the determinants of these trait perceptions. While we have only presented data from 1992 in this section in order to save space, comparable data for all of the years are available elsewhere.[14] We regard the ANES trait items as good measures of voter perceptions of candidate character traits, but they have some limitations, which we discuss below.

One limitation of the ANES trait items is that the list of traits included in any given survey varies from year to year. Some traits questions, such as the ones about strong leadership or honesty, were asked in every election year. Other trait items, such as whether the candidates are inspiring or compassionate, appeared in some surveys but not in others. Therefore, comparisons across election years are not based on perfect matches. However, this is not a serious problem. Different trait items tap the same underlying trait dimension, so in each year, with the exception of empathy in 1980, we have measures of each of the four trait dimensions discussed above—leadership, competence, integrity, and empathy—even if the specific measures may not be identical. For example, from 1980 through 1996, respondents were asked whether the candidates were inspiring, but they were not asked that in 2000, 2004, or 2008. However, responses to the question about whether the candidate is inspiring are highly correlated with responses to the question asking about whether the candidate is a strong leader, which was asked in every year. Therefore, we can regard the question about being inspiring as one measure of a more general leadership dimension, which is measured in some fashion in each year. The same principle applies to the other trait dimensions—competence, integrity, and empathy.

A second limitation is that in two years, 2000 and 2004, a few items were worded negatively. In other words, respondents were asked whether the candidates were dishonest, rather than whether they were honest, which is what respondents were asked in previous and subsequent years. This might not seem to be a problem, as saying that a candidate is not dishonest seems equivalent to saying that he is honest. Unfortunately, that is not quite the case. Our analysis indicates that some respondents were confused by the negative wording of the questions, making these items less accurate measures of respondent attitudes.[15] Fortunately, there is at least one positively worded item for each of the four trait dimensions available to us for each election year, and we can rely on these items to compare the effect of perceptions of particular traits on the vote across elections. For example, the question about the morality of the candidates was worded positively in every year. Therefore, it can be used to compare the impact of integrity on the vote across years, which helps to mitigate the problems created by asking the question about honesty in a positive fashion in most years but a negative fashion in some years.

A third problem is that in 2008 the ANES experimented with a new set of response categories for the trait items. One-half of the respondents received the version of the question that had been asked in earlier years, which allowed the respondent to say that the phrase applied to the candidate extremely well, quite well, not so well, or not well at all. The other half were asked a new version of the question, one that had a different set of responses. These respondents were asked whether the trait characterized the candidate extremely well, very well, moderately well, slightly well, or not well at all. Including the "moderately well" category changes how respondents reply.[16] Some who would have chosen a more positive or negative response instead select the somewhat ambiguous "moderately well" response. While this new set of response categories may be just as good as the old version, it makes comparisons across the years more difficult.[17] For that reason, when it is important to compare identical items across the years, our analysis of the 2008 data relies on the old question wording. In 2012, the ANES used only the new version of the trait questions; because of the problems of comparability to earlier years, we analyze the 2012 data in a separate chapter.

TRAIT DIMENSIONS

Our theoretical conceptualization of presidential candidate character traits has defined four trait dimensions that are relevant to voters. While these four dimensions—leadership, competence, integrity, and empathy—make theoretical sense, we also want to know if they match the empirical evidence. Do the voters group traits into these four categories? To answer that question, we examine the relationships among the various trait items that have been asked in the ANES surveys. Naturally, responses to all of the trait items tend to be intercorrelated. Respondents who rank a candidate high on one trait are likely to rate that candidate high on the other traits as well. However, the strength of these correlations varies, and we can see whether the strongest correlations are between the items that define a specific dimension.

To illustrate this analysis, we examine responses to the trait items that were asked in the 1992 ANES survey, which are displayed in Table 2.1. As we noted earlier, this is a good year to analyze patterns of responses among these items because respondents were asked to classify both major party candidates on nine different traits. Each of the four trait dimensions defined above is represented by at least two questions. In other years, fewer questions were asked, and some trait dimensions were represented by just one item. The correlations between each pair of items are in Table 2.3. The first three items in the list (whether the candidate is a strong leader, inspiring, and is someone who gets things done) are theoretically part of a leadership dimension. Responses to these three items are highly correlated, with all of the correlation coefficients equaling or exceeding .48, whereas responses to these items tend to be less strongly correlated with the other items. The one exception is the item asking whether the candidate really cares about people; that item is fairly highly correlated with the three leadership items. However, that item is even more strongly correlated with the question on compassion, which is what we would expect, given that both the "really cares" and the compassion items are theoretically part of an empathy dimension. The responses to the questions about the candidate's intelligence and knowledge, both of which are aspects of a competence dimension, are more highly correlated with each other than with any other items. This is also true for the items dealing with honesty and morality, both of which define an integrity dimension.[18]

We conducted the same analysis for several other election years (1996, 2000, and 2004) and the overall findings are similar to those in Table 2.3.[19] The items for each trait dimension tend to be more strongly correlated with each other than with the items from other trait dimensions. The exceptions to this pattern seem to be the result of some problems with the data, such

Table 2.3   Correlations among Candidate Traits, 1992

Bush								
	1	2	3	4	5	6	7	8
1. Strong leader								
2. Inspiring	.52							
3. Gets things done	.54	.50						
4. Knowledgeable	.35	.30	.25					
5. Intelligent	.36	.30	.26	.40				
6. Moral	.31	.28	.24	.31	.35			
7. Honest	.41	.40	.36	.34	.38	.49		
8. Really cares	.53	.52	.48	.29	.33	.32	.48	
9. Compassionate	.46	.42	.38	.30	.35	.42	.50	.57

Clinton								
	1	2	3	4	5	6	7	8
1. Strong leader								
2. Inspiring	.54							
3. Gets things done	.58	.48						
4. Knowledgeable	.37	.34	.41					
5. Intelligent	.30	.30	.34	.46				
6. Moral	.37	.42	.34	.26	.21			
7. Honest	.46	.48	.43	.30	.21	.57		
8. Really cares	.53	.53	.51	.33	.33	.43	.51	
9. Compassionate	.38	.41	.44	.33	.39	.36	.37	.54

Note: Entries are bivariate Pearson correlation coefficients.
Source: 1992 American National Election Study. Only major party voters are included in the analysis.

as the use of negative items in 2000 and 2004.[20] In the years in which all items are worded in a positive fashion, the two integrity variables, honesty and morality, are highly correlated, and they are more highly correlated with each other than with other trait items. However, when the question on honesty is negatively worded, then honesty and morality are not as highly correlated. The two or three leadership items asked in each of these years also are more strongly related to each other than to the other trait measures, as is the case for the two or three competence items asked in each of the years. The same pattern is generally true for the two empathy items asked in most of the years (whether the candidate is compassionate and cares about people). In sum, when the items are worded in a positive fashion, they fit the four theoretical dimensions that we outlined quite well, although there occasionally are a few anomalies.[21]

We conclude that leadership, competence, integrity, and empathy are theoretically relevant dimensions of character traits, but we recognize some problems in accurately measuring these trait dimensions in the two years when negatively worded items were used. Our solution to this problem is to rely on positively worded items to assess the effect of specific trait dimensions, but to use all of the trait items, positive and negative, to form any overall indices of trait perceptions. We use all of the trait questions to form the overall index in each year because we believe that the benefit of using all of the items outweighs the cost of including a couple of negatively worded items. However, when it comes to measuring specific traits, such as integrity, we prefer to use positively worded items. For example, if we +measured integrity in 2000 or 2004 by using the item on honesty or by combining the items on honesty and morality, we would not have results comparable to 1992 or 1996, when the item on honesty was positively worded. By using the item on morality to measure integrity, we have the same item, worded in a positive fashion for all four election years. Empirical analysis of our data supports these decisions.[22]

ALTERNATIVE MEASURES OF TRAIT PERCEPTIONS

A number of scholars have measured voter perceptions of presidential candidate character traits by relying on a different set of questions asked in the ANES election surveys. In each year, respondents were asked what they liked and disliked about the Democratic and Republican candidates, particularly as reasons to vote for or against either candidate. Respondents could provide up to five likes or dislikes about each candidate. These responses can be used to create measures of the perceptions of candidate character traits and of other reasons for liking or disliking a candidate. Before 1980, these were the only measures of trait perceptions that were available to users of the ANES data. The authors of *The American Voter,* for example, relied on these like/dislike questions in their analysis of the 1952 and 1956 presidential elections, and their analysis indicated that Eisenhower won those elections in large part because of his favorable personal image.[23]

Using the responses to the like/dislike items has advantages and disadvantages compared to using the closed items when it comes to measuring perceptions of candidate personal traits. When a voter provides reasons for liking or disliking a candidate in response to open-ended questions, these reasons are likely to be ones that are important to the voter and ones that the voter feels fairly confident about with regard to how the candidate should be classified. This is not necessarily true for the closed trait items. Individuals might provide a response to a specific question about a trait item even if it is something that they do not care much about. For example, a voter might respond that a candidate is compassionate if asked about that specific trait, even if the voter is not concerned very much about that trait or is not certain about how compassionate the candidate truly is.

On the other hand, the open-ended questions have some disadvantages. Many voters might not clearly and fully articulate their reasons for liking or disliking a candidate when asked an open-ended question. They might provide very general comments when they truly have more specific reasons in mind, and they could fail to mention some important factors. For example, if a voter does not volunteer an opinion that a candidate is knowledgeable, should we conclude that the voter does not think that the candidate possesses that trait? If a voter fails to mention anything about honesty or trust when asked what he or she likes or dislikes about a candidate, is it reasonable to conclude that the voter has no opinion about the candidate's integrity? The responses to the open-ended items may well be a somewhat incomplete picture of the respondent's true likes and dislikes about the candidates. The characteristics that a voter cites as a reason for voting for or against a candidate undoubtedly are important to that voter, but other characteristics that are somewhat less salient but still important to the voter may not be identified.

In order to compare methods of measuring perceptions of candidate character traits, we also used the responses to the open-ended like/dislike questions about the two candidates. We classified all mentions of candidate personal qualities into the following categories: leadership, competence, integrity, empathy, warmth, and other. These traits were defined in the terms discussed earlier. Leadership encompassed all positive and negative references to being a strong leader, decisive, inspiring, and so on. Competence included references to being experienced, capable, knowledgeable, intelligent, dependable, or their opposites. Integrity included references to being (dis)honest, (un)trustworthy, and (a)moral. Empathy included references to (not) caring about others, (not) being compassionate, and being (un)concerned. Warmth included references to being personally likeable, friendly, or gregarious, plus mentions of factors that indicate a lack of warmth, such as being aloof, cold, or lacking a personal touch. The "other" category included all responses that did not seem to fit anywhere else, including general favorable or unfavorable comments (e.g., he is the best candidate; he would do the best job) and a variety of idiosyncratic responses (e.g., undemocratic, negative campaign tactics). Also included in the other category are references to personal characteristics, such as mentions of demographic and other background characteristics (e.g., overcoming adversity in life).

Table 2.4 summarizes perceptions of the personal traits of the major-party presidential candidates in 1992. We use this year to provide a comparison to the results displayed in Table 2.1; results for other years are in the chapter appendix (see Table 2.A2).[24] The entries in the tables are the average number of responses in each category. For example, the average number of positive responses about Bush's leadership was .058, a score that would result from 5.8 percent of the respondents providing one positive response each.[25] The average number of negative responses about Bush's leadership was .084. We then calculated a net score for each trait, defined as the number of positive mentions (i.e., reasons for liking the candidate) minus the number of negative mentions (i.e., dislikes) for each trait. This measure combines both the number of mentions of each trait and the relative favorableness of the mentions. If there is a large number of mentions of a trait for a candidate, but the mentions are equally divided between likes and dislikes, the net score will be zero, just as it would be if there were no mentions of that trait. For example, Bush's net score for leadership is -.026, indicating more negative than positive responses. We also calculated the average number of responses in each category, which is the number in parentheses. The average number of leadership mentions for Bush is just .142, which is simply the sum of the number of positive and negative mentions. This number, shown in parentheses, indicates that most respondents failed to make a single comment, positive or negative, about Bush's leadership ability. The same is true for Clinton's leadership ability.

The data in Table 2.4 do not always match those in Tables 2.1 (or Table 2.2, if you prefer to look at mean scores). For example, Table 2.4 indicates that Clinton had only a very modest advantage on leadership over Bush in 1992. There were as many negative references to his leadership abilities as there were positive references, and his net score of zero only slightly exceeded Bush's weak negative score (-.026). But in Table 2.1 we can see that Clinton did far better than Bush on two of the three leadership items—being inspiring and getting things done. On integrity, Bush has a clear advantage in Table 2.4, but his advantage on this trait is greater in Table 2.1, especially for the question about morality. Finally, Clinton has little advantage on empathy in Table 2.4, simply because so few respondents made comments that fell into this category. In Table 2.1, we see a sizable advantage for Clinton on empathy. Similar comparisons for other years show some common patterns. The responses to the open-ended, like/dislike items often differ from the responses to the closed items. Candidate advantages that are present in the responses to the closed items are typically present in the open-ended responses as well, but the extent of the advantage sometimes differs substantially.

A comparison of the two measurement methods indicates an interesting pattern. There is a general tendency for responses to the open-ended items to be more negative. For example, the data in Table 2.4 indicate that

Table 2.4   References to Character Traits in the Candidate Like/Dislike Questions, 1992

	Bush			Clinton		
Trait	Likes	Dislikes	Net Score	Likes	Dislikes	Net Score
Leadership	.058	.084	−.026 (.142)	.083	.083	.000 (.165)
Competence	.300	.191	.109 (.491)	.135	.225	−.090 (.361)
Integrity	.078	.094	.016 (.173)	.040	.301	−.261 (.340)
Empathy	.010	.010	.000 (.020)	.000	.018	.018 (.018)
Warmth	.008	.012	−.004 (.020)	.013	.020	.006 (.033)
Other	.123	.114	.009 (.238)	.268	.111	.157 (.380)

Note: Entries in the Likes and Dislikes columns are the average number of responses in that category. For example, the average number of responses that mentioned leadership ability as a reason for liking Bush was .058 (i.e., for every 100 respondents, there were slightly fewer than six such responses). The net score is the difference between the average number of positive and negative responses, and the number in parentheses is the total number of mentions (positive and negative) of that trait for that candidate. For example, the average number of responses that identified leadership ability as a reason for either liking or disliking Bush was .142 (i.e., slightly more than 14 such responses for every 100 respondents), and the negative net score indicates that there were more negative than positive mentions of Bush's leadership ability.
Source: 1992 American National Election Study. Only major party voters are included in the analysis.

on leadership Clinton had a score of zero and Bush had a slightly negative score. The responses to the leadership items in Table 2.1 are more favorable for both candidates. Similarly, Clinton has a negative score on competence in Table 2.4, but in Table 2.1 he has a very positive set of responses, at least as positive as those for Bush. The same is true for integrity: Clinton has scores on the closed integrity items that are fairly evenly balanced between positive and negative responses, but on the open-ended items he has strongly negative scores; Bush has quite positive integrity scores on the closed items but only weakly positive integrity scores on the open-ended items. This suggests that when respondents mention a character trait as a reason for voting for or against a candidate, they are particularly likely to cite something that the candidate falls short on. For traits where the candidate simply meets normal expectations, a voter is not as likely to mention that fact. If, for example, a voter thinks that a candidate is basically honest or knowledgeable, but not exceptionally so, the voter may not mention being honest or knowledgeable as a reason for liking the candidate. On the other hand, if a voter thinks that a candidate is dishonest or lacks knowledge, the voter is more likely to mention this, as the candidate is falling short of normal expectations. In years when a candidate was portrayed in the media as falling short on leadership, competence, or integrity, voters tended to offer the same criticisms in their responses to the open-ended items: Kerry did poorly on leadership in 2004; Bush did poorly on competence in 2000; and Clinton did poorly on integrity in 1996, for example (see Table 2.A2).

Because we have alternative methods for measuring trait perceptions, it is worthwhile to determine which is better: the responses to the closed trait items or the responses to the open-ended candidate like/dislike questions. We have compared both measurement methods and have found that measures of trait perceptions that are based on the closed items do a better job of predicting the vote than the measures that are based on the open-ended questions.[26] For that reason, we rely more on the closed trait items in our subsequent analysis.

Although the closed items are at least slightly better predictors of the vote, the open-ended questions are useful for determining how important various trait items are to the electorate. In particular, it is notable that very few respondents mentioned anything about warmth or empathy as a reason for liking or disliking either candidate in 1992.[27] Adding together the positive and negative responses for both candidates that refer to warmth or likability yields a score of about .05, a score that we would get if 5 percent of the respondents provided one response each in this category (or if fewer than 5 percent provided more than one response each). If every voter had made just one response, positive or negative, about the warmth of either candidate, the average score would have been 1.0. The paucity of mentions of warmth or likability casts doubt on the conventional wisdom that voters are strongly attracted to, or repelled from, candidates on the basis of this characteristic. If this characteristic truly was one of the most important traits to voters, we would expect that voters would cite it as much as they cite other characteristics, such as leadership or competence. Warmth or likability may not be irrelevant to voters, but it seems far from the top of their list of important personal characteristics for a president.

Of course, the 1992 figures may not be typical. Perhaps more references to warmth occurred in other years. To investigate that possibility, we calculated the average number of references to each trait dimension (leadership, competence, integrity, empathy, and warmth) for a number of years; this average includes positive and negative responses to either the Democratic or the Republican candidate. The results of this analysis are presented in Figure 2.1. References to leadership, competence, and integrity vary across the years. In 1996, there was a particularly high number of integrity responses; in 2004, there was a high number of leadership responses. On the other hand, references to warmth are relatively low in every year. The highest number is in 2000, when there were 140 such mentions per 1,000 respondents. Warmth seems to matter to some voters, but this candidate character trait ranks well below leadership, competence, and integrity in importance. If likability mattered as much as many pundits claim, we would expect to see many more mentions of this trait by voters, especially in years when the political commentators and columnists so uniformly identified one candidate as lacking warmth.[28]

The discrepancy between these data and the views of many pundits probably stems from some misinterpretation of public opinion data. Polls generally ask respondents whether they like or have a favorable view of a candidate. Not surprisingly, voters are strongly inclined to vote for the candidate that they like more or have a more favorable view of. The question is what voters mean when they say that they have a favorable view of a candidate. More careful analysis of the data suggests that voters often are referring to such things as being honest, forthright, inspiring, dynamic, and concerned about people like them. When voters say that they do not like a candidate, this does not necessarily mean that they do not find the candidate to be a friendly, jovial individual. More likely, it means that they see the candidate as insincere, uninspiring, weak, or unconcerned. Conversely, voters

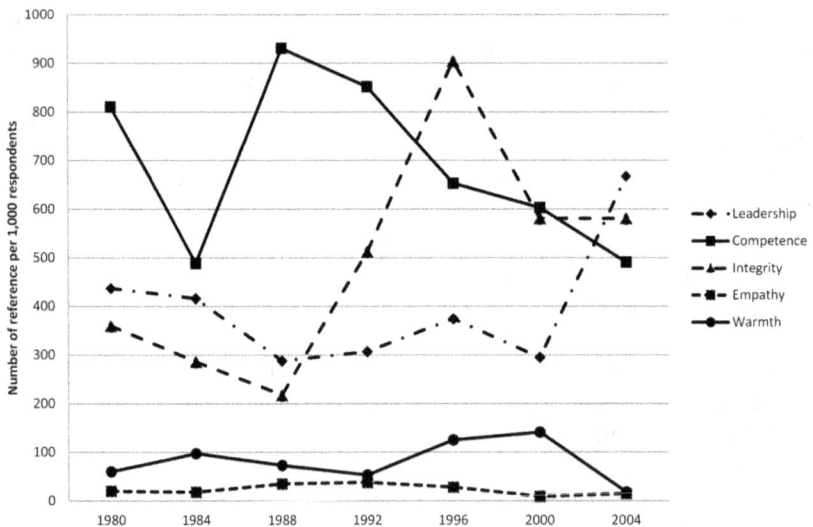

Figure 2.1   Total References to Each Character Trait in the Candidate Like/Dislike Questions, 1980–2004

Note: Lines represent the number of responses per 1,000 major party voters.

who say that they have a favorable view of a presidential candidate may be saying that the individual has the qualities to be a good president, not that the individual is a nice person to socialize with.

There also are relatively few references to empathy as a reason for preferring a candidate. The paucity of such mentions in the open-ended questions as reasons for liking or disliking candidates could be interpreted as indicating that voters are unconcerned about empathy. If asked to do so, they may rate a candidate on an empathy item, such as whether the candidate cares about people like them, but they do not use empathy as a basis for preferring one candidate over another. While this might seem to be a plausible interpretation, just as we reasoned in the above discussion of warmth or elitism, we believe that it is an incorrect one in this case. As later analysis will show, voters' responses to the closed empathy items do correlate strongly with their votes, even with other relevant variables (including the other traits) held constant. This is strong evidence that perceptions of empathy affect the vote. The reason why voters do not make references to empathy when asked open-ended, like/dislike questions, even though they seem to vote on the basis of such perceptions, is that they instead refer to a candidate being good for specific groups. Such responses are commonly made to the like/dislike questions about the presidential candidates. Respondents often say that a candidate is good (or bad) for working people, middle-class people, small businessmen, old people, women, blacks, and so on. Some responses are to more narrowly defined groups (e.g., farmers, veterans), but many are to far broader groups, such as middle-class or working-class people. Most of these responses can be interpreted as reflecting an empathy component. For example, if a middle-class voter sees one candidate as good for middle-class people and the other candidate as good for big business, the voter is likely to infer that the first candidate is the one who cares about people. In 2004, for example, about one voter in eight made some reference to a group or groups as a reason for liking or disliking Bush or Kerry, and about 90 percent of these references were favorable to Kerry (i.e., a reason for liking Kerry or disliking Bush), a pattern that is consistent with the fact that Kerry did better on the single closed item that measured empathy.

The interpretation that a number of voters infer empathy from their perceptions of the types of groups the candidate appears to favor also is consistent with the findings that Democratic candidates are generally perceived as more empathetic and that Democrats own issues related to the social safety net.[29] The responses to the open-ended items are not rich enough for us to understand fully the reasoning of voters, but it seems plausible that empathy is assessed by voters somewhat differently than leadership, integrity, or competence. When voters assess a candidate's empathy, they do not seem to be thinking about caring for someone personally, such as whether a candidate feels genuinely sorry about the misfortune of others. Instead, they have in mind concern about groups of people and how candidates would use the government to help them. All of this suggests that perceptions of empathy may have stronger public policy overtones than is the case for the other personal traits, an interpretation that fits with our earlier conceptual discussion of empathy.

CONCLUSION

Voters perceive character traits of presidential candidates. In doing so, they distinguish between different traits, sometimes seeing a candidate favorably on some traits, but less favorably on others. For most voters, the relevant trait dimensions are leadership, competence, integrity, and empathy. Contrary to the views of many pundits, few voters seem to choose candidates on the basis of general warmth or likability. Rather, voters rely on more relevant character traits in assessing the candidates. In this sense, voters are not as shallow in their reasoning as many pundits claim. This does not necessarily mean that voters make their judgments about these character traits in a logical or sophisticated fashion, relying on considerable information. What it does mean is that even if voters form their assessments of candidate character in a superficial manner, they are attempting to assess relevant traits, such as leadership ability, not irrelevant ones, such as whether the candidate would be an affable companion.

We are able to measure voter perceptions of candidate character traits either by using questions that ask voters to rate candidates on specific traits or by using responses to open-ended, like/dislike questions about the presidential candidates. We find that the specific trait questions provide better measures of trait perceptions, at least in terms of how well they are related to the vote. We have data for these trait items from 1980 on, so we rely on these closed trait measures in our subsequent data analysis. In doing so, we do not treat these trait items as having four evenly-spaced responses. Rather, we regard the two positive responses ("extremely well" and "quite well") and the two negative responses ("not too well" and "not well at all") as both being closer together than the middle two responses ("quite well" and "not too well"), and we use a scoring system that reflects this view. Indeed, the ANES implicitly acknowledged that the four responses were not evenly spaced when it later modified the responses to the trait questions so that there was an additional response (moderately well) between the two positive and the two negative choices. The 2012 ANES survey only used this new, five-category set of responses for the trait questions, creating some lack of comparability to earlier years, and for that reason, we analyze the 2012 data in a separate chapter.[30]

Chapter 2
Appendix

Table 2.A1   Factor Analysis for Candidate Character Traits, 1992

	Bush			
	Factor			
Trait	1	2	3	4
Strong leader	**.707**	.288	.262	.123
Inspiring	**.698**	.323	.162	.094
Gets things done	**.859**	.099	.067	.157
Knowledgeable	.184	.078	**.850**	.114
Intelligent	.131	.206	**.790**	.194
Moral	.135	.135	.183	**.909**
Honest	.233	.475	.208	**.581**
Really cares	.455	**.723**	.138	.085
Compassionate	.195	**.814**	.166	.256

Proportion of variance explained by the factors = .74.

	Clinton			
	Factor			
Trait	1	2	3	4
Strong leader	**.825**	.192	.164	.107
Inspiring	**.647**	.336	.123	.243
Gets things done	**.754**	.122	.249	.211
Knowledgeable	.315	.185	**.820**	−.039
Intelligent	.088	.023	**.778**	.405
Moral	.133	**.878**	.115	.179

(*Continued*)

Table 2.A1   (*Continued*)

	Clinton			
	Factor			
Trait	1	2	3	4
Honest	.374	**.763**	.088	.135
Really cares	.527	.318	.073	**.572**
Compassionate	.228	.188	.201	**.845**

Proportion of variance explained by the factors = .75.
Note: Entries are factor loadings from a principal components analysis with varimax rotation. Numbers in bold identify the factor on which each trait loaded most heavily.
Source: 1992 American National Election Study. Only major party voters are included in the analysis.

Table 2.A2   References to Candidate Character Traits, 1980–2004

	2004		2000		1996		1992	
Trait	Bush	Kerry	Bush	Gore	Dole	Clinton	Bush	Clinton
Leadership	.105	−.284	−.062	−.084	−.065	−.089	−.026	.000
	(.263)	(.404)	(.136)	(.159)	(.175)	(.199)	(.142)	(.165)
Competence	−.052	.077	−.053	.171	.199	.106	.109	−.090
	(.189)	(.302)	(.303)	(.300)	(.423)	(.230)	(.491)	(.361)
Integrity	.110	−.129	.060	−.199	.175	−.572	.016	−.261
	(.356)	(.225)	(.253)	(.328)	(.265)	(.640)	(.173)	(.340)
Empathy	.001	.006	.001	.006	−.002	.012	.000	.018
	(.009)	(.006)	(.003)	(.006)	(.009)	(.019)	(.020)	(.018)
Warmth	.001	.001	.011	−.003	−.026	.024	−.004	.006
	(.009)	(.009)	(.075)	(.066)	(.063)	(.062)	(.020)	(.033)
Other	.014	−.012	.054	.011	−.257	.042	.009	.157
	(.187)	(.375)	(.381)	(.401)	(.555)	(.325)	(.238)	(.380)

	1988		1984		1980	
Trait	Bush	Dukakis	Reagan	Mondale	Reagan	Carter
Leadership	−.117	−.007	.068	−.170	−.031	−.157
	(.173)	(.115)	(.196)	(.220)	(.188)	(.249)
Competence	.315	−.128	.129	.002	.035	.125
	(.532)	(.399)	(.270)	(.215)	(.373)	(.438)

(*Continued*)

Table 2.A2 (*Continued*)

Trait	1988		1984		1980	
	Bush	Dukakis	Reagan	Mondale	Reagan	Carter
Integrity	−.004	.007	.044	.025	.018	.132
	(.122)	(.097)	(.152)	(.134)	(.098)	(.262)
Empathy	−.002	.021	−.002	.006	−.001	.001
	(.011)	(.024)	(.005)	(.006)	(.001)	(.001)
Warmth	−.003	−.014	.006	−.030	−.001	.007
	(.034)	(.039)	(.055)	(.041)	(.029)	(.032)
Other	−.055	.039	.036	−.014	−.055	−.041
	(.121)	(.080)	(.061)	(.130)	(.221)	(.167)

Note: Entries are the net mean scores for the candidate, which are calculated from responses to the candidate like-dislike items. Positive mean scores indicate more positive references than negative references to the specified trait. Mean total mentions of the trait for the candidate are in parentheses. See the text for details on the variables.

Source: 1980–2004 American National Election Studies. Only major party voters are included in the analysis.

NOTES

1. Donald R. Kinder, "Presidential Character Revisited," in *Political Cognition,* ed. Richard R. Lau and David O. Sears (Hillsdale, NJ: Lawrence Erlbaum, 1986), 233–255.
2. Paul Goren, "Character Weakness, Partisan Bias, and Presidential Evaluation," *American Journal of Political Science* 46 (2002): 627–641; James A. McCann, "Changing Electoral Contexts and Changing Candidate Images During the 1984 Presidential Campaign," *American Politics Quarterly* 18 (1990): 123–140; Warren E. Miller and J. Merrill Shanks, *The New American Voter* (Cambridge, MA: Harvard University Press, 1996); Patrick A. Pierce, "Political Sophistication and the Use of Candidate Traits in Candidate Evaluation," *Political Psychology* 14 (1993): 21–35.
3. Carolyn L. Funk, "Bringing the Candidate into Models of Candidate Evaluation," *Journal of Politics* 61 (1999): 700–720.
4. Steven Greene, "The Role of Character Assessments in Presidential Approval," *American Politics Research* 29 (2001): 196–210.
5. Gregory B. Markus, "Political Attitudes during an Election Year," *American Political Science Review* 76 (1982): 538–560.
6. Pamela J. Conover, "Political Cues and the Perception of Candidates," *American Politics Quarterly* 9 (1981): 427–448.
7. Arthur H. Miller, Martin P. Wattenberg, and Oksana Malanchuk, "Schematic Assessments of Presidential Candidates," *American Political Science Review* 80 (1986): 521–540.
8. David P. Glass, "Evaluating Presidential Candidates: Who Focuses on Their Personal Attributes?" *Public Opinion Quarterly* 49 (1985): 517–34.

9. James E. Campbell, "Candidate Image Evaluations: Influence and Rationalization in Presidential Primaries," *American Politics Quarterly* 11 (1983): 293–313.

10. Kathleen Parker, "The Likability Test," *Washington Post,* May 16, 2012.

11. Respondents in 1992 were asked how well the following phrases applied to each candidate: he would provide strong leadership; he is inspiring; he would get things done; he is knowledgeable; he is intelligent; he is moral; he is honest; he really cares about people like me; and he is compassionate.

12. Some empirical investigation of these items supports this claim. If we examine the presidential vote for each response category for each item, holding party identification constant, we find that there generally are only small differences in candidate choice between the "extremely well" and "quite well" groups and between the "not very well" and the "not at all" groups, but the difference between the "quite well" and "not very well" groups is relatively large. Furthermore, if we examine how party identification relates to these responses, we find an interesting pattern. Individuals who judge the candidate of their party negatively on a trait are much more likely to select "not very well" than "not at all." Similarly, those who judge the candidate of the opposing party positively on a trait are more likely to select "quite well" than "extremely well." See Charles Prysby and David Holian, "Studying Voter Perceptions of the Character Traits of Presidential Candidates: Methodological Questions and Problems" (paper presented at the annual meeting of the Southern Political Science Association, New Orleans, LA, January 5–8, 2011) for a more thorough discussion.

13. Specifically, for positively-worded questions, "extremely well" is assigned a score of +2, "quite well" a score of +1, no response a score of 0, "not very well" a score of –1, and "not at all" a score of –2. The small number of respondents who did not provide a valid response to the question (i.e., said that they did not know how well the trait characterized the candidate) are scored as zero on the grounds that this response is less positive than saying that the trait characterized the candidate quite well, but more positive than saying that the trait characterized the candidate not very well. However, if these cases are treated as missing data and eliminated from the analysis, very similar results are obtained. For negatively worded questions, the scoring is reversed. Negatively worded questions are discussed in more detail later. We also used a scoring system that ran from +1 to –1; in this system, the two positive responses were combined and scored as +1, while the two negative responses were combined and scored as –1. We received very similar results for all of our analyses regardless of the scoring method employed.

14. Tables comparable to Tables 2.1 and 2.2 for other years can be found at http://charles.prysby.com.

15. The evidence for this conclusion comes from several findings. First, honesty and morality are not as highly correlated in 2000 or 2004 as they are in other years, as we discuss later. Second, in both 2000 and 2004, honesty does not correlate with the vote as well as does morality, but in other years it does. See Prysby and Holian, "Studying Voter Perceptions" for a more thorough discussion.

16. Prysby and Holian, "Studying Voter Perceptions."

17. The new set of response categories was introduced because of concerns that the old set did not constitute four equally spaced categories, a problem that we have discussed. Including the "moderately well" response option does seem to make the responses more evenly spaced. However, scoring the old response categories from +2 to –2 also handles this problem, with the additional virtue of maintaining continuity in question wording across the years.

18. A more sophisticated method for uncovering underlying dimensions is factor analysis. Factor analysis is a statistical method that attempts to reduce a set of variables down to a smaller number of dimensions or factors by analyzing the relationships among the variables. We conducted a principal components factor analysis with varimax rotation. In such an analysis, the number of factors extracted often is limited to those that have an eigenvalue that is greater than 1, which means that the factor accounts for more variance than what a single variable would account for. That method turned out to extract just one factor in most cases. Since we were interested in determining whether the trait items grouped into the four theoretical dimensions previously outlined, we specified the extraction of four factors, even if some of the factors had eigenvalues less than 1. For both Bush and Clinton, responses to the items load onto the four dimensions in the predicted fashion. The first three items load very heavily onto the first factor, which clearly captures a leadership dimension. The next two items, which are aspects of competence, load heavily onto the third factor; none of the other items loads very heavily onto this factor. The items dealing with honesty and morality, both aspects of integrity, load the strongest onto one factor (the second factor for Clinton and the fourth factor for Bush), as do the final two items, which are conceptually part of an empathy dimension. Thus, the factor analysis confirms our theoretical conceptualization. Voters see these specific traits as falling along the four dimensions of leadership, competence, integrity, and empathy. The results of this analysis are in the chapter appendix (see Table 2.A1).

19. We did not conduct this analysis for 2008 because of the problems introduced by the use of two different question versions in that year, a problem that we outlined earlier. We also did not analyze the 1984 data because in that year the ANES survey asked a number of trait items that conceptually did not seem related to the character aspects that we have outlined, nor did we analyze the 1980 data because there were no questions about empathy in that survey, so we cannot determine if that dimension fits that year. The correlation matrices and factor analyses for the years we did analyze are available at http://charles.prysby.com.

20. The problem in these two cases has to do with the fact that some questions were worded in a negative fashion in 2000 and 2004, as we discussed earlier. The problems introduced by the negative wording of the items can be illustrated by looking at the bivariate correlations among the trait items for each candidate for the 2004 election. Variables that should tap similar trait dimensions, and thus be highly correlated, sometimes are not. The problems are with two negatively worded items, one asking whether the candidate was indecisive and the other asking whether the candidate was dishonest. For example, being a strong leader and being decisive (specifically, not being indecisive) correlate less than we would expect, given that these are supposed to be highly related aspects of a more general leadership dimension. A similar pattern exists for the integrity measures, being moral and being honest (again, not being dishonest). These two items do not correlate as strongly as we would expect, given that both are aspects of a more general integrity dimension.

    Similar problems exist in 2000. In 2000, the question about honesty also was asked in a negative fashion, and it fails to correlate as strongly as we might expect with the other integrity item (whether the candidate is moral). Also, one of the two questions about empathy that were asked in 2000 was negatively worded. Respondents were asked whether "not being in touch with ordinary Americans" characterized the candidates. Responses to this question do not correlate that strongly with the other empathy item, which was worded in a positive fashion (whether the candidate really cares about people). In contrast, no such problems exist for the two measures of competence, both of which are positively worded in every year; they are very highly correlated with each other.

Our analysis of the data from 2000 and 2004 indicates that error was introduced by wording the questions in a negative fashion. The negative wording seems to have confused some respondents, which led them to respond in a direction opposite of what they intended. It also appears that the error is more likely to be random than systematic. In 2004, Bush is substantially ahead on being decisive, which corresponds to his advantage on being a strong leader. On being honest, Bush and Kerry are judged about even overall, which corresponds to the pattern for the other integrity item, which asked about their morality. Also, in 2000, Bush was seen as more honest than Gore, which matches our prior expectations, drawn from how the candidates were characterized during that presidential campaign. Thus, it seems that there were errors in both directions, leaving mean scores as fairly representative of true overall sentiment but weakening the correlations between the negatively worded items and other variables.

21. In 2008, all seven trait items were worded in a positive fashion. In this year, however, they did not fit into the four theoretical dimensions very well. The trait items for 2008 are difficult to analyze because they were asked in two different versions, as we explained earlier. Also, two of the theoretical dimensions, leadership and empathy, are represented by a single question. Furthermore, a new trait item, whether or not the candidate was optimistic, was introduced. This item was fairly weakly correlated with all of the other trait items, suggesting that it might represent a fifth relevant dimension, but since the question about optimism was not asked in previous years, we are reluctant to conclude that this is the case based on such limited evidence.

22. Our analysis of the vote in 2000 and 2004, the two years when negative items appeared, shows that an overall index based on all seven items is a better predictor of the vote than an index based on just the positively worded items. On the other hand, when we analyze the relationship of individual traits to the vote in these years, we find that the single item on morality, which was positively worded, is a better predictor of the vote in than the single item on honesty, which was negatively worded.

23. Angus Campbell, Philip E. Converse, Warren E. Miller, and Donald E. Stokes, *The American Voter* (New York: John Wiley, 1960), 44–58.

24. The responses to the candidate like/dislike questions are not available for 2008. The questions were asked in the 2008 ANES survey, but there have been lengthy delays in coding all of the open-ended items, and it is unclear when the coded responses to the candidate like/dislike questions will be available to the academic community.

25. Of course, there are other ways that a score of .058 could be obtained; it could result from fewer than 5.8 percent of the respondents making more than one mention each on average.

26. Charles Prysby and David Holian, "Perceptions of Candidate Personal Traits and Voting in Presidential Elections, 1996–2004," (paper presented at the annual meeting of the American Political Science Association, Chicago, IL, August 29 to September 2, 2007); Prysby and Holian, "Studying Voter Perceptions."

27. We were generous in counting responses as representing warmth. Any reference to having or not having a sense of humor, to being warm, kind, likeable, friendly, outgoing, or nice (or their opposites), to being or not being high-brow or high-fallutin', or to being able talk to the common man were

considered references to candidate warmth, along with very vague mention of just liking or disliking the candidate.

28. Furthermore, we see little evidence that elitism is a trait that voters think is important, at least in the sense that media pundits have frequently used the term. While many commentators may have thought that Kerry's elitism was a contributing factor to his 2004 defeat, there were few responses to the open-ended questions that could be classified in this category. Furthermore, the open-ended responses indicated that Kerry was seen by voters as far better than Bush for the average person. If Kerry really had been seen by voters as too aloof and elitist, and if voters truly thought that these characteristics were important, it seems unlikely that they would see Kerry as best for the ordinary voter or as the candidate who really cared about people like them. It is possible that voters have perceptions of how elitist the candidates are, but we see little evidence that they use these perceptions in determining which candidate is better suited to be president.

29. Danny Hayes, "Candidate Qualities through a Partisan Lens: A Theory of Trait Ownership," *American Journal of Political Science* 49 (2005): 908–923; John R. Petrocik, "Issue Ownership in Presidential Elections, with a 1980 Case Study," *American Journal of Political Science* 40 (1996): 825–850.

30. The new, five-category version of the trait questions was introduced in 2008; half of the respondents were given the new version of the trait questions, while half were given the old version. In 2012, only the new version was used.

3 Voter Perceptions of Candidate Character Traits

Voter perceptions of candidates' character traits vary from election to election, often quite dramatically. Even when the same person is a candidate in successive elections, the electorate's assessment of that candidate frequently changes. For example, from 1992 to 1996 positive views of Bill Clinton's integrity declined substantially from already low levels. From 2000 to 2004, views of George W. Bush's competence also fell a great deal; strangely, after four years in the White House, voters considered Bush to be not only less intelligent, but also less knowledgeable, despite the time invested in climbing the learning curve. In 1988, respondents gave George H. W. Bush, who was proclaiming a "kinder, gentler" Republican Party, the highest positive rating received by any Republican candidate in this analysis on the question of whether he really cared about people like the voter. Four years later, this reasonably favorable perception dropped so much that Bush received the lowest empathy-related assessment among all candidates in this analysis. Of course, voter perceptions do not always become more negative over the course of a president's first four years. Perceptions of Ronald Reagan's leadership skills, both in terms of providing strong leadership and being inspiring became far more positive in 1984 compared to 1980, and assessments of Clinton's competence, already impressive in 1992, moved to greater heights in 1996. Perceptions, moreover, do not merely follow election results. If trait perceptions were simply the product of one's vote intention, rather than one factor to consider among many, Bob Dole would have won the presidency in 1996, and the 1988 election would have been far closer than the actual result.

Furthermore, voter perceptions of character traits—often helped along by campaigns offering competing interpretations of events—do not always accord with the conventional wisdom established by media pundits. On the one hand, yes, the first President Bush suffered a leadership problem—"the wimp factor"—that plagued him from his 1980 Republican primary loss through his years as vice president and president. And, yes, about half of the public considered John Kerry to be a flip-flopper, at least according to the responses to the statement that Kerry "can't make up his own mind," a question that seemed to be included in the survey specifically for the senator's candidacy.[1] In these cases, the public and the pundits agreed. On the other hand, while the media and the Bush campaign criticized Al Gore's integrity by portraying him as a serial exaggerator, if not an outright liar, two-thirds of the public believed him to be honest and more than that rated him positively on morality, scores well in line with those of other candidates in the analysis. The most interesting case of divergence between conventional wisdom and public opinion concerns empathy. As we suggested in Chapter 2, pundits tend to conflate empathy with personal displays of sympathy as well as affability, charm, and warmth. In other words, for a candidate to "really care about people like the voter," many pundits argue that candidates must project a certain gregariousness that would lead the typical voter to want to have dinner and swap stories with them. Democratic candidates Michael Dukakis, Gore, and Kerry were all condemned as elitists who did not understand or felt superior to ordinary people, yet the public considered them to be more empathetic than their Republican counterparts. Clearly the public discerns more of a policy component to empathy than the pundits do, which helps explain the Democratic advantage on this trait.

The examples and conclusions in the previous paragraphs come from Table 3.1, which presents the percentage of voters stating that the specified trait described each candidate "extremely well" or "quite well."[2] The table displays all trait measures included in at least two of the election year surveys from 1980 to 2008.[3] Because the trait questions employed a different response set in 2012, one that makes the results not directly comparable to those from earlier years, as explained in the previous chapter, the 2012 data are not included in this table, but they are discussed in Chapter 6. In Table 3.1, individual traits are grouped by the underlying character dimension they are most closely associated with, following the conceptualization discussed in Chapter 2. Of the 13 traits listed in the table, only three were included in the ANES surveys of all eight election years: whether candidates could be described as strong leaders, knowledgeable, and moral. In seven of the eight election years, the ANES included at least one trait question that corresponded to each of the four underlying trait dimensions. The exception is 1980, a year in which no item related to empathy was included in the survey.

We can also get a sense of the role of voter perceptions of character traits over this time span by considering the boxplots displayed in Figure 3.1. Each boxplot displays the range, median, and middle two quartiles for the net candidate scores on each of six trait questions: strong leadership, caring about people like the respondent, and being knowledgeable, intelligent, honest, and moral. These represent all of the trait questions included in at least six of the eight election surveys we are considering in this chapter. A median of zero for any trait would signify no net trait advantage for either party on a particular item, meaning that half of the voters saw one candidate as better on the trait and half saw the other candidate as better. The magnitude of the Republican Party's advantage can be identified by the

Table 3.1 Measures of Presidential Candidate Character Traits, 1988–2008

Trait	1980		1984		1988		1992	
	Reagan	Carter	Reagan	Mondale	Bush	Dukakis	Bush	Clinton
Leadership								
Strong leader	59.4	33.9	71.9	40.8	51.9	51.3	54.9	58.3
Inspiring	49.7	34.1	59.5	36.3	37.9	44.1	38.9	61.6
Gets things done	—	—	—	—	—	—	42.1	58.5
Decisive	—	—	—	—	—	—	—	—
Optimistic	—	—	—	—	—	—	—	—
Competence								
Knowledgeable	67.6	70.4	73.4	75.9	82.8	80.2	82.5	80.8
Intelligent	—	—	80.6	81.8	78.6	86.8	82.8	86.7
Integrity								
Moral	69.0	78.8	80.5	76.6	76.8	74.3	80.0	43.5
Honest	78.1	81.6	—	—	65.1	72.5	60.6	49.7
Decent	—	—	84.1	85.8	85.7	83.7	—	—
Empathy								
Really cares	—	—	49.1	57.9	50.3	62.3	37.0	63.7
Compassionate	—	—	59.6	72.4	61.3	69.5	57.3	75.7
In touch	—	—	38.2	62.1	—	—	—	—

(Continued)

Table 3.1 (Continued)

Trait	1996		2000		2004		2008	
	Dole	Clinton	Bush	Gore	Bush	Kerry	McCain	Obama
Leadership								
Strong leader	62.9	57.9	62.7	53.3	64.4	50.1	65.9	63.0
Inspiring	39.5	53.1	—	—	—	—	—	—
Gets things done	67.2	57.4	—	—	—	—	—	—
Decisive	—	—	—	—	74.5	52.8	—	—
Optimistic	—	—	—	—	—	—	63.8	86.7
Competence								
Knowledgeable	86.9	85.5	68.2	81.3	60.3	79.0	78.8	76.8
Intelligent	—	89.7	73.8	82.2	60.1	85.5	81.2	92.5
Integrity								
Moral	82.2	35.4	69.5	71.3	71.4	66.8	69.9	70.2
Honest	72.7	40.3	73.0	66.6	68.7	73.7	63.8	60.0
Decent	—	—	—	—	—	—	—	—

(*Continued*)

Table 3.1 (Continued)

Trait	1996		2000		2004		2008	
	Dole	Clinton	Bush	Gore	Bush	Kerry	McCain	Obama
Empathy								
Really cares	45.1	57.6	46.3	56.3	48.1	57.6	44.9	63.5
Compassionate	—	69.5	—	—	—	—	—	—
In touch	—	—	57.5	60.3	—	—	—	—

Note: Table entries are the percent of respondents who said that the specified trait characterized the candidate extremely well or quite well, except for the following cases: (a) the 2000 and 2004 figures for "honest" represent the percentage of respondents saying "dishonest" does not describe the candidate; (b) the 2004 figures for "decisive" represent the percentage of respondents saying that "can't make up his own mind" does not describe the candidate; and (c) the 2000 figures for "in touch" represent the percentage of respondents saying "out of touch with ordinary people" does not describe the candidate.
Source: 1980–2008 American National Election Studies. Only major-party voters are included in the analysis.

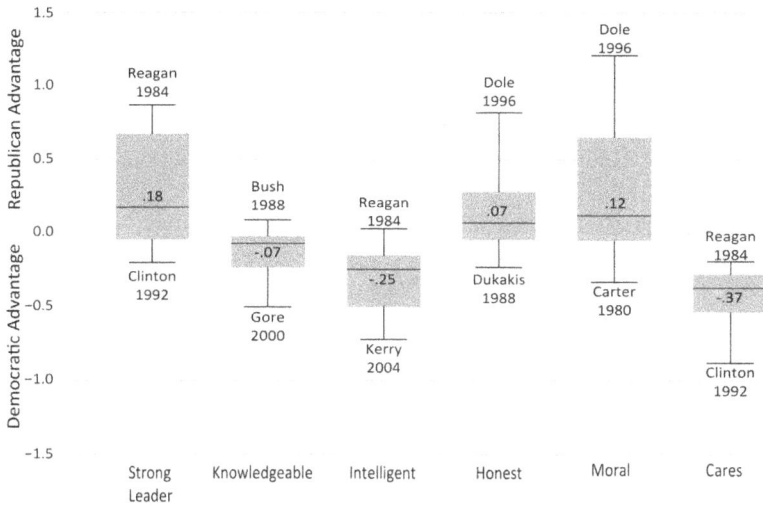

Figure 3.1   Boxplots of Net Candidate Advantage on Character Traits, 1980–2008
Note: The ANES did not include questions about caring or intelligence in 1980, or about honesty in 1984. In 1996, respondents were asked to assess President Clinton's intelligence, but not Robert Dole's

extent to which the median is above zero; a negative median indicates an advantage held by Democratic candidates. The range denotes each parties' largest net advantage on each trait, indicated in the figure by election year and the corresponding candidate who enjoyed the advantage for his party.[4] For example, Reagan benefitted from a net strong leadership advantage in 1984 of .87, which is the difference between Walter Mondale's mean leadership score (-.16) and Reagan's (.71).

From the figure, we can conclude that, first, the largest net advantage enjoyed by a candidate of either party on any trait in a given year is not necessarily earned by a winning candidate. For example, no Democrat enjoyed a larger advantage on the two competence items relative to his Republican opponent than Kerry did over Bush in 2004. Similarly, no Republican did better relative to a Democrat on either integrity item than Dole did versus Clinton in 1996. This would seem to suggest that while voters often perceive clear differences in candidate character, traits vary from election to election in terms of their centrality to the vote decision. As we will discuss in a more systematic fashion in the next chapter, Figure 3.1 also provides an initial indication that relative perceptions of leadership and empathy are especially important. The parties' best showings on both the strong leadership and caring questions include Reagan's 1984 reelection and Clinton's initial victory in 1992. The Republican triumph in 1984 was a landslide of historic proportions, and Clinton's comfortable win came at the expense of an incumbent president.

Second, the figure shows that one party held a distinct advantage on three traits—Republicans on strong leadership, Democrats on intelligence and caring—while neither party had much of an edge on knowledge and the two integrity items. The largest median net advantage on any trait is that enjoyed by Democrats on caring (-.37); Democratic candidates also held a reasonably large net advantage on intelligence (-.25), while the Republican edge on strong leadership represents the third largest gap (.18). That Democrats enjoy their largest advantage on an empathy item while Republicans do so on the leadership question is consistent with Hayes's discussion of trait ownership.[5] This concept, which derives from issue ownership, suggests that, over time, a party can become associated with a particular trait, thus conferring an advantage to its candidate, whomever that might be.[6] Hayes argues, in part, that because Republicans have built issue ownership advantages on national defense and civil and social order, the party's candidates are likely to be considered stronger leaders than their opponents. Similarly for Democrats, a reputation as the party of the working class, as the protector of the social safety net, and as a strong advocate for women and racial minorities has led to what we find to be a substantial empathy advantage for Democrats. Note that in the case of empathy, unlike the other traits, even the maximum value, which records a Republican's best showing on this trait relative to his Democratic opponent, is well below zero. Thus, in 1984 Reagan performed well for a Republican candidate on the caring item, but Mondale was still viewed as more caring by more voters.

More evidence of the extent of trait ownership can be seen in Table 3.1. No Republican candidate has bested a Democrat on any measure of empathy, from "really cares about people like you" to whether a candidate can be described as "compassionate" or "in touch with ordinary people." In fact, the difference between candidates in any given election has never been particularly narrow, with the exception of 2000 when Bush came within 3 points of Gore on whether the candidates were in touch with ordinary people. Other than this instance, no other Republican candidate since 1980 comes within 8 points of a Democrat's favorability on any empathy-related question.

The results for leadership across the years suggest a narrower Republican advantage on this trait than the Democrats enjoy on empathy. Republican candidates were viewed more favorably on "strong leadership" than their opponents in six of the eight elections since 1980, topped by Reagan's substantial 30-point advantage over Mondale in 1984. The two exceptions both involve the first President Bush. In 1988, Bush and Dukakis fought to a draw in terms of strong leadership perceptions, while in 1992, Bush again gave up the usual Republican advantage, narrowly trailing Clinton on this trait by 3 points. While Republicans tend to do well relative to Democrats on the specific "strong leadership" item, Democratic candidates perform better on other trait items related to the underlying leadership dimension. From 1980 to 1996, the ANES asked respondents whether the major party candidates could be described as "inspiring," a trait we show in Chapter 2 to be one aspect of leadership. Reagan was considered substantially more inspiring than either of his Democratic opponents, but the three Republican candidates after Reagan paled in terms of inspiring the electorate compared to their Democratic opponents, including the not-particularly-scintillating Michael Dukakis during a 1988 election season that saw neither side's partisans get especially excited about their candidates. Unfortunately, the ANES stopped asking respondents to assess the candidates' inspirational qualities in 2000. Thus we can only speculate on the extent to which the younger Bush may have had an inspiration advantage over Gore or Kerry, or whether Barack Obama parlayed his oratorical skills and campaign message into a substantial "inspiring" advantage over John McCain.[7] The Democrat certainly had the advantage, by over 20 points, on whether the candidates were "optimistic," an item included for the first time in the 2008 survey, and one that we believe overlaps conceptually with "inspiring."

Voter perceptions of the remaining traits displayed in both the figure and the table are more competitive from election to election. While Hayes argues that Republican Party ownership of issues related to traditional values leads to the party's ownership of the integrity trait, we see little evidence to support this.[9] Just as the party label confers certain advantages and imposes certain disadvantages on candidates, the candidates themselves—their experiences, reputations, and past actions—can also affect trait perceptions. Both Figure 3.1 and Table 3.1 provide evidence that from 1980 to 2008, Democratic candidates have fared about the same as their Republican counterparts on perceptions of morality and honesty, with the exception of one Democrat: Bill Clinton. The integrity gap favoring Bush in 1992 was large; in 1996, the advantage Dole enjoyed was chasm-like. The three largest advantages on any trait over the course of our study are the ones between Dole and Clinton on honesty (32.4 percent), Bush and Clinton on morality (36.5 percent), and Dole and Clinton on morality (46.8 percent). In this context, Clinton's 10.9 point deficit to Bush on honesty in 1992 has to be considered something of a victory. Other than this candidate effect, which happened to disadvantage a Democrat, Democratic candidates won as many perception battles over integrity as they lost. In fact, the Democrats most likely to suffer from Clinton integrity fatigue, thus turning a candidate effect into a party effect, were the Democratic candidates who came after Clinton, particularly his vice president, Al Gore. But this was not the case. Gore, for example, managed to outperform the younger Bush, albeit very narrowly, on morality, while trailing his opponent by only 6 points on honesty. Moreover, this honesty gap was as likely to be generated by Gore's behavior, including his involvement in well-publicized and questionable Democratic Party fundraising practices leading up to the 1996 election, as it was by guilt by association with Clinton. A final piece of evidence to suggest that neither party held a built-in integrity advantage comes from the fact that there were two larger honesty disparities in non-Clinton years, both of which favored Democrats over their Republican opponents: Dukakis (7.4 percent) in 1988 and Jimmy Carter (9.8 percent) in 1980.

Voters consistently give candidates the highest marks on the two measures of competence. In no case did more than 40 percent of voters rate any candidate negatively on knowledge or intelligence. With regard to knowledge, voters perceived the Republican candidate more knowledgeable in four elections and the Democratic candidate more knowledgeable in four. But with the exceptions of 2000 and 2004, at no time was the gap between the candidates more than 3 percentage points. On the intelligence item, the table shows that in the six elections that included this item for both candidates, the public always perceived the Democrat more positively. For the most part, however, this advantage wasn't particularly large. At least 80 percent of voters positively assessed every candidate's intelligence with the exceptions of the elder Bush in 1988 and the younger one in 2000 and 2004. Like Clinton's struggles with integrity perceptions, the younger Bush had a competence problem, which explains a good deal of the Democratic advantage on these items evident in Figure 3.1. However, unlike Clinton, whose integrity scores were under 50 percent, Bush's scores for competence bottomed out at about 60 percent positive in 2004.

Why are voters more likely to come to positive conclusions regarding candidate competence than any other character trait? During the general election campaign, when survey respondents are asked to assess competence, candidates have already demonstrated a great deal of it. Simply surviving the rigors of a primary season and accepting a party's presidential nomination with a triumphant convention speech likely allows most candidates to overcome competence-related concerns among most voters.

CANDIDATE CHARACTER TRAITS AND PRESIDENTIAL ELECTIONS, 1980–2008

We turn now to a discussion of each election year. We do so to provide some context for voter perceptions of candidate character. We examine how voters actually perceived the candidates, based on the ANES data, and how that compared to the judgments of political pundits and commentators at the time of the election. This will show when conventional wisdom about the effect of character traits on the election was on the mark and when it went awry. While we will investigate the question of the effect of perceptions of candidate character traits on the vote more thoroughly and systematically in the next chapter, the presence of a substantial gap between the candidates on a particular character trait provides some initial evidence for the potential influence of that trait and forms the basis of our expectations as we move forward.

1980

The 1980 campaign unfolded before an electorate that did not particularly like its choices. In July, a poll found that 70 percent of respondents agreed or strongly agreed that support for third-party candidate John Anderson had less to do with voter knowledge of Anderson than with voter dislike of President Jimmy Carter and his opponent, Ronald Reagan.[10] As election day neared, about 40 percent of poll respondents acknowledged voting against an opposing candidate rather than for their first choice.[11] Reagan's landslide victory was a better reflection of deep voter dissatisfaction with Carter, rather than widespread confidence in Reagan's ability to handle the job.[12]

We believe that the Democratic candidate disadvantage on providing strong leadership solidified with the 1980 election—with allowances for the dubious contributions of the unsuccessful Stevenson, Humphrey, and McGovern candidacies. In 1976, the leadership gap between Carter and Gerald Ford was in Ford's favor, but narrowly so.[13] Much as Republican candidates in the aftermath of the Great Depression were charged by Democrats with guilt by association with Herbert Hoover's ineffectual handling of the economy, Carter became the Republican rallying cry for Democratic weakness in the face of stagflation and an aggressive Soviet Union, thus turning an individual candidate disadvantage into a party effect. We cannot test this claim with ANES data, but our sense is that standard bearers for the party of Woodrow Wilson and Franklin Roosevelt, including Harry Truman, John Kennedy, and Lyndon Johnson, did not begin their campaigns suffering a leadership deficit simply because they were Democrats.

In 1980 Reagan's character trait advantage was built entirely on the two leadership items, the results of which demonstrated the challenger's clear advantage despite the electorate's uncertainty about other aspects of Reagan's character. Just short of 60 percent of ANES respondents expressed positive views of Reagan's ability to provide strong leadership; fewer than 50 percent identified him as inspiring. While each of these results place Reagan in the middle of the pack vis-á-vis other candidates in other election years on these items, the Republican candidate still enjoyed enormous advantages over Carter in this election year. Only 34 percent of ANES respondents held a favorable opinion of Carter's ability to provide strong leadership or to inspire. These results represent the worst performance on these measures by, not just a sitting president, but any candidate in this analysis. There were several reasons for Carter's low public esteem: four years of poor economic performance, including an election-year recession coupled with an annual inflation rate of over 13 percent; few major legislative successes despite large

Democratic majorities in both chambers of Congress; and the Iranian hostage crisis, which ground on without resolution during Carter's final 14 months in office and included a failed rescue attempt that resulted in the deaths of eight American military personnel.

Voter perceptions of Anderson's character traits are problematic in terms of their comparability to perceptions of the major party candidates because voters were, unsurprisingly, far more likely to express no opinion about the Illinois representative's character than they were about the president's or his Republican challenger's. However, while voters who expressed an opinion held net favorable impressions of Anderson's knowledge, morality, and honesty, Anderson, like Carter, failed to impress the public with his leadership or inspirational abilities. By about 10 percentage points, more voters viewed Anderson unfavorably than favorably on these leadership items in an election that likely turned on leadership.[14] As we shall see in the next chapter, not only were independents in 1980 powerfully influenced in their voting behavior by the candidates' character traits, so too were Democrats; both groups were drawn to Reagan because of the Republican candidate's leadership qualities.

This is likely the case because while Carter trailed badly on both of the leadership items, he was held in slightly higher esteem than Reagan on the other three trait-related measures included in the 1980 ANES: knowledge, morality, and honesty. Compared to other presidential election years, neither Carter nor Reagan fared particularly well on knowledge, the one 1980 item relating to competence. Carter was perceived more positively on this item by three percent of the public, a small advantage given that the incumbent Carter's campaign strategy hinged on raising concerns about Reagan's qualifications for the office. Such concerns, repeatedly reflected in polls taken over the course of the campaign, were that Reagan did not have the intellectual capacity necessary to be president and that—in part as a result of this perceived shortcoming and the candidate's often stark rhetoric concerning the Soviet Union—a Reagan administration would make war more likely.[15] The Carter campaign, however, was hard pressed to benefit from Reagan's perceived limitations in this area because, as we argued in Chapter 2, of the conceptual overlap between leadership and competence. Many of Carter's leadership failings, from his inability to work more effectively with a Democratic Congress, to his long and, at least by election day, unsuccessful efforts to free the hostages in Iran, likely led to more negative views of his competence.

Finally, Carter held the advantage on perceptions of his integrity, a characteristic he had emphasized during his 1976 victory as an antidote for the political and personal failings of Presidents Johnson and Nixon, which led to flaws in the prosecution of the Vietnam War as well as Nixon's downfall as a result of the Watergate scandal.[16] While there was little difference in the quite positive views of Carter's and Reagan's honesty, Carter enjoyed a 10-point edge in perceptions of morality. The

69 percent of respondents who held positive views of Reagan's morality placed him at the low end of the middle tier of candidates on this trait. He was viewed far more favorably than Clinton in either 1992 or 1996, but less positively than Bush in 1992, Dole in 1996, and Reagan himself in 1984. However, in the face of real concerns about an America in decline, Carter's advantage on integrity did not save him. The public seemed to believe that Carter was a good and decent man who was in over his head as president.

1984

The Great Communicator's first term did wonders for the esteem in which Americans held him as a person. Reagan's genial nature and "shining-city-on-a-hill" vision of the country's future, along with the return of economic growth and the steady retreat of inflation, contributed to his landslide victory. Reagan enjoyed gains in public perceptions across all four of the character trait questions repeated from 1980, gaining at least 10 points on three including the two leadership items. In fact, no candidate in this analysis held a larger leadership advantage than Reagan did over his opponent, Walter Mondale. Carter's former vice president, however, was viewed more positively on the three measures of empathy, which were included for the first time in the 1984 survey. The public held the two candidates in roughly equal and relatively high regard on competence and integrity. Thus, while Mondale lost a historically large landslide, he held his own on perceptions of character traits other than leadership.

Mondale joined Carter as the only candidates whose strong leadership qualities were judged unfavorably by more than 50 percent of the electorate. Mondale surely suffered guilt by association with the Carter administration, which plagued him not only in the general election contest, but also throughout his highly competitive primary campaign against fellow Democrat Gary Hart.[17] Mondale's leadership-related weakness was in stark contrast to Reagan, whose standing on strong leadership is the most positive of any candidate in Table 3.1. Reagan also fared well on the ability to inspire. Only Bill Clinton, during his first presidential run in 1992, was viewed more positively, although the ANES did not ask about inspiration after 1996.

On the other side of the trait spectrum, the electorate judged Mondale as clearly superior to Reagan on empathy. In 1984, the ANES included three questions that tapped this trait dimension: whether the candidates "really cared about people like" the voter, whether the term "compassionate" described the candidates, and whether the candidates were "in touch with ordinary people." Because the ANES included no empathy-related items in 1980, we cannot compare evaluations of Reagan over time. On the one hand, voters' perceptions of Reagan's empathy may have grown more positive over the course of his successful first term, similar to their perceptions of his knowledge, morality, and leadership qualities. However, as we noted in Chapter 2, we believe people's assessments of empathy reflect more than the belief that a candidate can relate to voters on a personal level or would escort an elderly person across the street or volunteer at a soup kitchen. Empathy also encompasses a significant policy component, and a prominent Democratic attack on Reagan in 1984 was that his economic policies had benefited the wealthy at the expense of the less fortunate, who were waiting in vain for prosperity to trickle down. The apotheosis of this Democratic argument came, not from Mondale, but from the keynote speaker at the 1984 Democratic National Convention, Mario Cuomo. The then Governor of New York juxtaposed Reagan's "shining city on a hill" rhetoric with Cuomo's own "Tale of Two Cities" convention speech, which blamed Reagan for shredding the social safety net with the resulting dire effects visited upon the "other America," the one left in the valley and therefore out of the Reagan recovery.[18] Mondale would go on to reprise this line of attack throughout the general election campaign, but to little avail. This is not particularly surprising given that the 1984 campaign, as with 1980, was likely to be more focused on retrospective evaluations of the incumbent's job performance, and less so on candidate character traits.

1988

Reagan's leadership qualities cast a long shadow over the campaign to succeed him. According to the 1988 ANES survey, 64 percent of the public favorably described the outgoing president as a strong leader. While Reagan continued to thrive in this area, both candidates running to replace him suffered by comparison. Only about half the voters perceived either of the 1988 nominees as a strong leader, a mediocre result relative to the other candidates in Table 3.1. Besides the aforementioned Carter and Mondale, the electorate held only John Kerry's leadership qualities in marginally lower regard than those of the 1988 presidential candidates, George H. W. Bush and Michael Dukakis. This result reflected several factors. Both Bush and Dukakis were seen by a solid majority of voters as uninspiring, which likely derived in large part from their oratorical shortcomings. Dukakis was considered a technocrat who spoke in prose, not poetry; Bush was prone to mangling his syntax. However, common weaknesses on this trait did not prevent the candidates, the vice president in particular, from trying to bring leadership potential to the forefront of the campaign.

Despite his World War II service, Navy fighter pilot credentials, and a distinguished political career that included a one-year stint as Director of Central Intelligence during the Ford administration, Bush struggled against a perception of weakness throughout his years as vice president. Several commentators felt that Bush did not seem presidential to many voters, especially in comparison to Reagan.[19] Bush's difficulty in projecting himself as a strong and decisive leader were reflected in a provocative and widely discussed

Newsweek cover story titled "George Bush, Fighting the 'Wimp Factor'." As a 1980 Republican primary candidate, Bush judged Reagan's economic proposals to be based on "voodoo," but then quickly endorsed them once he fell short of the nomination. Bush had also supported abortion rights and the Equal Rights Amendment, but promptly switched these positions in order to serve more comfortably as Reagan's running mate. "Bush very nearly did not become vice president in 1980 because Reagan also doubted his toughness. Yet he ultimately cinched the job precisely because Reagan realized that Bush—unlike first choice Gerald Ford—would gracefully and gratefully accept the subservience the post demands. Bush did not disappoint him."[20]

Part of the Bush campaign's approach to the electorate's doubts about its own candidate was to run a relentlessly negative campaign against Dukakis, in order to hang the wimp charge around the Democrat's neck. One claim was that Dukakis was soft on crime. In one particularly notable case, the candidate played into his opponent's hands on this issue when, in the second and final presidential debate, Dukakis prosaically restated his lifelong opposition to capital punishment via an answer to a hypothetical question outlining the rape and murder of his wife.[21] The soft-on-crime attack was also highlighted by two of the more notorious—and devastating—television ads of this or any election cycle.[22] The subject of each was Dukakis's opposition to the death penalty, Massachusetts's prison furlough program, and the Democrat's supposed desire to hand out "weekend passes" to murderers. One ad told the story of Willie Horton, an African American prominently pictured in a menacing mug shot, which added a racial undertone to the attack. While on a prison furlough in 1987, Horton kidnaped a Maryland couple and committed a series of crimes that included rape. A second ad highlighted the weekend pass theme by showing a long line of prisoners marching in and immediately out of jail through a revolving door. Despite Dukakis's defense that the furlough program had begun under the previous governor, a Republican, and that he did not personally approve prisoners for furloughs, the damage was done.

The Bush campaign also exploited the foreign policy advantage held by the vice president over the governor. This attack culminated in another memorable ad, which made use of a photo opportunity, arranged by the Dukakis campaign, designed to highlight the governor's commander-in-chief credentials. The video showed Dukakis smiling from beneath an oversized helmet while standing in the turret of an M1 Abrams tank. The Bush campaign used the visuals to mock Dukakis as a cartoonish potential steward of the nation's foreign policy, while a laundry list of weapons systems and military decisions the governor had opposed scrolled across the screen.[23] While that ad was partly policy criticism, it also attempted to portray Dukakis in an unfavorable personal light.

Most observers felt that Dukakis failed to counter the Republican attacks effectively, leaving him on the defensive throughout much of the campaign, and further undermining his claims to strength and fortitude. Thus, the inability, reticence, or unwillingness to respond forcefully led some analysts to argue that voters felt that Dukakis was not a person who would fight back when challenged.[24] Bush's reputation as vice president combined with his campaign's devastating portrayal of Dukakis as a weak challenger unworthy of the office resulted in an electorate that perceived neither candidate as a particularly strong leader.

Dukakis tried to dismiss these Republican attacks by pivoting to competence. The former Massachusetts governor argued that the election was, in fact, about competence, not ideology, and that his record in Massachusetts of balanced budgets and job growth was evidence of his ability to manage government well.[25] Voters seemed to receive this message. Over 80 percent of respondents reported positive perceptions of Dukakis's knowledge and intelligence. His debate performances and campaign speeches contributed to these perceptions. While his campaign style was "cool, unemotional, cerebral, even bland," he communicated a thorough understanding of policy issues.[26] During the first debate, one panelist referred to him as the "smartest clerk in the world," a characterization that captured doubts about his leadership abilities as much as it praised his knowledge and intelligence.[27] Bush also did well on competence, which is unsurprising, given his considerable political and governmental experience, from vice president and head of the CIA to ambassador to both the United Nations and China to chairman of the Republican National Committee and two-term member of the U.S. House of Representatives.

The area where Dukakis had his greatest advantage was empathy. Voters were much more likely to see him as someone who was compassionate and who really cared about people like them. This might seem surprising in light of the widespread portrait of Dukakis as passionless, or in these wide ranging descriptions of the candidate in a Newsweek profile: "a colorless drone," "an earnest nerd," "poetic as a slide rule," and the "Mr. Spock of politics."[28] Rather, Dukakis's favorable marks on empathy make sense in the context of Democratic Party trait ownership and the related policy foundation of empathy perceptions. During the campaign, Dukakis spoke repeatedly about the need for economic policies to help ordinary Americans who he claimed, in an echo of the 1984 campaign, had not benefitted much from the economic policies of the Reagan administration. For his efforts, 62.3 percent of the public said that Dukakis really cared. This was a favorable rate about on par with Clinton in 1992 and Obama in 2008, which were the best scores on this item. Unfortunately for Dukakis, Bush also scored well on the really cares item, at least for a Republican. The vice president was the only Republican candidate in this analysis to be considered favorably by a majority of the American public—albeit a slight one—on the really cares question. During a campaign in which Bush stressed he would "stay the course" set by the popular Reagan in almost every way, the one exception was an attempt to smooth the hard edges of the Reagan Revolution by promising a "kinder, gentler nation," one that would emphasize helping the truly needy through volunteerism and private efforts rather than government programs.[29] Nevertheless, the public clearly saw Dukakis in more positive terms on empathy. Furthermore, while many media pundits thought that Dukakis lost in large part because he lacked warmth and embodied elitist values, we saw in Chapter 2 (Table 2.A2) that voters made very few references to personal warmth or elitist values in their responses to the open-ended, like/dislike questions about these two candidates. This finding suggests to us that voters did not care about these things nearly as much as pundits thought that they did.

Finally, both candidates did well on integrity, which also is not surprising, as no major questions were raised about the personal trustworthiness or morality of either candidate during the campaign. Democrats hoped to use the Iran-Contra scandal to call into question Bush's integrity, but Bush argued that he was not involved in these decisions. This answer may have dealt satisfactorily with the integrity question, but it did little to bolster his leadership credentials. In sum, Dukakis did somewhat better overall than Bush on candidate character traits, as perceived by the voters. He was about even with Bush on leadership, competence, and integrity, and he was clearly ahead on empathy. Nevertheless, Dukakis lost the election handily, largely because voters saw him as too liberal and because they were happy to give Reagan a third term by promoting his vice president. While pundits may have attributed Dukakis's defeat largely to his personal failings, these data undermine that conclusion.

1992

In 1992, the public was not enamored with its choices for president. In April of that year, only 31 percent of Americans reported being satisfied with their options: an increasingly unpopular Republican president and a scandal-plagued governor of Arkansas.[30] According to an April Gallup Poll, President Bush's public approval stood at 39 percent, a result in the late stages of what would be a 60-point decline from his high of 89 percent, recorded just 14 months earlier during the first Iraq War. As for the Democratic challenger, the same Gallup Poll indicated that Bill Clinton's bruising path through the primary calendar left his favorable rating underwater at 34 percent favorable versus 47 percent unfavorable, a result that concerned Democrats, many of whom felt that Clinton's character-related problems would doom his general election campaign and cost the party the White House despite the opportunity provided by the sluggish economy and Bush's unpopularity.[31]

Such abysmal assessments of the major party candidates left open the possibility of a legitimately competitive third-party campaign, particularly as Pat Buchanan's insurgent Republican primary candidacy and the various

Democratic alternatives to Clinton began to fade.[32] Texas billionaire H. Ross Perot indicated he would consider filling the vacuum created by widespread voter discontent in a February appearance on *Larry King Live*. On the eve of the Democratic National Convention, a July 9–10 Gallup/Newsweek poll showed Perot (25 percent) in a statistical tie with Bush (29 percent) and Clinton (26 percent). Perot's flirtation with, and subsequent launching, abandoning, and re-launching of his Reform Party candidacy helped shape the rest of the campaign.[33] Unfortunately, because of Perot's indecision, the ANES did not include any trait questions about him. The most proximate comparison that we can offer of Americans' perceptions of Perot's character traits relative to Bush's and Clinton's are the results of a Time/CNN survey of registered voters taken in late October. While the trait-related questions are not identical to ANES items, they suggest that Americans held Perot in high regard and presage his strong showing on election day when he received 19 percent of the popular vote, the best such showing for a third party candidate since Teddy Roosevelt's 27 percent in 1912.[34] A higher percentage of Americans agreed that Perot was the stronger leader and more caring and honest than either of his opponents.[35]

As for assessments of Bush and Clinton from ANES data, the public perceived large differences between them on three of the four trait dimensions we analyze. The one exception was competence. Both candidates were judged positively by over 80 percent of voters on both knowledge and intelligence. In contrast, the variation in candidate favorability on two of the three leadership items and all of the measures of integrity and empathy were quite large, ranging from just over 22 points in Clinton's favor on being inspiring (a leadership item) to Bush's enormous 36-point advantage on morality (an integrity item).

Part of the president's campaign strategy was to raise doubts about Clinton's integrity. Moreover, many pundits expressed doubts that the public would elect a president whose unsavory personal baggage had been so widely reported. Over the course of the Democratic primary campaign, questions arose about Clinton's marital fidelity, college-age marijuana use, and efforts to avoid military service in Vietnam, which led to exhaustive and breathless media coverage that nearly derailed Clinton's campaign in advance of the New Hampshire primary.[36] By the general election, the challenger's weaknesses on this score were well known, well vetted and, to the great frustration of the Bush team, old news in light of growing concern about the state of the economy. Overall, less than 50 percent of voters viewed Clinton positively on the two integrity items. No candidate in this analysis, other than Clinton again in 1996, scored lower than 60 percent favorable on either of these items.

Beyond attacking Clinton's integrity, the Bush campaign dusted off criticisms similar to those they had lodged against Dukakis's leadership credentials four years earlier. First, the Bush team tried to brand Clinton a failed leader of a small, poor, and insignificant state. This allowed Republicans to argue that their opponent was unqualified to handle the nation's foreign policy, national defense, and, therefore, any international crises that might emerge, such as Iraq's invasion of Kuwait, the successful reversal of which formed the basis for Bush's own claims to strong leadership. However, as Bush lurched from one attack to the next, the campaign found that Clinton, unlike Dukakis, was anything but a passive target.[37] The Democratic candidate's rapid response "War Room" was primed to both answer attacks immediately, instead of letting them fester as the Dukakis campaign had, and to refocus the debate on the election's overarching issue: anemic economic performance. One particularly effective Clinton campaign ad combined these themes by both accusing the president of engaging in unfair negative advertising, a charge supported by pulled quotations from newspaper stories criticizing Bush on this score, while also seamlessly reminding voters of Bush's unpopular economic stewardship. The ad ended with a voiceover intoning, "George Bush is trying to scare you about Bill Clinton, but nothing could be more frightening than four more years."[38] In 1980, Bush rode Reagan's coattails to the vice presidency on the power of the electorate's overwhelmingly negative response to the question: Are you better off now than you were four years ago? In 1992, the Clinton team won the White House in part by asking the same question and receiving the same answer.

Despite the Bush campaign's efforts to undermine public confidence in the challenger's readiness to lead, about 58 percent of respondents had a positive impression of Clinton on the strong leadership item; only 55 percent said the same about the incumbent president. The flipside of Republican trait ownership of leadership, as we noted above with regard to issue trespassing, is that when the Republican candidate does no better or only modestly so than his Democratic opponent on the strong leadership item, the Democrat tends to win. This was the case in 1992. Beyond eclipsing Bush in public perceptions of a strong leader, the public favored Clinton even more relative to the president on the two other leadership questions included in the 1992 survey: inspiring voters and getting things done. Clinton bested Bush by over 22 percentage points in the former case, and 16 in the latter. Bush's low across-the-board marks on this character dimension resulted in part from the economic recession and ensuing slow recovery that characterized the last half of his term in office. Surprisingly, it seems that the successful ousting of Saddam Hussein from Kuwait was not enough to overcome the wimp label that dogged Bush as vice president. The fact that third-party candidate Ross Perot heaped more criticism on the president, which served to reinforce some of the attacks made by Clinton, did not help matters.[39]

Clinton also had a large advantage on empathy. Bush received the lowest empathy marks of any candidate in this analysis, while Clinton enjoyed the most positive voter perceptions on both the "really cares" and "compassionate" items. For the Bush team, this was a sad bookend to the

1988 campaign, during which the electorate had given its candidate the highest positive rating on empathy of any Republican candidate in this analysis. A number of incidents, minor by themselves but consequential in tandem, reinforced the notion that Bush was out of touch. Media accounts of the president's February 1992 appearance at a meeting of the National Grocers Association, made to demonstrate Bush's concern about the weak economy and to announce proposals to stimulate it, became consumed with Bush's supposed astonishment with a bar code scanner, technology that had over the course of the previous decade become commonplace to the average American.[40] The president's campaign faced similar difficulties during the second of three presidential debates, which was run in a town hall format that played to the strengths of the more personally affable and rhetorically lucid Clinton. The challenger exuded the empathy and confidence of a television evangelist, moving close to the questioners and urging one woman to repeat her question about whether Mr. Bush was out of touch. Moreover, Bush seemed unable to understand an awkwardly worded question about how people had been affected by the recession, whereas Clinton handled it adroitly, with a hint of emotion for good measure.[41] Late in the debate, viewers saw the president checking his watch, an innocent enough action that came to symbolize a candidate bored with a debate that had been focused primarily on the voters' primary concern: the economy.[42]

Voters in 1992 perceived stark differences between the candidates on three of the four trait dimensions. Overall the combination of a faltering economy and Clinton's solid standing with the public on leadership and excellent showing on empathy allowed the challenger to overcome the incumbent by a comfortable margin in this three-man race. While neither the primary nor the general election campaigns lacked for details on Clinton's personal inadequacies, the Clinton team did an effective job of answering the charges and pivoting back to the economy. The public certainly expressed its doubts about the Democrat's integrity, but President Bush was unable to leverage this advantage into enough votes to compensate for Clinton's advantages elsewhere.

1996

Clinton's first term was a roller coaster ride. While the economy steadily improved and the nation continued to enjoy a post–Cold War peace dividend, the nation's politics moved from one highly charged partisan confrontation to another, including numerous accusations of scandal, most of which had their origins in Clinton's Arkansas days; the administration's botched attempt to remove restrictions on gay men and women from serving openly in the military; a health care reform plan that failed in spectacular fashion; a midterm election that resulted in simultaneous Republican control of both chambers of Congress for the first time in 40 years; and brinkmanship over a government shutdown out of which Clinton emerged as the defender of the middle class—in contrast to his "extremist" Republican foils—and the odds-on favorite to win a second term.[43] Out of this crucible, Clinton became slightly less personally appealing to Americans on every leadership, integrity, and empathy item. The exception was competence. Positive perceptions of Clinton's knowledge and intelligence grew a few points each from already impressive heights. Nearly 90 percent of Americans agreed that "he is intelligent" described the president either extremely or quite well. Although the ANES did not ask about the intelligence of Clinton's Republican opponent, Senator Robert Dole, 87 percent of respondents considered the veteran lawmaker to be knowledgeable, suggesting a likely draw on this trait.

In contrast, the public held Dole in higher regard relative to Clinton on two of the leadership measures and—by vast margins—on both measures of integrity. On the other hand, the positive impression Ross Perot made on the electorate ebbed considerably, along with the Reform Party candidate's percentage of the national popular vote, which declined 11 points from his 1992 showing to under 9 percent.[44] In Dole's case, the Republican's background as a decorated World War II veteran gravely wounded by Nazi gunfire provided a stark contrast with Clinton's machinations to avoid the Vietnam War–era draft. Dole bested Clinton by 5 points on the strong leader attribute and by nearly 10 points on the ability to get things done. While the leadership advantage was small relative to those enjoyed by most successful Republican candidates, the advantage on getting things done has to be considered particularly impressive for anyone whose résumé included Senate Majority Leader, given the Senate's well-earned reputation as averse to strong leadership, and as a place where accomplishments—when anything is accomplished at all—come at an excruciatingly slow pace. Dole's overall trait advantage likely gave Republicans some hope that, despite the improving economy, a campaign focused on the personal character of the candidates would put the challenger in position to win. While that may have been the plan, the campaign unfolded otherwise. As election day drew near and Clinton maintained a consistent and significant advantage in the polls, Dole, at a late October campaign stop, was reduced to imploring his audience with the question, "Where is the outrage?"[45] While Dole's specific attack in this speech concerned his charge that the media was failing to report various Clinton administration scandals, including the lengths to which the Clinton campaign went to raise campaign cash, his more general complaint was that of a candidate about to lose an election despite his enormous advantage on personal integrity.

Dole, however, was not without liabilities. The senator's age—he would have been 73 on Inauguration Day—and poor public speaking skills were drawbacks, particularly given the obvious contrasts with Clinton, whose allusions to building a bridge to the future were as incessant as they were obvious reminders of Dole's advancing years.[46] Not surprisingly, the one aspect of leadership for which Clinton held the advantage was on being the more inspiring candidate, which probably reflected differences in age and oratorical abilities.[47] Dole also suffered the usual Republican handicap on empathy. While the empathy gap narrowed considerably from 1992 to 1996, Clinton still enjoyed a 12.5-point advantage on whether or not the candidates "really cared."

Finally, Dole's attempt to stir up voter outrage in the face of a steadily improving economy was a reasonable tactic given the president's persistent Achilles's heel: the public's overwhelmingly negative assessment of his integrity. Many Republicans felt that the questions raised about Clinton's integrity provided a clear advantage to Dole, who did not have charges of unethical or dishonest personal behavior clouding his candidacy.[48] In terms of honesty and forthrightness in public life, many critics questioned how Dole could argue that one of the centerpieces of his platform, a proposed 15 percent across-the-board income tax cut, could be implemented without increasing the budget deficit or cutting important government programs, as Dole seemed to imply.[49] However, fairly run-of-the-mill tall tales from the campaign trail paled in comparison to the integrity-related questions that shadowed the Clinton campaign. Besides the charges aired repeatedly during the 1992 campaign, such as marital infidelity, marijuana use, and draft evasion, others gained steam during the first term, especially in the wake of the appointment of independent counsel Kenneth Starr. Initially, Starr's investigation of Clinton encompassed alleged financial improprieties arising out of the Whitewater land development deal. Soon, Starr's brief expanded to, among other things, allegations of improper terminations of White House travel office personnel and the improper use of confidential FBI files.[50] These alleged scandals also involved Hillary Rodham Clinton, who was far more controversial than most first ladies.[51] Starr was also granted authority to investigate the president's alleged sexual harassment of a former Arkansas state employee, Paula Jones. The Jones lawsuit ultimately led prosecutors to Monica Lewinsky, the White House intern whose intimate relationship with Clinton was made public early in the second term and led to the president's impeachment by the House and acquittal in the Senate.

The public considered Clinton and Dole about equally competent and gave Dole the advantage on leadership. Clinton's advantage over Dole on empathy was substantial, but it was considerably smaller than Dole's advantage on integrity. Overall Dole bested Clinton on candidate character traits. Nevertheless, Dole lost. The 1996 outcome resembles the situation in 1988, when Dukakis lost despite a similarly modest advantage on personal traits. A key difference was that in 1996, the incumbent president was running for reelection, and in such situations it is extremely difficult to defeat the sitting president absent substantial dissatisfaction with administration policies and performance. Satisfaction with Clinton's role in strengthening the economy simply trumped the widespread acceptance that the president was no exemplar of personal honesty and moral rectitude.

2000

Candidate character traits played an important role during the 2000 presidential election for two reasons. First, each side believed that the opposing candidate had a fatal weakness waiting to be exploited. Democrats were convinced that George W. Bush could be presented to the public as out of his depth, a friendly enough guy with whom voters could imagine enjoying a lively conversation about baseball, but someone who could not be so easily envisioned as president. Republicans were equally sure that Al Gore could be portrayed as a duplicitous and serial exaggerator whose interpersonal skills rendered him unable to connect with the average voter.

Second, with no incumbent president running for reelection, the campaign did not automatically focus on the record of the past four years. Gore, as the sitting vice president, could have made the Clinton administration's record a central issue in the campaign. This would have been a reasonable approach given that the record was one of peace and prosperity and that Clinton's approval rating was well over 50 percent throughout his second term. Under similar circumstances, the elder Bush firmly embraced Reagan and did not let go until he won the White House. Gore, however, chose not to pursue this strategy in order to distance himself from the dark side of the Clinton years: the scandals, most notably the Lewinsky affair and the subsequent impeachment of the president.[52] Many analysts argued that Gore lost because he did not more effectively associate himself with the popular aspects of the Clinton administration. Others suggested that the vice president's "people versus the powerful" stab at populism undermined his ability to share in the credit for a robust economy. In the words of one observer, Gore's incongruous message boiled down to, "You've never had it so good, and I'm mad as hell about it."[53]

For his part, Bush was not anxious to focus on Clinton's record on the economy either given the success of the previous eight years—and distinct from the economic struggles of the first Bush presidency before that—because such a focus might give voters ample reason to keep the White House in Democratic hands. The result was that less attention was devoted to arguing whether the policies of the last four years should be continued than is usually the case in presidential election campaigns. In fact, media coverage of the election consistently framed the contest as one between "the gregarious chairman of the Inter-Fraternity Council" and the "earnest leader of the Science Club."[54]

Bush was the son of one president, but fashioned himself the heir of another. Like Ronald Reagan—and unlike his father—the public's perception of Bush was that of a strong leader who was competence challenged.

In 2000, Bush did almost 10 points better than Gore on the sole leadership item, whether each candidate could be described as a strong leader. Almost 63 percent of ANES respondents had a favorable impression of Bush in this regard; only 53 percent said the same about Gore. During the campaign, Bush presented himself as a governor willing to reach across the aisle and work with Democratic state legislators who controlled the Texas House of Representatives throughout his time in office. In his acceptance speech at the Republican National Convention, Bush presented himself as a "uniter, not a divider."[55] He repeatedly stressed his bipartisan approach to governing during the debates.[56] Moreover, as someone who was not part of the federal government, he could criticize the partisan squabbling in Washington, to which his opponent presumably contributed. Gore, on the other hand, was unable to convince voters of his leadership potential. Perhaps serving as the vice president for eight years did not afford Gore many opportunities to display leadership skills.[57] Gore's struggles to project strength were similar to those of the other former vice presidents in this analysis, Mondale and the elder Bush, both of whom also suffered below average leadership ratings.

With regard to competence, the Republican candidate was characterized by many pundits as gregarious but uniformed.[58] Some questioned his qualifications to be president. During both the primary and general elections, Bush frequently projected a shallow understanding of national and foreign affairs. Proving that he was indeed his father's son, he also was prone to verbal gaffes.[59] His sole governmental experience consisted of being governor of Texas for six years. By itself, that was not much different from the experience of some previous presidents, including Reagan, but when combined with serious questions about his knowledge and intelligence, these doubts formed a picture of someone who was not yet ready to be president. Indeed, some observers felt that Bush would not have been able to capture the Republican nomination—or become governor of Texas in the first place—were it not for the family name.

Gore benefitted from a famous family name as well but, again like the elder Bush, had a great deal of experience in the federal government. For Gore, this included three terms in the House of Representatives and 16 years split equally between the Senate and the vice presidency. Unlike his opponent, and in fact quite the opposite of his opponent, Gore's reputation was that of an extremely knowledgeable candidate who was personally cold and aloof, similar to the characterization of Dukakis in 1988—and John Kerry and Barack Obama in the two subsequent elections.[60] Pundits frequently described Gore as a "policy wonk" who lacked personal warmth and charm. During the debates, he displayed his mastery of the details of public policy. On the other hand, this knowledge of governmental affairs, especially as it was displayed in the first debate, led many to characterize Gore as a know-it-all.[61] Whereas Bush was often criticized for knowing too little, pundits flayed Gore, it seems, for knowing too much—and being insufferable about it.

During the general election campaign, misstatements by Bush or Gore that fit these stereotypes became fodder for the pundits. Small errors, including mispronunciations and garbled syntax were inflated to illustrate Bush's deficient brain power. An examination of the treatment of the candidates by late-night television comedians, such as Jay Leno and David Letterman, found that Bush was the subject of an inordinate amount of jokes about his intelligence, knowledge, and verbal blunders.[62] With regard to the vice president, Gore's credit claiming for his role on a House committee that provided seed money for the commercial development of the Internet morphed into the persistent but demonstrably false assertion that Gore claimed he had "invented the Internet." This line was repeated verbatim and referred to so often that it became widely accepted as fact. During their first debate, Bush jokingly accused Gore of "inventing the calculator" in response to the vice president's abundant use of statistics.[63] Throughout the election season, the media, prodded by the Bush campaign, portrayed Gore as someone who exaggerated and distorted the truth as a means of self-promotion.[64] The Republican strategy was a successful one as minor misstatements by the vice president became fodder for media "truth squads." In some typical examples, Gore was criticized for stating in the first presidential debate that he had never suggested that his opponent did not have the necessary experience to be president when he in fact had done so, albeit seven months earlier, and for claiming that his mother-in-law's out-of-pocket expenses for a particular drug were three times what Gore paid for the same drug for his dog, when in reality Gore was referring to the wholesale price, not the retail price of either prescription.

Despite the emerging picture of Gore as someone who not only stretched the truth, but was also stiff and impersonal, voter perceptions of Gore's empathy were quite positive, although not quite as positive as Clinton's. Bush did much worse than Gore on the question of whether the candidate "cares about people like you," and slightly worse on the question of who was more "in touch with ordinary people."[65] Bush attempted to present himself as a "compassionate conservative" during the campaign, but this did not produce very favorable assessments of his empathy. As we argued earlier, judgments by the voters about a candidate's empathy are based in large part on policy positions and related arguments, not on purely personal displays of compassion or affability. In comparison, Gore stressed his desire to fight for policies that would benefit the middle class and ordinary working Americans.[66] His party affiliation and emphasis on these themes contributed to positive assessments of his empathy.

As the data in Table 3.1 show, these characterizations of the candidates were reflected in public opinion. Bush's scores for being knowledgeable and intelligent were the lowest received by any candidate, except for his scores four years later. Voter perceptions of Gore's competence were quite positive, which is what we would expect to find given the prevailing characterizations of him in the media and his eight years as vice president. Positive perceptions of Gore's integrity likely suffered, although the vice president did almost as well with the public as Bush. Despite the pundits, Gore seemed to outperform their assessments of his integrity in that solid majorities of voters thought that he was honest and moral. If Bush had an advantage on this trait, it was a very small one. When we add in the fact that Gore had sizable advantages on competence and empathy, advantages that appear to have outweighed his disadvantage on leadership, the net result is that Gore had a small overall advantage on character traits. Furthermore, while Bush may have displayed more personal warmth than Gore, few voters offered this as a reason for choosing between the candidates, as we noted in Chapter 2. (See Table 2.A2.) Thus, Gore did not seem to be disadvantaged by being less personally charming. Nevertheless, Gore, like Dukakis and Dole before him, was unable to convert a modest advantage on personal traits into electoral victory, although he did capture a very narrow plurality of the popular vote.

2004

The 2004 election was the first after the September 11 terrorist attacks and ensuing American military interventions in Afghanistan and Iraq. The attacks focused public attention on leadership in the face of the threat of terrorism at home and abroad. This served the Bush campaign well as the president outperformed his Democratic opponent, John Kerry, by a substantial margin on both leadership questions: providing strong leadership and being decisive.[67] Nearly 65 percent of respondents considered the president a strong leader; only a bare majority held a similarly favorable impression of Kerry. This gap was the largest between two candidates in this analysis save for advantages enjoyed by Ronald Reagan in 1980 and 1984. The other ANES question that dealt with leadership had never before been included among the character trait battery. Respondents were asked to judge the degree to which the candidates were decisive. This was likely in response to questions raised about Kerry by the Bush campaign, questions that seem to have resonated with the public, given that the president's advantage on being decisive was about 22 points. The impression of Kerry as flip-flopper was underscored by a Bush campaign ad reminiscent of the first President Bush's attack on another Democratic nominee from Massachusetts. Like the elder Bush's tank takedown of Michael Dukakis, the son's campaign used ostensibly positive video, this time of a vacationing, physically fit Kerry windsurfing, as a metaphor for Kerry's alleged on-a-dime position shifting on the Iraq War and its funding.[68]

The ad also underscored another Bush campaign critique of its opponent: the cultural gap between the decisive, straight-shooting, regular guy president and his elitist, all-too-highbrow challenger.[69] As election day neared, the Kerry campaign decided to contest the hardening conventional wisdom that its candidate was a little too elitist, a little too European or, even worse, French, by sending Kerry hunting in order to highlight his macho credentials. Just eleven precious days before votes were cast at the end of this competitive campaign, Kerry trudged, double-barreled shotgun in hand, into an eastern Ohio cornfield. The hunting foray resulted in four dead geese, but no measurable regular-guy surge to the Democratic nominee.[70] However, the outcome of this campaign event probably was irrelevant, as our analysis in Chapter 2 indicates that voters are not influenced much by perceptions of elitism.

With the exception of leadership, Kerry more than held his own with the incumbent. The Democrat's greatest trait advantage came on public perceptions of competence, Bush's biggest weakness as a candidate. Favorable assessments of the president's knowledge and intelligence declined substantially from 2000 to 2004. Questions concerning the president's lack of engagement and interest in the details of public policy, and the specific ways in which this shortcoming may have contributed to major failures concerning Iraq policy once the president declared "mission accomplished," likely fueled these doubts. On the other hand, the public held Kerry's knowledge and intelligence in high regard. While barely 60 percent of respondents reported favorable impressions of the president's competence, 79 percent perceived Kerry as knowledgeable and over 85 percent described him as intelligent. Besides his two decades of Senate service, Kerry was also well served by his performance in the three presidential debates. Polls showed that the public considered Kerry the winner of each contest.[71] The Democrat appeared "confident, competent, and more informed than the incumbent president."[72] Kerry's competence may have narrowed the gap between the candidates. Bush, after all, won by a slender margin compared to most incumbents who have successfully sought reelection.

Kerry was also viewed more favorably by the public on empathy. Nearly 10 percent more respondents viewed the Democrat as someone who "really cared" about people like them. Like Gore four years earlier, Kerry's aloof personal nature and often remarked on difficulty connecting with voters did not undermine his—and his party's—reputation for empathy. Nearly 58 percent of the public viewed the senator favorably on this trait. However, four years into the Bush administration, the president's empathy rating improved marginally from his first election. Thus, while Kerry did better than Bush on really caring, this advantage was much smaller than Clinton's in 1992 and Obama's four years later.

Finally, neither candidate held an edge on integrity. Bush held about a 5-point lead on morality; Kerry enjoyed a similar advantage on honesty. The favorability levels of both candidates on each trait were about average compared to other candidates in the analysis. For Bush, who had campaigned in 2000 on his promise to restore integrity to a White House brought low by the Clinton years, the issue that threatened to undermine the president's reputation for integrity was the increasingly tenuous justification for invading Iraq. The continued failure to find weapons of mass destruction and increasingly prevalent reports of cherry-picked intelligence threatened to undermine public perceptions of Bush's honesty, or, to the extent that voters perceived the hidden hand of Vice President Richard Cheney as the driving force behind the rush to war, to undercut perceptions of Bush's competence.

One of Kerry's strengths as a candidate was his presumed ability to go toe-to-toe with the president on national security issues. While the Democrat's claims to leadership were undermined by his Senate record—and the Bush campaign's unrelenting exploitation of that record—Kerry could point to his highly decorated service in the Vietnam War. The contrasts with the Republican ticket were striking. Bush served in the Air National Guard during the war. However, the legitimacy of that service became an issue late in the campaign when questions arose over whether Bush had actually fulfilled his obligation to the military. Cheney received five deferments from military service, during years when he was a student and when his wife became pregnant. In contrast, Kerry volunteered for duty and served with distinction, despite being a child of the kind of privilege that enabled many of his generation to avoid service. Yet Kerry's opponents, with the blessing of the Bush campaign, challenged Kerry's claims to heroism, and therefore his integrity, by raising questions about the veracity of Kerry's war record. The Swift Boat Veterans for Truth (SBVT), backed by millions of dollars in anti-Kerry money, claimed that Kerry had distorted his war record and did not deserve the medals conferred on him by the military. Despite the fact that SBVT produced no evidence to substantiate its claims, and that most fellow veterans who had actually served under Kerry's command disputed its charges, the doubts raised about Kerry's service hounded him through election day. Kerry's failure to respond more quickly and forcefully to these attacks may well have cost him in terms of perceptions of his integrity, leadership, or both.[73] Furthermore, the lack of response brought with it one more unwanted comparison to the Dukakis campaign's ineptness at answering charges lodged against it.

Many media pundits explained Bush's victory in 2004 as due in large part to the advantage that he held over Kerry on character traits. Kerry was described as aloof, humorless, and indecisive. In contrast, Bush was viewed as warm, authentic, and a strong leader. Our data show something different. Overall, Kerry was about even with Bush on character traits. The advantage that Bush had on leadership was balanced by Kerry's advantages on empathy and competence. Bush may have been seen by voters as personally warmer and friendlier, but these traits do not influence voters very much. Kerry's defeat most likely reflects the difficulty of defeating an incumbent president with an approval rating around 50 percent, especially in an election in which as many Republicans as Democrats went to the polls.

2008

An anemic and, ultimately, collapsing economy set the tone for the 2008 campaign. Only 1980, the first presidential election in this analysis, comes close to the economic fears and dislocation that Americans faced in 2008. Unlike the 1980 election, however, during which Americans expressed more ambivalence about the character traits of Carter and Reagan, the electorate held the 2008 candidates' leadership skills and competence in higher regard. Given the context of the 2008 election, which so heavily favored the Democratic Party, John McCain's inability to raise doubts about his opponent's readiness to be president, in terms of leadership ability and competence, stands as a stark failure.

When Barack Obama finally became the presumptive nominee of the Democratic Party on June 3, 2008, after a long, achingly close, and extremely hard fought primary season, one thing seemed clear to politicians and pundits alike: McCain, would enjoy a substantial strong leadership advantage over his much younger, largely untested opponent. McCain's prospects for realizing the kind of leadership gap that usually portends a Republican general election victory rested not only on the usual Republican leadership advantage, but also on McCain's personal story. The Arizona senator served with distinction in Vietnam as a naval pilot, flying more than 20 missions over North Vietnam before being shot down and captured. As a prisoner of war for more than five years, McCain displayed heroism in refusing the early release offered him as the son of a Navy admiral and in enduring brutal treatment from his captors.

The obvious contrast with Obama was that the Democrat had never served in the military. Moreover, the Democratic primary seemed to provide the McCain campaign with an opportunity to cement its candidate's strong leadership advantage by building on a message conveniently introduced to the public from within the Democratic Party by Obama's primary rival, Senator Hillary Clinton. The Clinton campaign tried to undermine the excitement building around Obama by emphasizing the degree to which the first-term senator was new to the world stage and, therefore, unproven. The culmination of this strategy was Clinton's "3:00 a.m. Phone Call" advertisement, launched in advance of the Texas primary in early March 2008. The ad argued that Clinton was—and, implicitly, Obama was not—prepared to lead the country and keep it safe in a dangerous world. Hence, the Clinton campaign saw advantage in contrasting its candidate's 15-plus battle-tested years on the national stage, nearly equally split between time spent as First Lady and senator from New York, with the "overnight success" nature of Obama's emergence into the national spotlight. The Clinton strategy failed. But McCain's biography and reputation—war hero, long-serving member of Congress, party-bucking maverick—represented a greater threat to Obama's legitimacy as a potential commander in chief. The McCain campaign raised questions about Obama's lack of experience and leadership skills by attempting to turn the large and enthusiastic crowds Obama routinely drew into a negative. McCain's argument was that Obama's appeal was that of a celebrity without substance. One ad intercut glimpses of Britney Spears and Paris Hilton amidst shots of Obama addressing enormous—and foreign—crowds while the question, "Is He Ready to Lead?" flashed across the screen.[74]

Unfortunately for McCain, as Table 3.1 shows, over 60 percent of Americans seem to have answered "yes" to that question, and a strong leadership gap never materialized. McCain's favorable "strong leadership" rating bested every candidate in this analysis with the exception of Reagan in 1984. This accomplishment was mitigated, however, by the fact that Obama was the only Democrat to exceed 60 percent favorability on this trait. McCain's attempts to take advantage of what seemed to be a strong built-in advantage on this trait were largely futile. Furthermore, on the second indicator of leadership, whether "he is optimistic" described the candidates, Obama enjoyed a lead of about 23 points over McCain. This was the first time the ANES asked voters to assess candidates' optimism, and it seems appropriate given that Americans seem to appreciate optimism in their presidents, particularly during trying times. The obvious comparisons are to Franklin Roosevelt and Ronald Reagan, who each came to power in difficult, or in FDR's case cataclysmic, economies, yet were admired for providing much needed reassurance while leading the nation through great difficulties.

A second trait McCain seemed in an excellent position to exploit was competence. Yet, like leadership, the McCain campaign failed to press its built-in advantage. Any hope that the electorate would turn to McCain's decades of governmental experience in response to the growing threat to the global economy was likely extinguished by McCain's decision to name Sarah Palin as his running mate in order to provide a spark for his candidacy, a decision that likely did more harm than good.[75] To parry the charges of inexperience the McCain campaign managed to make, Obama highlighted his own judgment, from his decision to oppose President Bush's preemptive invasion of Iraq when doing so was politically risky, to his approach to the financial sector collapse, the aftermath of which saw McCain calling for a suspension of the campaign and a postponement of the first presidential debate. In response, Obama calmly observed that presidents often have to do more than one thing at a time. The Obama campaign deftly used the deepening economic crisis to portray McCain's actions as politically motivated and erratic, the latter a word that also served as a none-too-subtle reminder of the Republican candidate's advancing age. Moreover, some ill-considered comments over the course of the campaign haunted McCain. At one point, the Republican admitted to a limited understanding of the economy; later, he declared that the fundamentals of the economy were strong even as grim economic news continued to pile up. Such statements undermined McCain's claim of a competence advantage over his much younger and less experienced opponent.

As Table 3.1 shows, voters held quite favorable views of both candidates' knowledge and intelligence. While McCain enjoyed a slight edge on knowledge, more than three-quarters of the electorate considered both candidates favorably on this trait. Perceptions of each candidate's intelligence were also quite positive. Just over 81 percent of respondents viewed McCain favorably in this regard. Yet this fell over 10 points short of Obama's rating. Over

92 percent of those surveyed perceived Obama's intelligence favorably. This was not only the highest favorable rating for any candidate on this trait, but on any trait displayed in Table 3.1. Moreover, Obama's favorability on intelligence was the only candidate rating to exceed 90 percent. Clearly, the electorate rewarded McCain's experience by perceiving him as quite competent. Equally clearly, the McCain campaign failed to call into question the competence of a young presidential candidate who just over four years earlier was a little known state senator.

Neither candidate held an advantage on integrity. The honesty ratings, about 64 percent for McCain and 60 percent for Obama, were low relative to the average presidential contest in the other years in this analysis. Each campaign made charges designed to stimulate distrust of its opponent. Obama responded to the McCain campaign's assertion that the Democrat was little more than a celebrity with a light résumé by highlighting McCain's supposed hypocrisy on a number of fronts. One Obama ad in particular tried to undermine McCain's integrity by accusing the Republican of a routine willingness to say one thing and do another. In response to the McCain campaign's celebrity attack, the Obama ad pointed to McCain's own pursuit of celebrity, particularly his many appearances on shows such as *The View*, *Saturday Night Live*, and *Late Night with David Letterman*. To McCain's reputation as a political maverick independent of and above the partisan fray, Obama accused his opponent of cozying up to lobbyists and embracing—literally and on numerous occasions—the unpopular President Bush.[76] McCain also had to deal with the echoes of the so-called "Keating Five" scandal, which occurred in the aftermath of the government bailout of the savings and loan industry in the 1980s. McCain was cleared of the most serious charges of influence peddling, but the appearance of impropriety that his association with Keating produced served to further undermine his reputation for being superior to the average Washington politician.[77]

Unfavorable public perceptions of Obama's honesty were likely generated by questions about the candidate's past. First among these was Obama's association with his adopted hometown, Chicago. While Obama framed his Chicago years as in the service of seeking a better life for the city's poor via community organizing, his opponents argued that Obama was guilty by association with the city's notoriously bare knuckle politics. In the ad "The Chicago Way: Shady Politics," created by the Republican National Committee, a narrator brought together three threads from Obama's past: his relationship with William Daley, an Obama adviser and in the ad's words, "heir to the Chicago machine;" his dealings with Tony Rezko, who was convicted of fraud and bribery in 2008, three years after allegedly helping Obama purchase his home on Chicago's South Side; and Obama's association with Bill Ayers, a Chicago-area academic who helped found the Weather Underground, a radical group that engaged in a series of bombings of public buildings to protest the Vietnam War.[78] Separately, these charges did not amount to much. Together, they were meant to suggest that Obama would bring Chicago-style politics to Washington.

And then there was the matter of the Rev. Jeremiah Wright. The McCain campaign joined in the chorus of charges regarding Obama's Chicago roots and his associations with Rezko and Ayers, especially Palin, who seemed to relish the running mate's traditional attacking role by repeatedly charging that Obama consorted with terrorists, in reference to Ayers. However, the McCain campaign steered clear of the Wright controversy. Rev. Wright, who married the Obamas and baptized their children, gave a series of incendiary sermons regarding race in America. The revelation of these speeches and the repeated airing of their most provocative claims during the Democratic primary threatened to derail Obama's campaign by raising questions about how familiar Obama was with these sermons, whether he had denounced them at the time they were given, and whether it was appropriate for him and his family to remain members of Wright's congregation. Given that these questions raised concerns about Obama's integrity and that the Wright videos received an enormous amount of media attention, perceptions of Obama's honesty surely suffered regardless of McCain's decision to avoid discussing the issue in light of the delicate racial politics at work.

Finally, Obama enjoyed a substantial advantage on the only empathy question posed in 2008: did respondents feel that McCain and Obama really cared about people like them? Obama faced charges similar to those made about past Democratic nominees Dukakis, Gore, and Kerry. Could Obama connect with the American public? Was he too much the "liberal elitist" to understand the problems ordinary people faced? While Obama, like those previous candidates, may have had trouble overcoming doubts about his ability to relate to "real folks" at the individual level, we have shown repeatedly in this analysis that when Americans assess empathy, they seem far more concerned with public policy than personal displays of sympathy or geniality. As such, the combination of Democratic trait ownership and an economic free fall overseen by a Republican administration led to a substantial Obama advantage on empathy. Clinton's lead on empathy in 1992 was larger, but only because George H. W. Bush was perceived so negatively on the "really cares" indicator. Favorable perceptions of Obama's empathy were essentially equal to those of Clinton during his first campaign for the presidency.

CONCLUSION

Our analysis of individual elections from 1980 to 2008 demonstrates the great deal of variation that exists in voter perceptions of the character traits of presidential candidates. For the most part, this variation occurs across specific traits within any given election year. In other words, we have no example of a candidate, even landslide winners, who held an advantage on all four character trait dimensions—leadership, competence, integrity, and empathy—discussed in this analysis. In part, this can be explained by trait ownership. Voters held every Democratic candidate in higher regard than their Republican opponents on every survey item related to empathy. Conversely, most Republicans received more favorable ratings on the strong leadership item, often by substantial margins. Republicans who lessened the empathy gap and Democrats who minimized the leadership gap tended to win their elections.

Besides party effects, certain candidates, given their backgrounds, reputations, and campaign messages, also influenced trait perceptions. Clinton and the second President Bush suffered from public doubts about their integrity and competence, respectively. Carter, Mondale, and the first President Bush were considered particularly weak in terms of leadership, Bush especially so given his built-in party advantage. Furthermore, incumbent performance affected trait perceptions. The public evolved from being suspicious of Reagan's character in 1980, in the form of middling ratings on each of the trait items, to far more confident in 1984. Bush's favorability on empathy and his son's standing on competence fell from election to reelection. So did perceptions of Clinton's integrity and, to a lesser extent, his empathy, although favorable perceptions of his competence increased a bit from already high levels.

While trait perceptions varied in interesting ways and often became central to the narrative as the campaigns unfolded, our survey data do not always support the political pundits' conventional view of each race. Democratic candidates Dukakis, Gore, and Kerry had their weaknesses, which included relatively low favorability on the ability to provide strong leadership. But this weakness did not include an overall character deficit vis-à-vis their opponents, as the pundits suggested. Each held his own by balancing poor performance on leadership with the typical Democratic advantage on empathy. And each was viewed about as favorably as his opponent on competence and integrity. Even Gore, who suffered a barrage of criticism regarding his honesty, both from the Bush campaign and the media, still did almost as well as Bush on this trait, and bested him on the other integrity measure, morality.

It also is important to note that perceptions of candidate character traits are not decisive in a presidential election. Clinton won reelection in 1996 by a comfortable margin even though Dole was seen as somewhat better overall on personal traits, capturing advantages on integrity and leadership to more than make up for his deficit on empathy. Similarly, George H. W. Bush won election in 1988 without an advantage on character traits, as did his son in 2000 and 2004. Media commentators and analysts often are quick to ascribe the outcome of a presidential election to the character traits of the candidates. The loser is the one who fails to connect with the voters on a personal level. Often, the winner is the candidate who has a clear advantage on character traits, but in several recent elections this was not the case.

With this descriptive account of the role of candidate character trait perceptions in presidential elections in hand, we now turn to a systematic analysis of these traits. How much do perceptions of character traits affect the vote when we take into account other important factors, such as partisanship, ideology, issues, and retrospective evaluations of incumbent performance? Which individual trait dimensions—leadership, competence, integrity, or empathy—seem to matter most in any given election? Finally, are these perceptions simply a product of rationalization undertaken by voters who have already decided how they would cast their votes, or is there evidence to support character trait perceptions as exerting both direct and indirect effects on the vote? We turn to these questions in the next chapter.

NOTES

1. The ANES has not included a decisiveness item among the candidate trait measures before or since 2004.
2. As we discussed in the last chapter, in a few years the ANES used negative wording to assess voter perceptions of candidate traits. These included questions asking respondents to assess whether the candidates were dishonest, indecisive, or out of touch with ordinary people. In these cases, we include the percentage who answered that, for example, dishonest described the candidates "not too well," or "not well at all."
3. To save space we do not display any trait measures that the ANES asked about just once, with the following two exceptions. These come from two of the more recent presidential elections, 2004 and 2008. In 2004, respondents were asked to assess the extent to which Bush and Kerry could be described as "indecisive." In 2008, respondents were asked whether "optimistic" described McCain and Obama.
4. As we detailed in Chapter 2, we code responses as to whether the individual trait describes the candidate in the following manner: "Extremely well" is coded +2; "quite well," +1; "not too well," −1; and "not well at all," −2. A mean score of zero suggests that positive and negative references to a candidate balance out. By this measure, the highest mean score for any candidate on any trait is Obama's score of 1.29 for intelligence in 2008, followed closely by Reagan's score of 1.27 for honesty in 1980. Respondents gave the lowest mean scores to Carter for leadership in 1980 (-.47), and Bush for "cares about people" in 1992 and Clinton for morality in 1996 (-.43).
5. Danny Hayes, "Candidate Qualities through a Partisan Lens: A Theory of Trait Ownership," *American Journal of Political Science* 49 (2005): 908–923.
6. For a discussion of issue ownership, see John R. Petrocik, "Issue Ownership in Presidential Elections, with a 1980 Case Study," *American Journal of Political Science* 40 (1996): 825–850.
7. An October 2008 Pew Research Center for the People & the Press survey found that 71 percent of respondents answered "yes" when asked the following question: "As I name some traits, please tell me whether you think each one describes Barack Obama. . . . Inspiring . . . Do you think of Barack Obama as inspiring or not?" Only 37 percent agreed that McCain possessed this trait. We could find no general election polls in 2000 or 2004 that asked respondents to assess the inspirational qualities of the candidates.
8. Hayes, "Candidate Qualities through a Partisan Lens," 2005, 920.

9. Hayes, "Candidate Qualities through a Partisan Lens," 2005.
10. A July 1980 national survey conducted by Cambridge Reports/Research International included the following question: "Some people say that most of the support for John Anderson (for President) that has emerged in recent months is based more on dislike of Jimmy Carter and Ronald Reagan rather than on any real knowledge of, or support for, Anderson. Would you strongly agree, somewhat agree, somewhat disagree, or strongly disagree with this idea?" The 70 percent who expressed some level of agreement in July was up from the 63 percent who expressed agreement when asked the same question as part of an April 1980 poll.
11. Kathleen A. Frankovic, "Public Opinion Trends," in *The Election of 1980,* ed. Gerald Pomper (Chatham, NJ: Chatham House Publishers, 1981).
12. Frankovic, "Public Opinion Trends,"103.
13. While we have no ANES data relevant to this trait, four CBS News/New York Times polls taken in September and October of that year included the following question: "Now, I would like to read you a list of sentences that people have used about candidates for public office. For each sentence, I would like you to tell me whether it fits Gerald Ford or Jimmy Carter better. If you feel the sentence fits neither person, or fits both people equally, just say so. . . . He's more of a leader." This is obviously not the same as the ANES questions we are dealing with in this research, in that it forces a comparison on respondents, some of whom may have positive (or negative) impressions of both candidates' leadership skills. In any event, Carter trailed Ford in these direct comparisons by anywhere from 2 to 7 points across the four polls, a small gap as likely to be explained by the fact that Carter was still relatively new to the national political scene while Ford was the incumbent president, as by Republican trait ownership.
14. The percentage of all voters who viewed Anderson favorably was 30.7 percent on being a strong leader; 31.2 percent on being inspiring; 54.7 percent on being knowledgeable; 55.7 percent on being moral; and 64.8 percent on being honest. These results are low relative to Carter and Reagan in part because anywhere from 25 percent to one-third of voters expressed no opinion about the less well known Anderson's character traits.
15. Frankovic, "Public Opinion Trends," 103.
16. Ross K. Baker, "The Outlook for the Carter Administration," In *The Election of 1976,* ed. Gerald Pomper (New York: David McKay Company, 1977), 146.
17. Gary R. Orren, "The Nomination Process: The Vicissitudes of Candidate Selection," in *The Elections of 1984,* ed. Michael Nelson (Washington, DC: CQ Press, 1985), 68, 73.
18. Henry A. Plotkin, "Issues in the Campaign," in *The Election of 1984,* ed. Gerald Pomper (Chatham, NJ: Chatham House Publishers, 1985), 39.
19. Marjorie Randon Hershey, "The Campaign and the Media," in *The Election of 1988,* ed. Gerald M. Pomper (Chatham, NJ: Chatham House Publishers, 1989), 77.
20. Margaret Garrard Warner, "Bush Battles the 'Wimp Factor,'" *Newsweek,* October 19, 1987.
21. Paul R. Abramson, John H. Aldrich, and David W. Rohde, *Change and Continuity in the 1988 Elections* (Washington, DC: CQ Press, 1989), 50.
22. Hershey, "The Campaign and the Media," 86.
23. "Willie Horton," "Revolving Door," and "Tank Ride" are available at http://www.livingroomcandidate.org/commercials/1988. While the latter two ads were created and aired directly by the Bush campaign, the "Willie Horton" ad was the work of the National Security Political Action Committee,

an organization that was technically independent of the Bush campaign. The Horton ad and the role that it played in the campaign are discussed in Jamieson (1992, 16–42).

24. Paul J. Quirk, "The Election," in *The Elections of 1988,* ed. Michael Nelson (Washington, DC: CQ Press, 1989), 76.
25. Quirk, "The Election," 72.
26. Hershey, "The Campaign and the Media," 78.
27. American Presidency Project, "Presidential Debate in Winston-Salem, North Carolina" (September 25, 1988), http://www.presidency.ucsb.edu/ws/index.php?pid=29411 (accessed March 14, 2012).
28. Larry Martz, "Dukakis: By the People Who Know Him Best," *Newsweek,* July 25, 1988.
29. Barbara G. Farrah and Ethel Klein, "Public Opinion Trends," in *The Election of 1988,* ed., Gerald M. Pomper (Chatham, NJ: Chatham House Publishers, 1989), 109.
30. This result is from an ABC News poll conducted on April 8 and 9, just after April 7 victories in the Wisconsin and New York primaries made it increasingly clear that Clinton would be the Democratic nominee.
31. Abramson, Aldrich, and Rohde, *Change and Continuity in the 1992 Elections,* 38.
32. Ryan J. Barilleaux and Randall E. Adkins, "The Nominations: Process and Patterns," in *The Elections of 1992,* ed. Michael Nelson (Washington, DC: CQ Press, 1993), 45–46.
33. After announcing his willingness to run, Perot spent the rest of the spring and early summer assembling a high-profile campaign staff. On July 16, as Clinton prepared to give his acceptance speech at the Democratic National Convention in New York City, Perot announced that he would not be a candidate for president, citing a reluctance to allow the election to be decided by the House of Representatives in the event that no candidate were to receive a majority of the Electoral College vote. As election day approached, after he had jumped back into the race in September, Perot claimed that the actual reason for his July exit was to avoid a Republican Party-orchestrated dirty tricks campaign aimed at his daughter's approaching wedding. An account of Perot's evolving explanations of his quitting the race can be found in Richard L. Berke, "Perot Says He Quit In July To Thwart G.O.P. 'Dirty Tricks'," *New York Times,* October 26, 1992, national edition.
34. The Time/CNN questions were worded as follows: "In your view, which of these descriptions apply and which do not apply to [Candidate Name]: . . ." The relevant traits included in the survey were "a strong and decisive leader," "cares about the average American," and "would say anything to get elected president." A final question asked "Do you think [Candidate Name] is honest and trustworthy enough to be president, or don't you think so?" Thus, the survey included one leadership, one empathy, and two integrity items.
35. The Time/CNN results for Bush and Clinton on the empathy and both integrity items are very similar to ANES results. Respondents in both cases suggested a substantial empathy advantage for Clinton and the reverse on integrity. The exception is the leadership item. Among registered voters in late October, the Time/CNN poll showed that Bush held a 12-point lead on Clinton, 63 percent to 51 percent, with regard to whether "strong and decisive leader" applied to each candidate. In contrast, as displayed in Table 3.1, slightly more major party voters viewed Clinton as likely to provide strong leadership, 58 percent to 55 percent. Including Perot voters narrows this advantage to 56 percent to 55 percent.

36. Abramson, Aldrich, and Rohde, *Change and Continuity in the 1992 Elections,* 51–53.
37. F. Christopher Arterton, "Campaign '92: Strategies and Tactics," in *The Election of 1992,* ed. Gerald M. Pomper (Chatham, NJ: Chatham House Publishers, 1993), 76.
38. The Clinton ad "Scary" is available at http://www.livingroomcandidate.org/commercials/ 1992.
39. James Ceaser and Andrew Busch, *Upside Down and Inside Out: The 1992 Elections and American Politics* (Lanham, MD: Rowman and Littlefield Publishers, 1993), 22.
40. See, e.g., John E. Yang, "Bush Says Tax Plan Critics Are Divisive; President Goes to Grocers to Seek Support for Economic Incentives," *Washington Post,* February 5, 1992.
41. Paul J. Quirk and Jon K. Dalager, "The 1992 Presidential Election: A 'New Democrat' and a New Kind of Presidential Campaign," in *The Elections of 1992,* ed. Michael Nelson (Washington, DC: CQ Press, 1993), 73.
42. Maureen Dowd, "A No-Nonsense Sort of Talk Show," *New York Times,* October 16, 1992.
43. Walter Dean Burnham, "Bill Clinton: Riding the Tiger," in *The Election of 1996,* ed. Gerald M. Pomper (Chatham, NJ: Chatham House Publishers, 1997), 12–13.
44. The voting public viewed Perot less positively than Dole on every trait measure and bested Clinton only on the presidents' glaring weakness: the two integrity items. The percentage of all voters who viewed Perot favorably on each of the items was 35.3 percent on strong leadership; 31.5 percent on being inspiring; 49.8 percent on getting things done; 67.3 percent on being knowledgeable; 62.7 percent on being moral; 56.7 percent on being honest; and 37.8 percent on caring about people like the respondent.
45. Katherine Q. Seelye, "Dole Is Imploring Reporters to 'Rise Up' Against the Press," *New York Times,* October 26, 1996.
46. The Dole campaign had only itself to blame for Clinton's bridge metaphor. In his Republican National Convention acceptance speech, Dole offered himself as a bridge to the America of the 1920s, the America into which he was born. The president responded in kind during his acceptance speech. In the words of a *New York Times* editorial, "It was an odd line coming from the party of Ronald Reagan, the arch-angel of American optimism, and Mr. Clinton served notice that Mr. Dole would not be allowed to forget his blunder. 'We do not need to build a bridge to the past, we need to build a bridge to the future,' Mr. Clinton said in elaborating his theme that he and the Democrats are the best leaders for the next century" See, "Mr. Clinton's Bridge," *New York Times* (August 31, 1996).
47. Marion R. Just, "Candidate Strategies and the Media Campaign," in *The Election of 1996,* ed. Gerald M. Pomper (Chatham, NJ: Chatham House Publishers, 1997), 80; Michael Nelson, "The Election: Turbulence and Tranquility in Contemporary American Politics," in *The Elections of 1996,* ed. Michael Nelson (Washington, DC: CQ Press, 1997), 58.
48. There was an exception, the effect of which influenced the Dole campaign more than it did the American public. *The Washington Post* uncovered evidence of an extra-marital affair decades in the candidate's past and before his marriage to his second wife, Elizabeth Dole. While the *Post* decided against running the story, the threat that it would likely led the Dole campaign to tone down some of its criticisms of Clinton's personal behavior. A behind-the-scenes account of this story is provided by Leonard Downie, Jr., and Robert G. Kaiser, *The News About the News: American Journalism in Peril* (New York: Vintage Books, 2002).

49. Harold W. Stanley, "The Nominations: Republican Doldrums, Democratic Revival," in *The Elections of 1996*, ed. Michael Nelson (Washington, DC: CQ Press, 1997), 37.

50. James Ceaser and Andrew Busch, *Losing to Win: The 1996 Elections and American Politics*, (Lanham, MD: Rowman and Littlefield Publishers, 1993), 93–94; Just," Candidate Strategies and the Media Campaign," 93–94.

51. Charles Prysby and Carmine Scavo, "Who Hates Hillary? Public Opinion Toward the First Lady," *Politics and Policy* 29 (2001): 521–544.

52. Margaret Tseng, "The Clinton Effect: How a Lame-Duck President Impacted His Vice President's Election Prospects," in *The Election of the Century*, eds. Stephen J. Wayne and Clyde Wilcox (Armonk, NY: M. E. Sharpe, 2002).

53. Michael Kinsley, "The Art of Finger-Pointing: Why Wait Until Next Week? Let's Start Now," *Slate* (October 31, 2000), http://www.slate.com/articles/news_and_politics/readme/2000/ 10/the_art_of_fingerpointing.html (accessed September 30, 2013).

54. Marjorie Randon Hershey, "The Campaign and the Media," in *The Election of 2000*, ed. Gerald M. Pomper (Chatham, NJ: Chatham House Publishers, 2001), 70.

55. This was a promise that rang true during the campaign, but one that Bush proved unable to deliver on once in office. See Gary C. Jacobson, *A Uniter, Not a Divider: George W. Bush and the American People* (New York: Pearson Longman, 2007).

56. Hershey, "The Campaign and the Media," 60–62.

57. Michael Nelson, "The Election: Ordinary Politics, Extraordinary Outcome," in *The Elections of 2000*, ed. Michael Nelson (Washington, DC: CQ Press, 2001), 57–61.

58. James W. Ceaser and Andrew E. Busch, *The Perfect Tie: The True Story of the 2000 Presidential Election* (New York: Rowman & Littlefield Publishers, 2001), 33.

59. Hershey, "The Campaign and the Media," 58; Paul J. Quirk and Sean C. Matheson, "The Presidency: The Election and the Prospects for Leadership," in *The Elections of 2000*, ed. Michael Nelson (Washington, DC: CQ Press, 2001), 170.

60. Wilson Carey McWilliams, "The Meaning of the Election," in *The Election of 2000*, ed., Gerald M. Pomper (Chatham, NJ: Chatham House Publishers, 2001), 180.

61. Ceaser and Busch, *The Perfect Tie*, 150; Hershey, "The Campaign and the Media," 62.

62. Marshall Sella, "The Stiff Guy vs. the Dumb Guy," *New York Times Magazine* (September 24, 2000), 72.

63. Scott Rosenberg, "Did Gore Invent the Internet?" *Salon* (October 5, 2000), http://www.salon. com/2000/10/05/gore_internet/ (accessed October 16, 2012).

64. For a typical example, see Carter M. Yang, "Al Gore Prone to Exaggeration," *ABC News* (October 7, 2000), http://abcnews.go.com/Politics/story?id=122765&page=1 (accessed September 27, 2013).

65. This question was negatively worded. Respondents in 2000 were asked whether the phrase he is "out of touch with ordinary people" characterized each candidate. Table 3.1 reports the percent of people who said that the statement characterized the candidate "not too well" or "not well at all."

66. Ceaser and Busch, *The Perfect Tie*, 125–127.

67. This question was worded negatively. Respondents in 2004 were asked whether the phrase he "can't make up his own mind" described the candidates. Table 3.1 reports the percentage of people who said that the statement characterized the candidate "not too well" or "not well at all."

68. See "Windsurfing" at http://www.livingroomcandidate.org/commercials/2004.

69. James W. Ceaser and Andrew E. Busch, *Red Over Blue: The 2004 Elections and American Politics,* (Lanham, MD: Rowman & Littlefield Publishers, 2005), 17.

70. On October 21, 2004, a panel of pundits on CNN's *Lou Dobbs Tonight* discussed how Kerry's hunting foray would play with conservatives, suburban women, and the "Bubba" vote. Mark Warren of *Esquire* magazine remarked that Kerry's photo opportunity had "less to do with gun control, more to do with regular guy. Which is . . . the regular guy gap with Kerry. That he's just trying to convince you that he can have a beer with you, he can shoot a gun with you."

71. The average responses to survey questions that asked the public who won each debate in the week after each contest show that the public believed Kerry won the first and third debates by about a 10-point margin. This gap widened to over 30 points for the second debate.

72. Gerald M. Pomper, "The Presidential Election: The Ills of American Politics After 9/11," in *The Elections of 2004,* ed., Michael Nelson (Washington, DC: CQ Press, 2005), 57.

73. Pomper, "The Presidential Election," 66–67.

74. See "Celeb at http://www.livingroomcandidate.org/commercials/2008.

75. Gerald M. Pomper, "The Presidential Election," in in *The Elections of 2008,* ed., Michael Nelson (Washington, DC: CQ Press, 2010), 59.

76. See "Embrace" at http://www.livingroomcandidate.org/commercials/2008.

77. Kate Kenski, Bruce W. Hardy, and Kathleen Hall Jamieson, *The Obama Victory: How Media, Money, and Message Shaped the 2008 Election* (Oxford: Oxford University Press, 2010), 31.

78. Kenski, Hardy, and Jamieson, *The Obama Victory,* 96–97.

4 The Impact of Candidate Character Trait Perceptions on the Vote

Voters care about character. As previous chapters show, voters develop perceptions of the character traits of presidential candidates, perceptions that tend to fall along four dimensions of character: leadership, competence, integrity, and empathy. In every year, there is considerable variation among the voters in their evaluations of these traits: some voters rate a candidate highly on a number of traits, while others have unfavorable perceptions. Not only is there variation among the voters in each year; there also is considerable variation across the years in the overall assessment of the character traits of the presidential candidates. As we discussed in Chapter 3, in some years, one candidate has a distinct overall advantage on character traits, but in other years, the candidates are assessed more evenly by the electorate. Regardless of what overall advantage on character traits exists, differences on individual trait dimensions are often pronounced in each year. Republican presidential candidates usually are viewed more favorably by the voters on providing strong leadership, and Democratic candidates are seen as more empathetic, although these partisan advantages vary across the years, as the previous chapter demonstrated. While the Republican candidate was seen as a stronger leader in most of the years that we examined, in 1988 and 1992 he held little or no advantage. The magnitude of the advantage possessed by the Democratic candidate on empathy similarly varied across elections, from moderate in 1984 and 2000 to very substantial in 1992 and 2008. Perceptions of integrity and competence display no systematic partisan advantage, but they too vary considerably across elections, sometimes providing sizable advantages to specific candidates, such as Bob Dole's enormous superiority on integrity in 1996 or John Kerry's great advantage on competence in 2004.

These observations lead to a central question: how much do perceptions of candidate character traits affect the presidential vote? Does having a more favorable personal assessment of one candidate make a voter significantly more likely to vote for that candidate? When one candidate is evaluated more favorably than the other by the electorate, does this translate into significantly more votes? Do some traits count more in the minds of most voters? We investigate these questions in this chapter, relying again on the

ANES survey data from 1980 through 2008. The data for the 2012 election are analyzed in a separate chapter because the trait questions were asked in a different format in that year. As we shall see, our findings indicate that voter perceptions of the character traits of the presidential candidates have a substantial effect on the vote. A candidate who is seen as superior to his opponent on character traits overall does benefit significantly in the vote. Furthermore, some character traits tend to matter more than others. Leadership and empathy usually are the traits that have the greatest impact, although there is considerable variation across the years in the impact of individual trait dimensions on the vote, which also is an interesting finding.

THE ANALYSIS OF TRAIT PERCEPTIONS AND THE VOTE

Any analysis of the effect that perceptions of the character traits of presidential candidates have on voting must consider the fact that these perceptions are associated with a variety of other political attitudes that may affect the vote. This point often is ignored by media pundits, who frequently look just at the simple association between trait perceptions and the vote and conclude that character traits play a big role in the presidential election without considering the possibility that these relationships could represent the confounding effect of other variables. Party identification is at the top of this list of possible confounding factors, not surprisingly, since partisanship affects how people see the political world in so many ways.[1] Democrats are prone to see the Democratic candidate in more positive personal terms, and Republicans have a similar partisan bias. Beyond party identification, perceptions of candidate character traits are correlated with ideology, issue orientations, and assessments of the performance of the president, all of which are also related to party identification and to the presidential vote. We include measures of all of these attitudes in our analysis to determine the independent, direct effect that trait perceptions have on the vote. Since the analysis only examines the vote for the two major-party candidates, the dependent variable (the vote) is dichotomous, making logistic regression the appropriate statistical analysis.[2]

It would be too repetitive to report the details of the logistic regression of the vote for each election from 1980 to 2008 (the analysis of the 2012 election is reserved for a later chapter). Instead, we provide a more detailed report for three elections: 1980, 1996, and 2008. These three elections span the time period that we analyze, so we can see whether similar effects were present for more recent elections as for elections 30 years ago. Moreover, these three years capture three types of presidential elections: one where an incumbent was defeated, one where an incumbent was reelected, and one that did not involve an incumbent seeking reelection. After a more careful analysis of the impact of candidate character trait perceptions on the vote in these three presidential elections, we provide a summarized report of these relationships for all eight elections held during this time span.

Candidate Character Traits in the 1980 Presidential Election

To begin, we look at an analysis of the 1980 presidential vote. As Chapter 3 discussed, this was an election in which the Republican challenger, Ronald Reagan, had a huge advantage over the incumbent president, Jimmy Carter, on the leadership dimension. While Carter did as well or better than Reagan on other character traits, Reagan still came out ahead on the voters' overall assessment of character. Moreover, Reagan's personal characteristics were widely viewed in the media as contributing to his victory. In this analysis, we predict the 1980 presidential vote from the overall candidate character trait index, along with party identification, ideological orientation, retrospective evaluations of President Carter's handling of the presidency, and attitudes on social welfare and moral issues.[3] The character trait index is the average net score across all of the candidate character trait items asked in that year, and it runs from –4.0 (most favorable to the Democratic candidate) to +4.0 (most favorable to the Republican candidate), as explained in Chapter 2.

The results of the logistic regression analysis are in Table 4.1. The first column (model 1) shows the prediction of the vote using just party identification and ideology. As we can see, relying on just these two variables, we are able to predict the presidential vote fairly well: almost 82 percent of the cases are correctly predicted, and the pseudo $R^2 = .55$. The analysis in the second column (model 2) adds the evaluation of Carter's job performance and orientations on social welfare and moral issues to the equation. This improves our ability to predict the vote, showing that while voting was heavily influenced by party identification and ideology, these additional attitudes also influenced the presidential vote. Finally, we include the candidate character trait index in the analysis (model 3), which increases our ability to predict the vote even more: about 90 percent of the cases are correctly predicted, and the pseudo $R^2 = .78$. The coefficient for the trait index is both statistically significant at the .001 level and substantively large. Even with other relevant political attitudes held constant, change in a voter's evaluation of the character traits of the candidates, as measured by the trait index, has a strong effect on his or her vote.

The approach that we employ here is a conservative one. We assume that perceptions of the character traits of the presidential candidates can be influenced by the other variables in the equation, but that trait perceptions do not affect these other variables.[4] In other words, while trait perceptions have a direct effect on the vote, they do not have any indirect effects through the other variables. If trait perceptions do affect any of these other attitudes—if, for example, perceptions of Carter's character traits influenced how voters evaluated his handling of the presidency, rather than the other way around—then there would be both direct and indirect effects on the

Table 4.1 Logistic Regression of Presidential Vote, 1980

Independent variable	Model 1	Model 2	Model 3
Party identification	.855**	.669**	.476**
	(.064)	(.077)	(.088)
Ideology	.348**	.292**	.278*
	(.085)	(.116)	(.130)
Approval of Carter's job performance		1.308**	.763**
		(.137)	(.157)
Social welfare issues index		.447**	.291*
		(.111)	(.134)
Moral issues index		.556	.414
		(.371)	(.414)
Candidate trait index			1.489**
			(.196)
Nagelkerke pseudo R^2	.55	.71	.78
% cases correctly predicted	81.7	86.8	89.7

**p < .01, *p < .05 (one-tailed tests).

Note: Bolded entries are logistic regression coefficients, with standard errors in parentheses. The dependent variable is the presidential vote. See the text for details on the independent variables. Positive coefficients indicate that the likelihood of voting for Reagan is increased by having a stronger Republican identification, a more conservative ideological orientation, more conservative orientations on the two issue indices, greater disapproval of Carter's presidential job performance, and more positive views of Reagan's character traits relative to Carter's.

Source: 1980 American National Election Study. Only major party voters are included in the analysis.

vote, which would make the total impact of character trait perceptions even greater than what we estimate.

If we compare the regression coefficients for the variables in model 3 with those for model 2, we see that when character trait perceptions are included in the analysis, the impact of a number of the other variables declines. For example, the coefficient for party identification in model 2 is .669, but in model 3 it is .476. This shows that some of the effect that party identification has on the vote is not a direct effect, but rather an indirect effect through perceptions of candidate character traits. This makes perfect theoretical sense. Both Democrats and Republicans naturally would be inclined to see their party's candidate in more favorable terms, which then would strengthen their desire to vote for him. However, perceptions of candidate character traits are not purely reflections of orientations such as party identification or ideology. As we discussed in Chapter 3, in some years the Democratic or Republican candidate is viewed more positively than in other years, both overall and on specific trait dimensions. These substantial differences across the years indicate that the candidates themselves influence these perceptions, and since trait perceptions affect the vote, candidates who are able to create more positive images will be rewarded in the election. That is exactly what happened in 1980. Even though more voters identified as Democrats than as Republicans, Reagan was seen by the voters in more favorable personal terms than was Carter, which helped him win the election.

Because logistic regression coefficients are difficult to interpret directly, we translate the regression results into the change in the likelihood of voting for the Republican candidate for average Democrats, independents, and Republicans, given different trait index scores. To calculate the predicted vote probabilities for average Democrats, we determined the attitudes of the average Democratic identifier on the other variables in the equation (ideology, assessments of presidential performance, and orientations on social welfare and moral issues) and then held these values constant to calculate how the expected vote of an average Democrat would change as his or her score on the candidate character trait index changed.[5] The same procedure was followed for average independents and average Republicans.[6] In doing this, we only calculated the vote probabilities for character trait index scores between –2.0 and +2.0. While the trait index scores run from –4.0 to +4.0, few voters had scores above +2.0 or below –2.0, scores that are extremely favorable to one candidate. Voters who had such trait index scores were almost exclusively strong partisans with a high predisposition to vote for their party's candidate anyway, so their voting behavior was scarcely altered as their evaluations of the personal qualities of the candidates became even more lopsided. In fact, most of the voters in 1980 were at best moderately favorable to one of the two candidates on this factor: about 53 percent had a candidate character trait index score that was between –1.0 and +1.0, a figure that is typical for other years as well, although the exact percentage varies from year to year.

The predicted probabilities of voting Republican for Democrats, independents, and Republicans are displayed in Figure 4.1. As we can see, the likelihood of voting for the Republican candidate, Ronald Reagan, increases substantially as the candidate character trait index score moves from –2.0 to +2.0. The greatest change occurs between –1.0 and +1.0, which represents over one-half of the voters, as pointed out above. Independents were strongly affected by their perceptions of the character traits of the presidential candidates. An average independent voter with a trait index score of –1.0, which would be moderately favorable to Carter, had only about a 36 percent likelihood of voting for Reagan, but with a trait index score of +1.0 (moderately favorable to Reagan), the same voter had about a 95 percent likelihood of voting for Reagan, an increase of almost 60 percentage points in the probability of a Reagan vote.

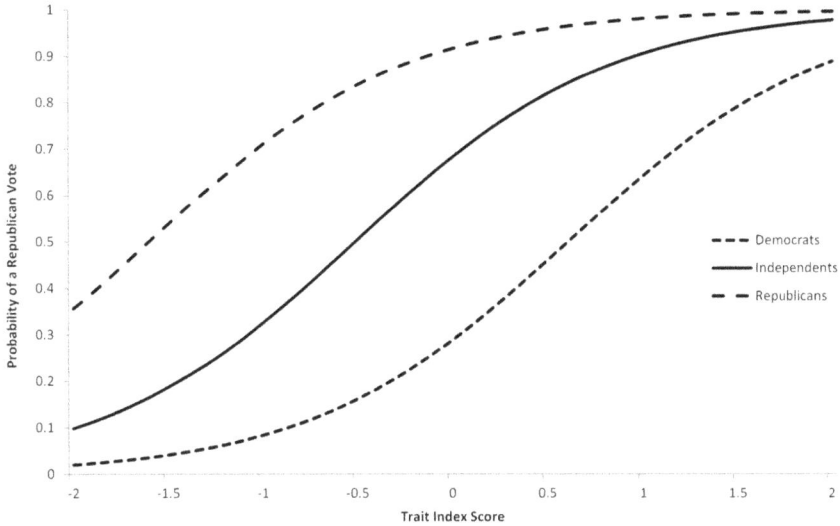

Figure 4.1   Presidential Voting by Trait Perceptions, 1980

Democrats also were substantially affected by their trait perceptions. We can see from Figure 4.1 that Democrats who thought that Reagan was superior to Carter on character traits were more likely to defect than were Democrats who thought the opposite. In fact, this analysis indicates that an average Democrat who perceived Carter and Reagan to be even overall in character traits (i.e., a character trait index score of 0) had about a 30 percent likelihood of voting for Reagan. This is a fairly high defection rate, and it reflects the fact that many Democrats were unsatisfied with Carter's job performance, especially regarding the economy, so they had reasons to vote for Reagan apart from questions of personal character. If that average Democrat also was moderately favorable to Reagan in trait perceptions—represented by a trait index score of 1.0, for example—then the likelihood of voting Republican skyrocketed to 70 percent. Moreover, it was not improbable that an average Democrat would see Reagan as superior to Carter in personal qualities. There were a significant number of Democrats who had exactly such views: about one-fourth of the Democrats had a character trait index score above zero, and 10 percent had a score that exceeded +1.0. Carter won only about 75 percent of the vote of Democrats; had he been viewed more favorably in personal terms, he would have captured more of these votes and thus made the election closer than it was.

Republicans were less influenced by trait perceptions, but they were not immune to such effects. An average Republican who had a candidate character trait index score of zero (not favorable to either candidate) had a 93 percent likelihood of voting for Reagan, but an average Republican with a trait index score of −1.0 (moderately favorable to Carter) had only a 70 percent likelihood of voting for Reagan. Republicans were strongly inclined to vote for Reagan on other grounds, so having a somewhat unfavorable view of his character traits, relative to those of Carter, did not diminish their enthusiasm for voting Republican nearly as much as was the case for Democrats and independents.

Perceptions of character traits contributed to Carter's defeat, although other factors were very important in that election.[7] Carter's approval rating in August 1980 was just 26 percent.[8] The worsening economic situation, which was marked by both high unemployment and inflation, the prolonged stalemate in the Iran hostage crisis, and the Soviet invasion of Afghanistan all contributed to a widespread feeling that Carter was managing neither the economy nor foreign affairs very well. These factors alone could have produced a Republican victory, but it helped that Reagan was eventually viewed in sufficiently favorable personal terms for voters to be confident that he could do a better job than the incumbent president.

There was a significant third-party candidate in this election: congressman John Anderson, who ran as an independent, received almost 7 percent of the vote. Even though few voters cast a ballot for him, Anderson was not perceived much more negatively than Carter and Reagan in personal terms by the electorate. Voters ranked him between Carter and Reagan on being inspiring and being a strong leader, and they thought that he was about as knowledgeable as Reagan and only slightly less honest than the two major candidates. The interesting finding is that the Anderson voters perceived the character traits of Carter and Reagan negatively. Anderson voters tended to be about as negative as the Carter voters in perceptions of Reagan and about as negative as the Reagan voters in perceptions of Carter. This suggests that voters are particularly motivated to cast a ballot for a minor-party candidate when they do not find either major-party candidate to be appealing in personal terms.

Candidate Character Traits in the 1996 Presidential Election

Another interesting election to examine is the 1996 contest between Bill Clinton and Bob Dole, a presidential election that differs from 1980 in two significant ways. First, the incumbent president was reelected, not defeated. Second, the candidate who was more highly rated on character by the voters, Dole, lost the election, as Chapter 3 pointed out. We ran a logistic regression of the presidential vote in 1996, using the candidate character trait index along with other relevant political attitudes, such as party identification and evaluations of presidential performance, just as we did for 1980.[9] These results are presented in Table 4.2, and the patterns are similar to those for 1980: the trait index has a strong impact on the vote, and the coefficients for the other variables decline when the trait index is included in the equation, indicating that the effect of party identification, ideology, and other attitudes on the vote is partly through their influence on the perception of candidate character traits.

Again, we translate the results of the logistic regression into predicted probabilities of voting for the Republican candidate, given different trait index scores. Figure 4.2 shows the predicted probabilities of voting for the Republican candidate in 1996 for average Democrats, independents, and Republicans, just as Figure 4.1 did for 1980. Comparing Figures 4.1 and 4.2, we see that candidate character trait perceptions played a smaller role in 1996 than they did in 1980. Democrats, independents, and Republicans all increased their likelihood of voting for Dole as their scores on the trait index

Table 4.2 Logistic Regression of Presidential Vote, 1996

Independent variable	Model 1	Model 2	Model 3
Party identification	.927** (.059)	.696** (.080)	.476** (.092)
Ideology	.689** (.099)	.500** (.140)	.374** (.159)
Approval of Clinton's handling of the economy		1.060** (.174)	.574** (.207)
Approval of Clinton's handling of national security		.856** (.143)	.669** (.163)
Social welfare issues index		.699** (.156)	.611** (.134)
Moral issues index		.552 (.464)	.573 (.527)
Candidate trait index			1.281** (.196)
Nagelkerke pseudo R^2	.72	.83	.87
% cases correctly predicted	88.4	91.2	93.9

**p < .01, *p < .05 (one-tailed tests).
Note: Bolded entries are logistic regression coefficients, with standard errors in parentheses. The dependent variable is the presidential vote. See the text for details on the independent variables. Positive coefficients indicate that the likelihood of voting for Dole is increased by having a stronger Republican identification, a more conservative ideological orientation, more conservative orientations on the two issue indices, greater disapproval of Clinton's presidential job performance, and more positive views of Dole's character traits relative to Clinton's.
Source: 1996 American National Election Study. Only major party voters are included in the analysis.

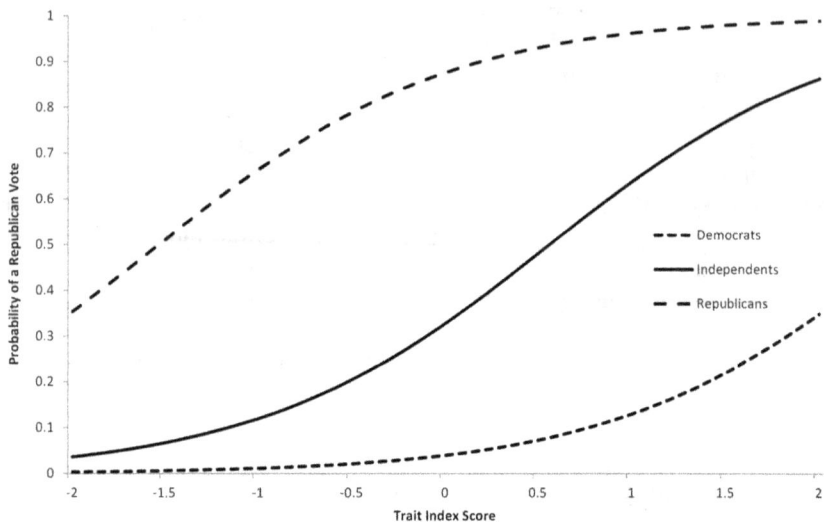

Figure 4.2   Presidential Voting by Trait Perceptions, 1996

increased, but the extent of the increase was considerably smaller than what we found for 1980. Perceptions of the character traits of Clinton and Dole had relatively little effect on Democrats, who were not prone to defect in that year. Even when an average Democrat had a character trait index score of +2.0, which would be quite favorable to Dole, such a voter had only a 35 percent likelihood of voting for the Republican candidate. Republicans were somewhat more affected by their trait perceptions: moving from a trait index score of +1.0 (moderately favorable to Dole) to −1.0 (moderately favorable to Clinton) lowered the likelihood that an average Republican would vote for Dole from about 95 percent down to 65 percent. Independents were the most affected by trait perceptions; a change from −1.0 to +1.0 in the character trait index increased the probability of a Republican vote for an average independent by over 50 percentage points.

Clinton had the advantage of running for reelection during a time of peace and prosperity, just the opposite of what Carter faced in 1980. Voters were generally pleased with the performance of the first Clinton administration, as reflected by an approval rating of over 50 percent in the summer of 1996. The best hope for Dole was to win over voters based on character, an area where Clinton had real weaknesses. But while Dole was seen as better overall on character traits, these perceptions did not affect the vote enough to change the outcome. Clinton did receive a smaller share of the vote than he would have if he had been perceived in more favorable personal terms, especially with regard to his integrity, but he nevertheless won by a comfortable margin.[10]

As in 1980, there was a significant third-party candidate in this presidential election. Reform Party candidate Ross Perot received about 8 percent of the vote, far less than he won in 1992, but still a strong showing for a third-party candidate. Unlike the Anderson voters in 1980, the 1996 Perot voters did not hold strongly negative views of the character traits of both candidates. The Perot voters were more positive in their assessments of Clinton's character traits than were the Dole voters and more positive in their assessments of Dole's character than were the Clinton voters. Overall, the Perot voters found Dole to be better than Clinton on integrity and leadership, but the reverse on empathy. Naturally, the Perot voters thought that their candidate was better than both Clinton and Dole on character, but their vote does not seem to be the result of a strong antipathy toward the character of both major party candidates, as we found for Anderson voters in 1980. The same pattern is true in 1992, when Perot won around 19 percent of the vote: the Perot voters had significantly more favorable views of Clinton than did the Bush voters and significantly more favorable views of Bush than did the Clinton voters. While evaluations of the character traits of the candidates played a role, the decision to vote for Perot appears to be influenced more by orientations toward policy issues and party performance.[11]

Candidate Character Traits in the 2008 Presidential Election

The 2008 presidential election is an equally interesting case.[12] Unlike 1980 and 1996, this election did not feature an incumbent president running for reelection. It also was an election in which the two candidates, Barack Obama and John McCain, differed enormously on a variety of personal characteristics, as Chapter 3 noted. Perhaps these circumstances would make character traits particularly important to the voters. To examine these effects, we ran a logistic regression of the presidential vote in 1996, using the candidate character trait index along with other relevant political attitudes, such as party identification and evaluations of presidential performance, just as we did for 1980 and 1996.[13] We included a measure of attitudes toward blacks in this analysis, something we did not do for the previous analyses, because several studies found that Obama lost votes because of his race.[14] Also, we excluded blacks from the analysis; blacks voted almost unanimously for Obama, and blacks had extremely favorable views of his personal traits, so including them in the analysis would inflate the relationship between trait perceptions and the vote. The results of the logistic regression are in Table 4.3, and they are similar to the results of the 1980 and 1996 analyses: the candidate trait index has a substantial effect on the vote even with other relevant attitudes taken into account.

Figure 4.3 shows the predicted probabilities, based on the logistic regression analysis of the vote, for average Democrats, independents, and

Table 4.3   Logistic Regression of Presidential Vote, 2008

Independent variable	Model 1	Model 2	Model 3
Party identification	**.865**** (.054)	**.631**** (.063)	**.609**** (.076)
Ideology	**.646**** (.084)	**.384**** (.105)	**.195** (.120)
Approval of Bush's handling of the economy		**.440**** (.181)	**−.004** (.201)
Approval of Bush's handling of national security		**1.195**** (.215)	**.640**** (.249)
Social welfare issues index		**.167** (.674)	**.172** (.232)
Moral issues index		**.674**** (.147)	**.771**** (.167)
Attitude toward blacks		**1.491**** (.263)	**.774**** (.297)
Candidate trait index			**1.579**** (.160)
Nagelkerke pseudo R^2	.70	.76	.83
% cases correctly predicted	88.4	89.4	92.9

**p < .01, *p < .05 (one-tailed tests).
Note: Bolded entries are logistic regression coefficients, with standard errors in parentheses. The dependent variable is the presidential vote. See the text for details on the independent variables. Positive coefficients indicate that the likelihood of voting for McCain is increased by having a stronger Republican identification, a more conservative ideological orientation, more conservative orientations on the two issue indices, greater approval of Bush's presidential job performance, and more positive views of McCain's character traits relative to Obama's.
Source: 2008 American National Election Study. Only white major party voters are included in the analysis.

Republicans, given different candidate character trait index scores. The impact of perceptions of candidate character traits in 2008 is more similar to what we found for 1980 than to 1996. All three groups—Democrats, independents, and Republicans—were substantially influenced by their trait perceptions. Independents were the most affected: a change in the character trait index score from −1.0 to +1.0 increased the likelihood that the average independent would vote for McCain by 65 percentage points. Democrats and Republicans were slightly less influenced, but there still was a sizable effect. Both average Democrats and average Republicans had their likelihood of voting for McCain shift by 50 percentage points as the trait index score went from −1.0 to +1.0. As we discussed in Chapter 3, any Democratic

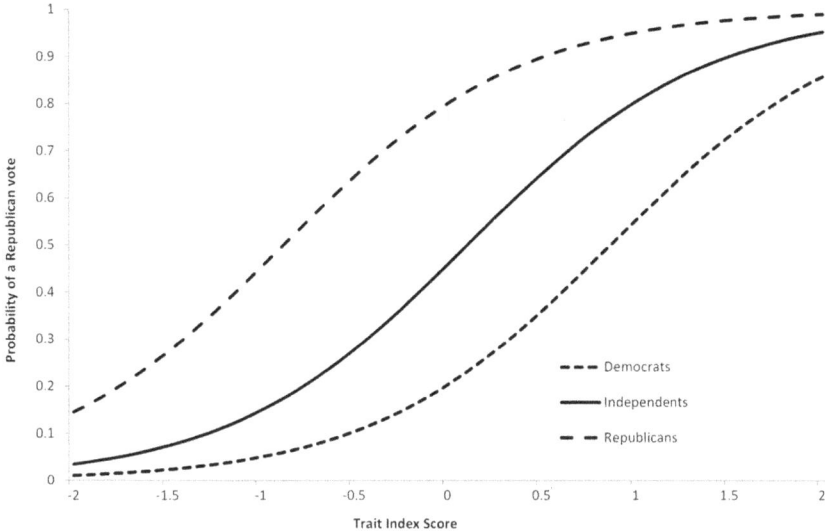

Figure 4.3   Presidential Voting by Trait Perceptions, 2008

presidential candidate would have started with a sizable advantage in 2008 given the low approval of the Bush administration, but Obama added to that advantage by doing better than McCain in overall trait perceptions, which clearly mattered to the voters.

Candidate Character Traits in Presidential Elections, 1980–2008

We conducted similar logistic regression analyses for the other presidential elections between 1980 and 2008.[15] Rather than display a separate table and chart for each year, we summarize the results of these analyses by reporting the change in the likelihood of voting for the Republican candidate for average Democrats, independents, and Republicans as the character trait index score moves from –1.0 to +1.0. As we pointed out, about one-half of the voters in each year had an index score in this range, so this method provides a good indication of the extent of influence that character traits have across elections. The results for all presidential elections from 1980 to 2008 are provided in Figure 4.4.

Several patterns appear in these data. First of all, in every year all three partisan groups are affected by trait perceptions. Democrats, independents, and Republicans always become more likely to vote for the Republican candidate as their perceptions of the character traits of the candidates become

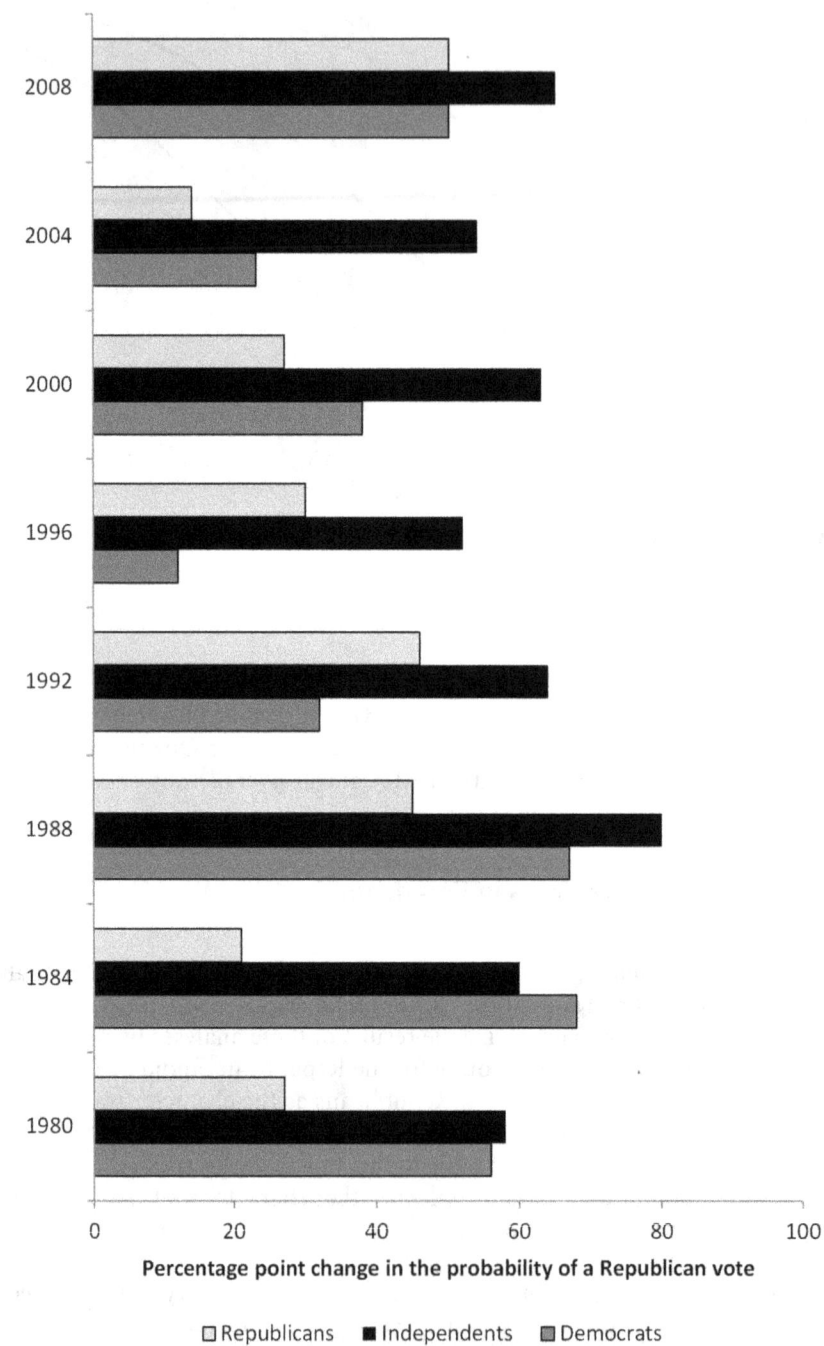

Figure 4.4 Impact of Change in the Trait Index on Voting Behavior, 1980–2008

more favorable to the Republican. However, independents are usually more influenced by character trait perceptions than are Democrats or Republicans. The exceptions to this pattern are the Democrats in 1980 and in 1984, who were slightly more affected than were independents. Whether Democrats in those two years decided to vote for their party's candidate or to defect and vote for Reagan depended very much on how they saw the candidates in personal terms. A significant number of Democrats voted for Reagan because they saw him as superior to his Democratic opponent in presidential character. Still, the general pattern over these eight presidential elections is that trait perceptions have considerably more influence on the voting behavior of independents. This is not surprising. Independents are more likely to have conflicting evaluations of the candidates on other factors, such as presidential performance or issue positions, making their evaluations of the character traits of the candidates more likely to sway their vote. Also, independents lack an inherent partisan disposition that would incline them to vote in a certain direction, so they are more likely to be influenced by election-specific factors, such as candidate character.

With regard to partisan voters, Democrats were more affected by character trait perceptions in the 1980s, but Republicans were more affected in the 1990s. This suggests that there is a tendency for the identifiers of the party that loses the election to be more affected by trait perceptions. Such a pattern seems quite logical. A presidential candidate who is able to convince voters who identify with the other party to vote for him is more likely to win, and one way of convincing those voters to defect is to be seen as superior on character traits and to persuade people to vote on that basis. As we discussed in Chapter 1, such a strategy is nearly as old as the republic and is perfectly captured by the campaign slogan of the candidate of the minority Republican Party in 1952: I Like Ike. Conversely, a candidate who is unable to convince voters from the other party that they should defect on the basis of character traits is less likely to win.

Another interesting pattern in Figure 4.4 is that the years in which no incumbent president was running for reelection seem to be ones where the effect of trait perceptions on the vote is more pronounced.[16] Identifying the years that are above average in trait effects is complicated by the fact that there are three partisan groups for each election, and these three groups normally vary considerably in the extent to which their vote is influenced by character traits. If we simply average the change in the probability of a Republican vote that is calculated for the three partisan groups in each year, and then compare these averages across years, we find that the top two years are 1988 and 2008, both years in which there was no incumbent president running. Interestingly, in 2000, another year with no incumbent running, the effect of trait perceptions on the vote of independents was quite strong, but the effect on Democrats and Republicans was weaker than normal. The two years in which voters were least affected by trait perceptions are 1996 and 2004, both years in which the incumbent president was reelected.

When no incumbent president is running for reelection, it may be that the election becomes less of a referendum on the performance of the sitting president and more of a contest between two candidates, with personal qualities playing a significant role in the evaluation of the candidates. In the years in which an incumbent president is reelected, voter satisfaction with the performance of the incumbent seems to diminish the impact of character traits on the vote. In 1996, for example, Democrats who thought that Dole was better on character traits were only modestly more likely to vote for him than were Democrats who thought that Clinton was superior on character traits. A very similar pattern exists for Republican voters in 2004. However, in 1984, Democrats and independents were strongly affected, although Republicans were not, so there are differences among elections in which the incumbent president wins. In the two elections in which an incumbent president was defeated—1980 and 1992—the impact of trait perceptions on the vote was about average. In both of these years, a failing economy was a major factor in the defeat of the incumbent president, but it seems that voters, especially independents and supporters of the other party, were not willing to replace that president unless they also had confidence in the personal qualities of the challenger. Of course, we should be cautious about accepting all of the above generalizations, as they are based on a small number of presidential elections, but they suggest some possible reasons why the impact of candidate character traits on the vote varies across election years. At the same time, it is important to remember that in no year did the perception of candidate character traits fail to have a significant effect on the vote.

THE IMPACT OF INDIVIDUAL CHARACTER TRAITS ON THE VOTE

The preceding analysis tells us about the impact that overall character trait perceptions have on the presidential vote, but it does not explore the effect that specific trait perceptions have. This is a relevant topic to investigate because candidates almost always are more advantaged on some traits than on others, as Chapter 3 discussed.[17] If the character trait that a candidate does really well on is also a particularly important trait to the voters in that year, then the candidate is advantaged much more than if that trait is considered unimportant by the voters. If, for example, one candidate has a large advantage on integrity, it certainly makes a difference how much voters consider this trait in determining their vote.

Figure 4.5 shows the effect that perceptions of the four trait dimensions—leadership, competence, integrity, and empathy—had on the presidential vote for the 1984 to 2008 elections. These four trait dimensions are measured by four questions that were asked in an identical fashion in each year: to what extent were voters willing to describe each candidate as a strong leader, as knowledgeable, as moral, and as someone who cares about people like the voter. There are other questions that were asked about leadership,

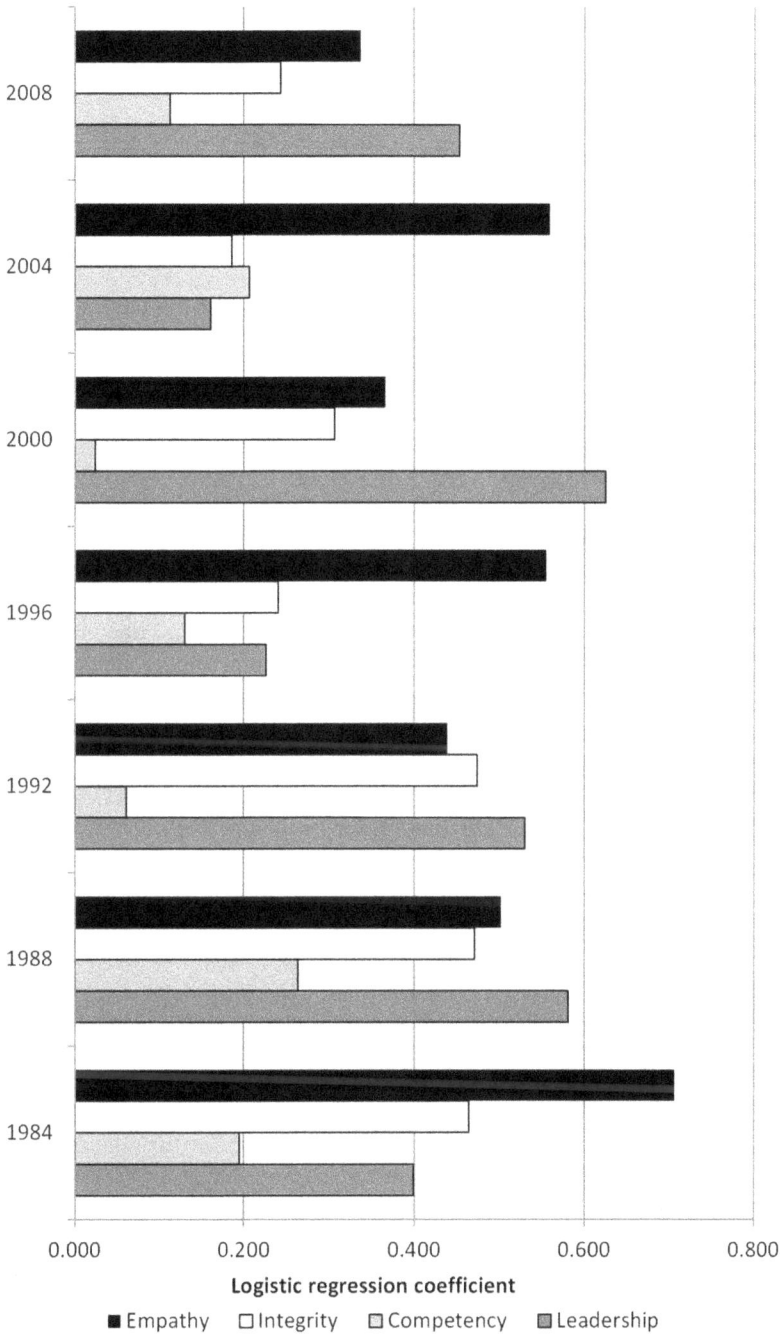

Figure 4.5 Impact of Individual Traits on Voting Behavior, 1984–2008

competence, integrity, and empathy, but only these four were asked in every year in exactly the same manner (data from 1980 are not included in this analysis because no question about empathy was asked in that year). To determine the relative effect of each of the four trait dimensions in each year, we ran logistic regressions that were similar to the ones run for the previous analysis, except that the overall character trait index was replaced by the measures of the four specific trait dimensions.[18] The bar chart shows the size of the logistic regression coefficients for each of the four traits for each year; the larger the coefficient, the greater the effect of the trait on the vote.[19]

Several patterns are present in these data. First of all, leadership and empathy emerge as the two most important traits.[20] One of these two is always the most important; in three of the years, they are the top two. Competency, on the other hand, is almost always the least important trait; only in 2004 did it fail to rank fourth. Integrity falls slightly behind leadership and empathy in importance; it ranks third in four of the years and second in three of the years.

It is hardly surprising that leadership is usually an important trait to voters. The nature of the modern presidency, especially regarding foreign affairs and national security, demands an individual who can be in control, act decisively, and get things done. Presidential candidates often have been criticized for failing to display strong leadership skills. Presidential campaigns frequently tout the leadership abilities of their candidate or denigrate those of the opponent, as the previous chapter pointed out. However, it is surprising that voters do not seem to take perceptions of competency into account very much in deciding which candidate to vote for, as such traits as being knowledgeable and intelligent certainly seem relevant. This puzzling result might be due to the relationship between leadership and competence, which we discussed in Chapter 2. The direct effect of perceptions of competence on the vote may be relatively weak compared to the effect of other trait perceptions, but perceptions of competence probably influence perceptions of leadership. Presidential candidates who are seen as lacking knowledge, experience, or intelligence are less likely to be seen as capable leaders. Thus, competence might have a substantial indirect effect on the vote.

Empathy is sometimes ignored as a relevant character trait by analysts, as we discussed in Chapter 2, but these data indicate that it is quite important to voters. Empathy ranks first or second among character traits in every year except 1992 in impact on voters. The more that a voter perceives a candidate to be superior to his opponent on this dimension, the more likely the voter is to vote for that candidate, even with other relevant attitudes such as party identification and ideology held constant. Because Democratic presidential candidates do well on this character trait, ignoring it results in an inaccurate estimate of how positively a candidate is seen by the voters. In 2004, for example, many media pundits claimed that George W. Bush was seen in more positive personal terms than John Kerry because the latter was seen as weak and indecisive. But while Kerry did poorly on the leadership dimension, he did quite well on empathy, and overall he was about even with Bush on character traits, as we discussed in Chapter 3. Republican presidential candidates who have been able to narrow the empathy gap, such as Bush in 2000, usually have been victorious.

Figure 4.5 shows that there is considerable variation in the effect of each of these traits across elections. Perceptions of leadership had a large effect on the presidential vote in 2000, but only a modest effect in 1996. Integrity was fairly important in 1984, 1988, and 1992, but it diminished in importance after that. Empathy was more important in 1996 and 2004 than it was in 2000. These variations help to explain some of the election outcomes, especially in light of how the popular media described the candidates, which we discussed in the previous chapter.

The 1996 presidential election represents one case where the outcome was seemingly at odds with the character evaluations of the candidates. Dole lost the election even though he was significantly advantaged on character traits. Not only was he seen as a stronger leader, which is usually the case for Republican candidates, but he also held an enormous advantage on integrity. Nevertheless, he was unable to make the election even reasonably close. The data in Figure 4.5 help to explain this anomaly. Neither leadership nor integrity mattered a great deal to voters in that year, so Dole only gained a small number of voters through his advantage on these traits. The trait that most influenced the vote in 1996 was empathy, which was the one area of character strength for Clinton. Had voters been influenced more by perceptions of integrity and less by perceptions of empathy, the election outcome undoubtedly would have been closer.

In 2000, Bush was widely portrayed as lacking in knowledge and intelligence. The popular media's characterization of Bush was, with just a little exaggeration, one of an amiable dunce. Al Gore, on the other hand, was widely considered to be extremely knowledgeable and intelligent. How then did Bush manage to win virtually the same share of the popular vote as did Gore? One answer to this question is that voters cared little about competence in 2000. Perceptions of the knowledge of the candidates did not have a statistically significant effect on the vote in that year. Conversely, perceptions of leadership had a large effect in 2000, greater than in any other year analyzed here, and this was the character trait dimension that Bush did best on. Despite being seen as lacking in knowledge, Bush still received strong marks for his leadership ability, which helps to explain his victory.

In 2004, Kerry came close to Bush in the popular vote, even though he was widely portrayed in the media as a weak and indecisive leader. However, we can see that perceptions of leadership had less effect on the vote in 2004 than in any other election examined here. Perceiving Kerry as a weaker leader than Bush made a voter only a little less likely to vote for him, so Kerry's disadvantage on this trait dimension was not crippling. On the other hand, perceptions of empathy had a strong effect on the vote, and this was an area of strength for Kerry. Had voters been relatively unconcerned about empathy and greatly concerned about leadership, Kerry would not have done as well as he did.

This leads to an interesting question: why were certain trait dimensions more important to the voters in some years than in others? This is not a question that we can answer conclusively with these data, in part because the data we present in Figure 4.5 must be interpreted with some caution. The individual trait dimensions are all intercorrelated, so estimates of the separate, independent effect of each trait dimension on the vote might not perfectly capture the true effect in each case. These intercorrelations are not so strong as to create multicolinearity problems, so we can have reasonable confidence in the results, although we should treat the coefficients with some caution.[21] The general patterns in the data, such as the consistently strong impact of leadership and empathy and the rather weak direct effect of competence, should reflect how voters incorporate character trait evaluations in their vote decisions, but the coefficients for any particular year might be imprecise estimates of the true effects of the trait dimensions.

Another point to consider is that we use a single item to measure each dimension in this analysis. As explained earlier, this is done to maintain a consistent measure across elections. For example, the trait dimension of competence is measured by the question about how knowledgeable the candidates are. However, competence includes more than knowledge, and while the various facets of competence are strongly interrelated, they do differ. Thus, somewhat different results might be present for a given year if we had used a different question to measure competence, such as a question on the experience of the candidates, or a question on the ability of the candidates to "get things done." Unfortunately, these questions were not asked in most years, so we cannot determine how much of a difference this would make. The same qualifications apply to the measures of leadership, integrity, and empathy.

With these caveats in mind, there are some thought provoking patterns evident in Figure 4.5. First, in all three open seat elections over the course of this time span (1988, 2000, and 2008), perceptions of leadership most influenced the vote, followed in each case by empathy. With no incumbent in the race, which results in a context characterized by greater uncertainty, voters seem to base their votes more on their relative perceptions of the two candidates' leadership qualities, thus paying attention to the core responsibility of the modern presidency—providing leadership at home and abroad.

On the other hand, in the three years in which incumbents won reelection (1984, 1996, and 2004), perceptions of leadership exerted much less influence on the voters, and empathy was more influential. This suggests that when incumbent presidents are reelected, it usually is because there is sufficient voter satisfaction with their handling of the economy and foreign affairs, so fewer voters are likely to feel that inadequate leadership is a reason to vote the incumbent out of office. Instead, voters seem to be more influenced by their perceptions of each candidate's empathy, a trait that we have suggested includes a significant policy component. In this context, voter dissatisfaction with the president is likely to be based more on policy considerations and less on retrospective evaluations of performance. In 1984, for example, while many voters felt that Reagan had done a good job of handling the economy, a number of those voters also felt that Reagan's economic policies did not benefit ordinary individuals enough, leading these voters to be influenced by their perceptions of Reagan's concern for the average man or woman.

Finally, we have the elections in which an incumbent president was defeated. In one of those years, 1992, leadership exhibits the largest coefficient, albeit by a modest amount over integrity and empathy. Unlike the three cases in which the incumbent won, voters harbored considerable doubts about the first President Bush's leadership qualities. He trailed Clinton in terms of public favorability on the strong leadership item, a particularly devastating state of affairs for a Republican candidate, as we outlined in Chapter 3.[22] We did not include data for 1980, another election when an incumbent president was defeated, because no question about empathy was asked in that year, thus making it impossible to compare the impact of all four trait dimensions in that election. However, our analysis of the 1980 data shows that leadership was more important than the other traits asked about in that year and that it had a powerful effect on the vote: the regression coefficient is very large in comparison to other years, eclipsed only by the 2000 coefficient. It appears that an incumbent president is most likely to be defeated when the electorate combines considerable doubt about his or her leadership with heavy emphasis on that character trait, exactly the mix found in 1980 and 1992.

While integrity and, especially, competence tend to exert less influence than leadership and empathy, elections in which perceptions of these traits are more influential seem sensible. This is particularly the case for integrity. In the three elections from 1984 to 1992, the coefficient for integrity, regardless of its relative importance among the other three traits, averages about .47. From 1996 on, the integrity coefficient averages about half that amount. It seems plausible that once Clinton, the most integrity-challenged candidate in this analysis, won and proved successful in office—despite growing concerns over his morality and honesty from 1992 to 1996—the result was to diminish voter concern with integrity. With regard to competence, this trait is particularly important in two elections, 1988 (in terms of the competence coefficient's absolute value) and 2004 (in terms of this coefficient's second place rank relative to the other three traits). In 1988, one of the candidates, Michael Dukakis, made competence a central theme of his campaign, arguing, in fact, that the election was about competence, not ideology. In 2004, the competence gap between the two candidates is the largest of any election. As Figure 3.1 (Chapter 3) makes clear, no candidate's knowledge and intelligence were viewed more positively relative to his opponent's than Kerry's were versus Bush's. This gap surely resulted in more—but ultimately not enough—votes for the Democrat.

We can only speculate about all of the reasons why individual traits vary in importance across the years, partly because our analysis encompasses a limited number of elections, and partly because we lack the data to test possible hypotheses. One possibility is that these patterns reflect the nature of the campaigns, given the particular context of the election, which is a crucial variable in setting expectations and determining campaign strategy.[23] Another possibility is that these patterns are influenced by the nature of the media coverage of the campaigns, which may frame different traits in different years. The events and circumstances of each particular election year also could shape these patterns, partly by influencing campaign strategies, candidate behavior, and media coverage. All of these factors are interrelated, and it may be that it is the complex interaction of these factors that determines the importance of each trait in a given year. Investigating these possibilities is beyond the scope of this book, but these speculations suggest worthwhile areas for future research.

DO PERCEPTIONS OF CANDIDATE CHARACTER TRAITS TRULY AFFECT THE VOTE?

The analysis in this chapter demonstrates that candidate character trait perceptions are related to the vote, even with other relevant attitudes held constant. While this is strong evidence that these perceptions affect the vote choice, we should consider the possibility that the causation is the other way around. Some scholars have suggested that voters first decide for whom they intend to vote, then form character trait perceptions that are consistent with that vote choice.[24] In this view, trait perceptions are simply rationalizations that support the vote decision, not influences on that decision. While it always is difficult to establish causality in social science research that uses cross-sectional analysis, there are several sound theoretical and substantive reasons to believe that our conceptualization is accurate.

One reason to conclude that perceptions of candidate character traits affect the vote is because it is easy for voters to form character trait perceptions and easy for them to choose among candidates on that basis. The media provide voters, even those who do not follow the campaign intensely, with plenty of information about the character and personalities of the candidates, and the presidential campaigns often highlight such factors, as we have discussed in previous chapters. On the basis of such information, voters can easily conclude that one candidate is a better leader, that one candidate is untrustworthy, or that one candidate is uninspiring. Whether these assessments accurately reflect the true nature of the candidates is another matter, one that is not relevant to the point here. Having formed these candidate character trait perceptions, it is easy for the voter to decide between the candidates on this basis. Given the relative ease of voting on the basis of trait perceptions, along with the fact that voters are encouraged to do so by both the media and the candidates, it would be surprising if voters ignored trait perceptions in choosing among the candidates.

Voters must decide to vote for a presidential candidate on some basis. If this decision is not influenced by candidate character trait perceptions, then it must be based on other attitudes. These other attitudes presumably include party identification, ideological and issue orientations, and evaluations of government performance. No one argues that people first decide how to vote, then form all of these other attitudes. Indeed, there is an extensive literature on the influence of both public policy issues and assessments of the economy on presidential voting.[25] But voting on the basis of policy issues or economic assessments is more demanding than voting on the basis of character trait perceptions. For example, voting on the basis of a public policy issue requires the voter to have an opinion on the issue, to understand where the candidates stand on the issue, and to perceive differences between the candidates on the issue.[26] Many voters fail to meet these conditions, even for fairly broad issues, such as whether there should be more or less government spending or services or whether defense spending should be increased or decreased.[27] Nevertheless, a substantial number of voters do base their vote on policy issues. If a significant number of voters spend the time and effort to form assessments of the candidates on the basis of policy issues and then vote at least partly on that basis, it is likely that many voters would also form candidate character trait perceptions before the vote decision, not afterward.

The description in Chapter 3 of how voters perceived presidential candidates provides further support for our view of causal direction. If candidate character trait perceptions are just a reflection or rationalization of the vote, then the popular vote winner always should have the most positive trait perceptions, which is not true for some elections. For example, voters in 1996 viewed Dole as clearly superior overall to Clinton in character traits. If voters were trying to rationalize their vote choice after the fact, Clinton voters, who outnumbered Dole voters, should have said that Clinton was better in personal terms, and Clinton should have come out ahead in character. That he did not is inconsistent with the view that vote choice determines trait perceptions. However, if trait perceptions influence the vote, along with other attitudes, the 1996 patterns make perfect sense. Clinton won in spite of his low integrity scores because he came out ahead on other factors, most notably on retrospective evaluations of government performance.

The discussion in Chapter 3 also shows that candidate character trait perceptions vary over time, even when the underlying vote stays the same. For example, Clinton received the same share of the two-party vote in 1992 and 1996, but he was seen as much better than Bush on character traits in 1992 but worse than Dole in 1996. If the vote choice determines trait perceptions, then when the aggregate vote changes little from one election to the next, aggregate trait perceptions should stay the same. In other words, Clinton should have had a similar advantage on trait perceptions in both years. That is not what happened between 1992 and 1996. Similarly, the Democratic share of the vote declined between 1996 and 2000, but we did not see a similar change in trait perceptions. In fact, Gore was seen in slightly more favorable terms than was Clinton, even though Gore won a smaller share of the vote. These patterns are more consistent with the conceptualization that character trait perceptions influence the vote, not that they are simply rationalizations of the vote.

Chapter 3 also shows that there is considerable variation across specific character traits in any given year. For example, in 2004, Bush did much better on leadership and integrity than he did on empathy. Kerry did better on competence and empathy than he did on leadership. Similar patterns exist in the other years that we have examined. For example, Obama in 2008 did very well when it came to perceptions of his intelligence but less well when it came to perceptions of his honesty. If voters form character trait perceptions to justify their vote after the fact, it seems unlikely that a candidate would do much better on some traits than on others. For example, if voters in 2004 first decided to vote for Bush, then formed character trait perceptions that were consistent with that vote, the views of Bush should be fairly uniform across all specific traits. If people were simply rationalizing their vote, they most likely would rationalize across the board. On the other hand, if character trait perceptions do influence the vote, and if these perceptions are in turn influenced by other factors, differences in how well the candidates score on different traits is to be expected.

Furthermore, our analysis in this chapter shows that the relationship between specific candidate character traits and the vote varies across the years. Leadership is almost always strongly related. Empathy usually is too. Sometimes integrity is important and sometimes it is not. Competence rarely is. If character trait perceptions were primarily or entirely rationalizations of the vote, we would expect all of these trait perceptions to be strongly related to the vote in each year. Having decided to vote for a candidate, the voter should then perceive the favored candidate to be clearly superior on each dimension, and thus the correlation between the vote and each trait should be similar. But if perceptions of candidate character traits affect the vote, and if some traits matter more than others to voters, then substantial variation in the strength of the relationships between the specific traits and the vote is to be expected.

Finally, candidate character traits are widely discussed in the media during a presidential campaign, in part because the presidential candidates and campaigns emphasize these characteristics. As we discussed in earlier chapters, the campaigns, including allied groups that spend on behalf of the candidate, frequently attack the opponent for being indecisive, a weak leader, lacking in empathy, inexperienced, or deceitful. Those who are involved in campaigns clearly believe that voters are influenced by candidate character trait perceptions, so much so that they spend considerable amounts of money trying to affect those perceptions. Perhaps they are completely mistaken on this point, but the widespread consensus among campaign professionals appears to support our view that the perceptions of the character traits of the candidates affect the vote and that these perceptions can be shaped by the candidates and the campaigns.

In sum, our existing theoretical knowledge of voting behavior, combined with the indirect evidence from the patterns of candidate character trait perceptions over time, as outlined in Chapter 3, provide a number of reasons to conclude that perceptions of candidate character traits do influence the vote for president. Additionally, there is some direct empirical evidence to support this conclusion. We analyzed the 2008 data to provide further information on the causal path between candidate character trait perceptions and the choice of presidential candidates in that election. In doing so, we considered two possible models of the relationship between party identification, ideology, candidate character trait perceptions, and candidate choice. These two models are depicted in Figure 4.6. As relatively stable political dispositions, party identification and ideology are commonly considered to be causally prior to both candidate character trait perceptions and the vote; the only question is whether character trait perceptions influence the vote or whether the vote affects trait perceptions. If the vote decision determines character trait perceptions, which we term the complete vote rationalization model (Model B), then party identification and ideology would affect the vote, but the effect of these two variables on character trait perceptions would only be indirect, through effects on the vote decision. If character trait perceptions affect the vote, but there is no voter rationalization (Model A), then party identification and ideology would have direct effects on trait perceptions. Only party identification and ideology are used in these models, rather than all of the independent variables that are used in our earlier analyses, for two reasons: (a) it keeps the models simple; and (b) party identification and ideology are more clearly causally prior to both trait perceptions and candidate preference. Even this simple model predicts

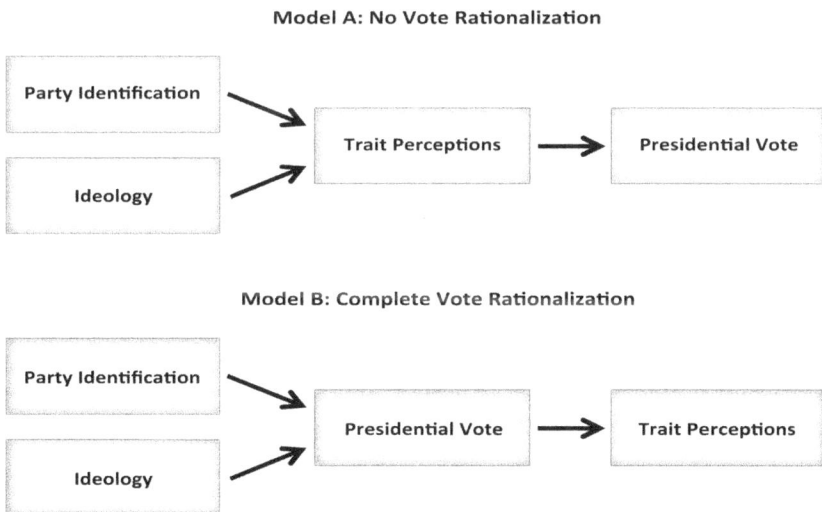

Figure 4.6 Two Models of Voting Behavior

the presidential vote fairly well, as we can see from model 1 in Tables 4.1, 4.2, and 4.3, partly because party identification and ideology are strongly related to the other variables that we considered, such as evaluations of the performance of the incumbent administration and orientations on issues of public policy. Nevertheless, the point here is not to predict the vote as well as we can, but to establish causal order, and the above models are appropriate for that purpose.

We then conducted two sets of analyses, first analyzing the effect of party identification and ideology on the presidential vote, with and without character trait perceptions included in the analysis, and then analyzing the effect party identification and ideology on trait perceptions, with and without vote included in the analysis. If Model A is accurate, then the coefficients that represent the effects of party identification and ideology on the vote should be stronger when candidate character trait perceptions are not included in the model. Once trait perceptions are included in the model, the coefficients for party identification and ideology should diminish to the degree that the influence of these two variables on the vote are indirect effects operating through trait perceptions. Our previous analysis concluded that trait perceptions were an important intervening variable between these two basic political orientations and the vote, so we would expect substantial reduction of these coefficients. Furthermore, the coefficients that reflect the effects of party identification and ideology on trait perceptions should remain the same regardless of whether presidential vote is in the equation, since Model A assumes that the vote has no effect on trait perceptions. If Model B is accurate, then the coefficients that represent the effects of party identification and ideology on the vote should not change when trait perceptions are included in the equation. Moreover, the effects of party identification and ideology on candidate trait perceptions should be reduced to zero when the vote is included in the model.

We test these expectations by examining changes in the coefficients. The results of our regression analyses are reported in Table 4.4. The first two columns of results (equations 1 and 2) use the presidential vote as the dependent variable and test the hypotheses that are based on Model A in Figure 4.6. Since the dependent variable is dichotomous, logistic regression is used for these analyses. The third and fourth columns (equations 3 and 4) use the candidate trait index as the dependent variable and test the hypotheses that are based on Model B. In this case, ordinary least squares regression is used because we have an interval-level dependent variable. While the logistic regression coefficients cannot be directly compared to the OLS regression coefficients, that presents no problem in this case, as the comparisons that we want to make are between equations 1 and 2 and between equations 3 and 4.

Comparing the results for equation 1 with those for equation 2, we see that the effects of both party identification and ideology on the vote are substantially diminished when the candidate trait index is introduced into

Table 4.4 Regression Analysis of Candidate Trait Perceptions and Presidential Vote, 2008

Independent variable	Presidential vote		Candidate trait index	
	Equation 1	Equation 2	Equation 3	Equation 4
Party identification	.865**	.668**	.362**	.168**
	(.054)	(.068)	(.018)	(.020)
Ideology	.646**	.358*	.274*	.178**
	(.084)	(.104)	(.027)	(.025)
Candidate trait index		1.793**		
		(.149)		
Presidential vote				1.398**
				(.086)
Adjusted-R^2	.70	.82	.52	.60

**p < .001, *p < .01

Note: Only major party voters are included in the analysis. Black voters are excluded from the analysis.

The dependent variable for equations 1 and 2 is the presidential vote, and the bolded cell entries are logistic regression coefficients, with standard errors are in parentheses. The R^2 for these two equations is the Nagelkerke pseudo R^2. The dependent variable for models 3 and 4 is the candidate trait index, and the bolded cell entries are unstandardized OLS regression coefficients, with standard errors in parentheses. See the text for details on the variables. Positive coefficients indicate that more positive perceptions of McCain relative to Obama are increased by having a stronger Republican identification and a more conservative ideological orientation.

Source: 2008 American National Election Study.

the analysis. The logistic regression coefficients for party identification and ideology in column 2 are considerably smaller than the corresponding coefficients in column 1. If trait perceptions had no causal effect, direct or indirect, on the vote, these coefficients should not diminish at all. The fact that they decline significantly is consistent with the expectations that we would have if Model A is the case, indicating that there is a true effect and that candidate character trait perceptions combine to form an intervening variable between these two fundamental political orientations and the presidential vote. Furthermore, the pseudo R^2 increases from equation 1 to equation 2, indicating that we are better able to predict the vote by using all three variables, which is consistent with the position that trait perceptions have an effect on the vote beyond that of party identification and ideology.

Comparing the results for equations 3 and 4, we also see substantial change in the coefficients once the vote is introduced into the equation. If the vote had no effect on trait perceptions, then the coefficients for party identification and ideology should not have changed from equation 3 to equation 4. The fact that they decline indicates that there is some effect of the presidential vote on candidate character trait perceptions. However, if trait perceptions were nothing more than rationalizations of the vote, then these coefficients should have disappeared completely. The fact that they do not, along with the results for equations 1 and 2, indicates that there also is a true effect of trait perceptions on the presidential vote.

Overall, the findings of this analysis lead us to conclude that reality is a blend of Model A and Model B. Both true direct effects and vote rationalization are present. To some extent, voters form or alter their perceptions of the personal characteristics of the candidates based on their intended vote. After having decided to vote for a given candidate, voters most likely interpret subsequent information that they receive in a manner that supports rather than undermines their decision. Such psychological processes probably influence how voters interpret information about the character traits of the candidates, as well as information about the issue positions of the candidates or about evaluations of the performance of the incumbent president. Nevertheless, it is evident that candidate character trait perceptions also affect the presidential vote, and the relationship between these two variables should not be dismissed as primarily or entirely voter rationalization.[28]

One objection to the analysis above might be that we cannot assume that party identification is completely unaffected by the vote. In particular, independents who say that they are closer to one party may not be indicating their long-term partisan disposition; instead, they might in some cases be true independents who say that they lean toward one party simply because they intend to vote for the presidential candidate of that party in that year.[29] To a lesser extent, the difference between strong and weak partisans could reflect similar considerations. Weak Democrats or weak Republicans might not be always be weak partisans in their basic, long-term orientation; they might be Democrats or Republicans who intend to vote for the candidate of the other party that year. One way to deal with this possibility is to use the simple trichotomization of party identification into Democrats, independents, and Republicans in the analysis. While voters might shift their orientation within each basic partisan category, they are unlikely to shift between categories based on their presidential vote choice. Independents who decide to vote for the Republican candidate may then become more likely to say that they lean toward the Republicans, but they are unlikely to state that they are now a Republican rather than an independent, for example. We replicated the analysis in Table 4.4 using a trichotomized version of party identification and found that the results were extremely similar, which provides more evidence for the conclusion that perceptions of candidate character traits affect the presidential vote.

Some of the confusion in the existing literature over whether there is a true effect of candidate character trait perceptions on the vote probably comes from confusing voter rationalization with partisan bias. There is no doubt that party identification has a strong effect on character trait perceptions, as we will demonstrate in the next chapter, but that does not constitute voter rationalization. Rather it indicates partisan bias, and it is exactly what we would expect from Model A in Figure 4.6. Perceptions of candidate character traits are not objective, dispassionate, unbiased assessments of the candidates. Democrats are very likely to see the candidate of their party in more favorable personal terms, which gives them a good reason to vote for that candidate; the same is true for Republicans. But other factors also affect how voters perceive these traits, and when Democrats or Republicans do not see the candidate of their party as possessing better character traits, which does happen, then their likelihood of defecting and voting for the candidate of the other party increases. That, of course, is why presidential campaigns try hard to convince voters, especially swing voters and weak supporters of the other candidate, that their candidate is superior in presidential character.

POLITICAL SOPHISTICATION, CHARACTER TRAITS, AND VOTING

When the pundits discuss—or more likely lament—the fact that many voters are too quick to rely on the personal likability or warmth of the candidates who run for president, the implicit premise is that this characterizes the less informed portion of the electorate. During the 2012 campaign, *Washington Post* columnist Kathleen Parker made this case in no uncertain terms when she compared voter decision making to a high school popularity contest.[30] Parker accused the Obama campaign of running as the nicer guy rather than as a president deserving of reelection. Worse still, she feared, a credulous public was buying this argument. Other commentators express similar views, implying that many voters base their vote on the character of the candidates rather than on more meaningful considerations.

Although such commentary is overly simplistic in its portrait of the average voter, there are theoretical reasons for expecting that those who are less politically sophisticated will base their votes relatively more on their perceptions of the character traits of the candidates. Very little information or knowledge is required for voters to form perceptions of the personal traits of candidates. Individuals form such judgments of other people routinely in their daily lives, and they can use the same methods to evaluate presidential candidates.[31] Both the campaigns and the reporters who cover them frequently emphasize the candidates' personal qualities so that even voters who pay only modest attention to advertisements, debates, and news stories about the campaigns will be able to absorb sufficient information to form perceptions of the personal traits of the candidates. Moreover, little background information about politics and governmental affairs is required to make personal judgments of the candidates. For these reasons, less politically sophisticated voters may well rely more heavily on trait perceptions in their vote decisions. By political sophistication, we mean the extent of the individual's knowledge about political and governmental affairs and the complexity of that knowledge. Individuals who are higher in political sophistication have both greater factual knowledge about government and politics and greater conceptual understanding of political issues. In other words, politically sophisticated voters have a deeper understanding of individual issues and a better comprehension of the interrelationship among issues.

Voters who are high in political sophistication will not necessarily think that candidate character is unimportant. There is every reason to think that even those who are very politically sophisticated will believe that personal qualities are important factors worth considering as part of vote choice. Clearly, as we outlined in Chapter 1, enough historical accounts of presidents have connected their successes or failures in part to their character; sophisticated voters are more likely than others to be well aware of such interpretations. What we suggest is that the politically sophisticated will also be concerned about policy issues and governmental performance and that they are likely to have the information necessary to choose between the candidates on the basis of these factors. Thus, the more sophisticated voters, as compared to their less sophisticated counterparts, will rely relatively more on policy issues in deciding on their vote. As a result, the more sophisticated voters will put less importance on questions of personal character.

Furthermore, more knowledgeable and sophisticated voters are more likely to conceptualize politics in a more ideological fashion or at least in terms of conflict among societal groups competing for scarce resources. *The American Voter* introduced the classification of citizens into different levels of conceptualization of politics, with the top category consisting of ideologues and near ideologues who tended to evaluate candidates in liberal-conservative terms.[32] Below this category are those who conceptualize politics in terms of group conflict; these voters distinguish Democrats and Republicans in terms of the groups that the parties benefit when in office. Voters who fall into one of these two categories would seem likely to base their vote decision substantially on how they evaluate the candidates in terms of ideology or group benefits, which should reduce the impact that candidate character traits have on their vote decision. A recent update of the levels of conceptualization in the American electorate estimated that about 25 percent of the voters in 2000 were in the top category (ideologues or near-ideologues) and another 30 percent were in the group benefits category; about 30 percent were in the retrospectively oriented "nature of the times" category, and 15 percent lacked a grasp of any issue content at all.[33] As one moves down this continuum from ideologues to no issue content voters, the influence of candidate characteristics on vote choice should increase.

However, the notion—both popular and scholarly—that the less sophisticated voters rely more on candidate character is not undisputed. One counterargument is that the more sophisticated among us recognize the potentially ephemeral nature of evaluating candidates on the basis of issue positions publicized during a hotly contested campaign.[34] Such voters understand that candidate Bush's promise never, under any circumstances, to raise taxes, or candidate Obama's disdain for health care reform that includes a mandate that individuals purchase a policy may be set aside in the face of the realities of governing. Confronted with what they suspect to be over-promising, savvy voters may well look to their perceptions of a candidate's honesty to judge the sincerity of a proposal.

Another argument suggests that more informed voters have richer political schema. In other words, such voters organize their thoughts about politics in a more logical manner, making connections among candidates, parties, and ideologies. This deeper understanding of the political process allows them to understand better the relevance of character traits to the job of being president, and thus to vote more on that basis.[35] Similarly, there is evidence to conclude that having a political schema that emphasizes candidate personalities is actually related to being more educated, not less.[36] Finally, other research has found little evidence that more and less sophisticated voters are any different in terms of their reliance on candidate traits.[37] In sum, while conventional wisdom and some sound theoretical reasons suggest that less sophisticated voters will be influenced more by their perceptions of candidate character, the limited scholarly research on this topic has not found much support for this hypothesis.

To investigate this question we focus on two recent presidential elections: 2000 and 2004. In both cases, the conventional wisdom, as expressed by many commentators, was that Bush was more appealing in personal terms than his Democratic opponents. As Chapter 3 discussed, pundits frequently derided both Gore and Kerry for being aloof elitists who lacked a common touch. Bush, on the other hand, supposedly related well to the ordinary person. If there is a tendency for less sophisticated voters to rely more on character traits, it should be present in these elections. To measure political sophistication, we use education, which is a frequently used surrogate for this variable. We conducted the same analysis of the vote reported earlier in this chapter, logistic regressions using the character trait index and other relevant variables to predict the vote, separately for three educational groups: those with no college education, with some college, and with a college degree. We again summarize the results by showing the change in the likelihood of voting for the Republican candidate as the character trait index score moves from –1.0 to + 1.0 for the average voter in each educational group. As we pointed out earlier, about one-half of the voters have a score in this range, and the greatest change in voting occurs here, so this is a good measure of the extent of influence that character traits have on voting.

The results are presented in Figure 4.7. In 2000, there is no support for the hypothesis that less sophisticated voters are affected more by trait perceptions. In fact, voters with no college education were the least affected by character trait perceptions, while those with some college education and

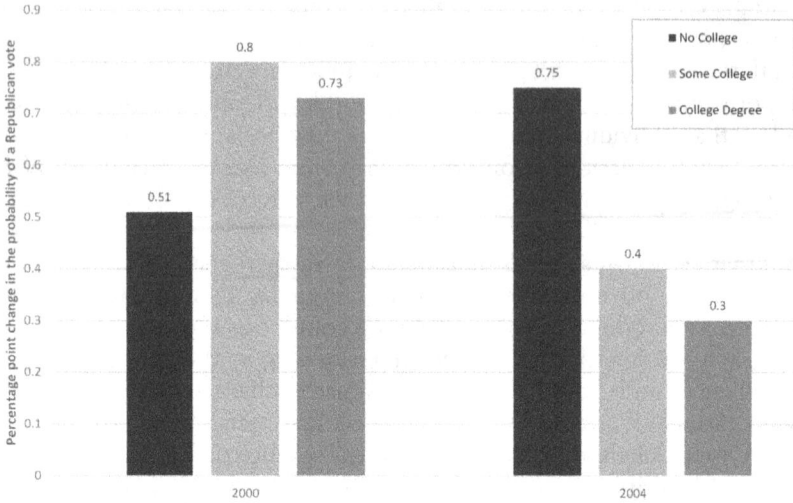

Figure 4.7   Impact of Change in the Trait Index on Voting Behavior, 2000 and 2004

those with a college degree were considerably more influenced. In 2004, however, there is support for the hypothesis. Those with the least amount of education were the most affected, and those with the most education were the least affected. The difference in the results for these two years suggests that there is no consistent relationship between political sophistication and reliance on candidate character traits. That conclusion is confirmed by similar analyses for the other presidential elections that we examine in this chapter. In only one other election, 1984, do we find a pattern similar to the one for 2004. In two of the years, 1980 and 1992, the college-educated were the ones most responsive to character trait perceptions. Given that other studies have found similar results, we conclude that voting on the basis of candidate character traits is not typically more prevalent among the less educated or the less politically sophisticated, although such a pattern may occur in a particular year.[38]

CONCLUSION

The perceptions that voters have of the character traits of the presidential candidates influence their voting behavior. Some of the correlation between trait perceptions and the presidential vote is a result of voters rationalizing their vote choice after the fact, but substantial direct effects exist. Independents generally are more strongly affected by their trait perceptions than are Democrats or Republicans, but partisans are influenced by the assessments they have of their party's candidate, relative to the opponent. While traits play a role in every presidential election, they appear to have a greater effect on voting behavior in elections in which no incumbent president is running for reelection, although some caution is warranted in making this generalization, since it is based on the patterns in a limited number of elections.

Perceptions of leadership and empathy tend to be more important than perceptions of competence or integrity in affecting the vote. These are the two trait dimensions that tend to be owned by one of the parties: leadership by Republicans and empathy by Democrats. The importance of each of the four trait dimension varies across the years. Leadership mattered a great deal to voters in 2000, but four years later, it was much less important. Voters were influenced more by their perceptions of empathy in 2004 than they were in 2008. Perceptions of the integrity of the candidates had a big effect on the vote in 1992, but much less so in 1996. Variations in the importance of the trait dimensions from one election to the next helps to explain why some candidates are able to win even when voters see them lacking on some trait dimension. Being seen as substantially worse on a trait dimension is not a great disadvantage if voters are not particularly concerned about that trait in that year.

NOTES

1. Larry M. Bartels, "Partisanship and Voting Behavior, 1952–1996," *American Journal of Political Science* 44 (2000): 35–50; Donald Green, Bradley Palmquist, and Eric Schickler, *Partisan Hearts and Minds* (New Haven, CT: Yale University Press, 2002), 204–229; Lewis-Beck et al., *The American Voter Revisited,* 111–137.
2. For discussions of logistic regression see: Gary King, *Unifying Political Methodology* (Cambridge: Cambridge University Press, 1989); David Knoke and George W. Bohrnstedt, *Statistics for Social Data Analysis,* 3rd edition (Itasca, IL: F. E. Peacock, 1994), 332–355; Lawrence S. Meyers, Glenn Gamst, and A. J. Guarino, *Applied Multivariate Research* (Thousand Oaks, CA: Sage Publications, 2006), 221–241.
3. Party identification is measured on a seven-point scale, from strong Democrat to strong Republican. Ideological orientation is measured on a seven-point scale, from very liberal to very conservative. Evaluations of Carter's handling of the presidency is measured on a four-point scale, from strongly approve to strongly disapprove. Attitudes on social welfare issues are measured by an index that combines several questions about social welfare programs and spending; the index runs from 1 (most favorable) to 7 (most unfavorable). A question about abortion is used to measure attitudes on moral issues, and the item is dichotomized into favor and oppose.
4. Our conceptualization of the causal order of the variables follows the one outlined by Warren E. Miller and J. Merrill Shanks, *The New American Voter* (Cambridge, MA: Harvard University Press, 1996), 189–211.
5. In 1980, an average Democrat had a score of 1.88 on the seven-point party identification scale, a score of 3.90 on the seven-point ideology scale, a score of 2.44 on the four-point Carter job approval scale, a score of 3.70 on the seven-point social welfare scale, and a score of 1.49 on the dichotomous

abortion item. For all items, the lowest score (1.0) is the most liberal or the most favorable to the Democrats.

6. An average independent had a score of 4.0 on the party identification scale, 4.22 on the ideology scale, 2.97 on the Carter job approval scale, 4.28 on the social welfare scale, and 1.49 on the abortion scale. An average Republican had a score of 5.95 on the party identification scale, 4.88 on the ideology scale, 3.37 on the Carter job approval scale, 4.86 on the social welfare scale, and 1.56 on the abortion scale.

7. For an analysis of the factors that affected voting behavior in the 1980 presidential election, see Paul R. Abramson, John H. Aldrich, and David W. Rohde, *Change and Continuity in the 1980 Elections* (Washington, DC: Congressional Quarterly Press, 1982).

8. Kathleen A. Frankovic, "Public Opinion Trends," in *The Election of 1980*, ed. Gerald Pomper (Chatham, NJ: Chatham House Publishers, 1981), 98.

9. The variables included in the logistic regression were: party identification (measured on a seven-point scale), ideology (a seven-point scale), approval of Clinton's handling of the economy (a four-point scale), approval of Clinton's handling of foreign affairs (a four-point scale), attitudes on social welfare issues (an index of several variables that runs from 1.0 to 7.0), attitudes on moral issues (an index of three items that runs from 1.0 to 2.0), and the candidate character trait index, which runs from –4.0 to +4.0.

10. For an analysis of the factors that affected voting behavior in the 1996 presidential election, see Paul R. Abramson, John H. Aldrich, and David W. Rohde, *Change and Continuity in the 1996 Elections* (Washington, DC: Congressional Quarterly Press, 1998). For an analysis of how trait perceptions influenced voting behavior in that election, see Garrett Glasgow and R. Michael Alvarez, "Uncertainty and Candidate Personality Traits," *American Politics Quarterly* 28 (2000): 26–49.

11. For an analysis of Perot activists, see Ronald B. Rapaport and Walter J. Stone, *Three's A Crowd: The Dynamics of Third Parties, Ross Perot, and Republican Resurgence* (Ann Arbor: University of Michigan Press, 2005).

12. For information on the 2008 election see Paul R. Abramson, John H. Aldrich, and David W. Rohde, *Change and Continuity in the 2008 and 2010 Elections* (Washington, DC: Congressional Quarterly Press, 2012); Janet M. Box-Steffensmeier and Steven E. Schier, eds., *The American Elections of 2008* (Lanham, MD: Rowman and Littlefield, 2009); James W. Ceaser, Andrew E. Busch, and John J. Pitney, Jr., *Epic Journey: The 2008 Elections and American Politics* (Lanham, MD: Rowman and Littlefield, 2009); William J. Crotty, ed., *Winning the Presidency 2008* (Boulder, CO: Paradigm Publishers, 2009); and Michael Nelson, ed., *The Elections of 2008* (Washington, DC: Congressional Quarterly Press, 2009).

13. The variables included in the logistic regression were: party identification (measured on a seven-point scale), ideology (a seven-point scale), approval of Bush's handling of the economy (a five-point scale), approval of Bush's handling of national security (a four-point scale), attitudes on social welfare issues (an index of several variables that runs from 1.0 to 5.0), attitudes on moral issues (an index of three items that runs from 1.0 to 4.0), attitudes towards blacks (an index of several items that runs from 1.0 to 3.0), and the candidate character trait index, which runs from –4.0 to +4.0.

14. Jonathan Knuckey, "Racial Resentment and Vote Choice in the 2008 U.S. Presidential Election," *Politics & Policy* 39 (2011): 559–582; Michael S. Lewis-Beck, Charles Tien, and Richard Nadeau, "Obama's Missed Landslide: A Racial Cost?" *PS: Political Science and Politics* 43 (2010): 69–76;

Spencer Piston, "How Explicit Racial Prejudice Hurt Obama in the 2008 Election," *Political Behavior* 32 (2010): 431–451.

15. The results of these logistic regressions are available at http://charles.prysby.com.

16. Donald R. Kinder, Mark D. Peters, Robert P. Abelson, and Susan T. Fiske, "Presidential Prototypes." *Political Behavior* 2 (1980): 315–337; and John L. Sullivan, John H. Aldrich, Eugene Borgida, and Wendy M. Rahn, "Candidate Appraisal and Human Nature: Man and Superman in the 1984 Election," *Political Psychology* 11 (1990): 459–484, argue that incumbent presidents are evaluated differently than non-incumbent presidential candidates.

17. Carolyn L. Funk, "Bringing the Candidate into Models of Candidate Evaluation," *Journal of Politics* 61 (1999): 700–720.

18. Respondents in each year were asked how well the following descriptions characterized each presidential candidate: (a) he would provide strong leadership; (b) he is knowledgeable; (c) he is moral; (d) he cares about people like me. The possible responses to each trait question were: extremely well, very well, not too well, or not well at all, which were scored as running from +2 to –2, as described in Chapter 2. For each trait, a net score was calculated by subtracting the score for the Democratic candidate from the score for the Republican candidate. The net scores run from +4 (the description fits the Republican candidate extremely well and the Democratic candidate not at all) to –4 (the description fits the Democratic candidate extremely well and the Republican candidate not at all).

19. It is legitimate to compare the logistic regression coefficient across traits and years because each coefficient indicates the change in the probability of a Republican (or Democratic) vote under specified conditions. For example, a coefficient of .40 would mean that if we have a voter who has a probability of .50 of voting for the Republican candidate and who also has a net score of zero on one of the trait items (i.e., the voter perceived both candidates to be equal on the character trait), then if that voter were to change his or her assessment of the candidates on the trait to be slightly more favorable to the Republican candidate (i.e., the voter's net score for that trait increases to 1.0), then the voter's probability of voting for the Republican candidate would increase to .60. Similarly, if that same voter were to change his assessment of the candidates on the trait to be slightly more favorable to the Democratic candidate (i.e., the voter's net score for that trait decreases to –1.0), then the voter's probability of voting for the Republican candidate would decrease to .40.

20. Paul Goren, "Character Weakness, Partisan Bias, and Presidential Evaluation: Modifications and Extensions," *Political Behavior* 29 (2007): 305–326, argues that this varies by party, with Democrats more concerned about empathy and Republicans more concerned about leadership.

21. The problem of multicolinearity is discussed in Lawrence S. Meyers, Glenn Gamst, and A. J. Guarino, *Applied Multivariate Research: Design and Interpretation* (Thousand Oaks, CA: Sage Publications, 2006), 180–182. They indicate that multicolinearity is a threat when the correlation between two independent variables exceeds .75. Most of the time, the correlations among the four trait dimensions are below this threshold, but occasionally they are slightly higher, though never above .80, a threshold suggested by other researchers.

22. Clinton also trailed Dole on strong leadership in 1996. However, this seems to be less a groundswell of concern about Clinton's abilities than the more typical Republican ownership of this trait. Furthermore, while Bush in 1992 trailed Clinton on all three measures of the underlying leadership dimension

(strong leadership, being inspiring, and getting things done), Clinton held a significant advantage over Dole on one of the same three measures, being inspiring (See Table 3.1 for details).

23. See Samuel L. Popkin, *What It Takes to Win—And Hold—the White House* (Oxford: Oxford University Press, 2012).
24. H. Whitt Kilburn, "Does the Candidate Really Matter?" *American Politics Research* 33 (2005): 335–356; Wendy M. Rahn, Jon A. Krosnick, and Marijke Breuning, "Rationalization and Derivation Processes in Survey Studies of Political Candidate Evaluation," *American Journal of Political Science* 38 (1994): 582–600.
25. For the influence of policy issues on voting, see R. Michael Alvarez, *Information and Elections* (Ann Arbor: University of Michigan Press, 1997); Edward G. Carmines and James A. Stimson, "The Two Faces of Issue Voting," *American Political Science Review* 74 (1980): 78–91; D. Sunshine Hillygus and Todd G. Shields, *The Persuadable Voter* (Princeton, NJ: Princeton University Press, 2008); John E. Jackson, "Issues, Party Choices, and Presidential Votes," *American Journal of Political Science* 19 (1975): 161–185; Samuel Merrill III and Bernard Grofman, *A Unified Theory of Voting* (Cambridge: Cambridge University Press, 1999).

For the influence of economic evaluations on voting, see Morris P. Fiorina, *Retrospective Voting in American National Elections* (New Haven, CT: Yale University Press, 1981); Douglas A. Hibbs, Jr., *The American Political Economy: Macroeconomics and Electoral Politics* (Cambridge, MA: Harvard University Press, 1987); D. Roderick Kiewiet, *Macroeconomics and Micropolitics: The Electoral Effects of Economic Issues* (Chicago: University of Chicago Press, 1983); Michael B. MacKuen, Robert S. Erikson, and James A. Stimson, "Peasants or Bankers? The American Electorate and the U.S. Economy," *American Political Science Review* 86 (1992): 597–611; Edward R. Tufte, *Political Control of the Economy* (Princeton, NJ: Princeton University Press, 1978).
26. Campbell, Angus, Philip E. Converse, Warren E. Miller, and Donald E. Stokes, *The American Voter* (New York: John Wiley, 1960), 169–187.
27. Lewis-Beck et al., *The American Voter Revisited*, 161–200.
28. James E. Campbell, "Candidate Image Evaluations: Influence and Rationalization in Presidential Primaries," *American Politics Quarterly* 11 (1983): 293–313, analyzes data during the 1976 presidential primaries at two points in time to address this question, and he finds that while candidate image has some effect on the vote intention, there is more influence in the other direction. Larry M. Bartels, "The Impact of Candidate Traits in American Presidential Elections," in *Leaders' Personalities and the Outcomes of Democratic Elections,* ed. Anthony King (Oxford: Oxford University Press, 2002) also used panel data to determine the direction of causality. Patrick J. Kenney and Tom W. Rice, "Presidential Prenomination Preferences and Candidate Evaluations," *American Political Science Review* 82 (1988): 1309–1319, use two-stage, least-squares regression to examine the direction of causality, and they conclude that trait perceptions affect the vote. Carolyn L. Funk, "The Impact of Scandal on Candidate Evaluations: An Experimental Test of the Role of Candidate Traits," *Political Behavior* 18 (1996): 1–24, using experimental data, found that trait evaluations truly affected overall candidate evaluations.
29. Bartels, "Partisanship and Voting Behavior," 46–48.
30. Kathleen Parker, "The Likability Test," *Washington Post,* May 16, 2012.
31. Carolyn L. Funk, "Understanding Trait Inferences in Candidate Images," in *Research in Micropolitics: Rethinking Rationality,* vol. 5, ed. Michael X.

Delli Carpini, Leonie Huddy, and Robert Y. Shapiro (Greenwich, CT: JAI, 1996). Wendy Rahn, John H. Aldrich, Eugene Borgida, and John L. Sullivan, "A Social-Cognitive Model of Candidate Appraisal," in *Information and Democratic Processes,* ed. John A. Ferejohn and James H. Kuklinski (Urbana: University of Illinois Press, 1990).

32. Campbell et al. *The American Voter.*
33. Lewis-Beck et al., *The American Voter Revisited,* 279.
34. David P. Glass, "Evaluating Presidential Candidates: Who Focuses on Their Personal Attributes?" *Public Opinion Quarterly* 49 (1985): 517–534.
35. Arthur H. Miller, Martin P. Wattenberg, and Oksana Malanchuk, "Schematic Assessments of Presidential Candidates," *American Political Science Review* 80 (1986): 521–540.
36. Richard R. Lau, "Political Schemata, Candidate Evaluations, and Voting Behavior," in *Political Cognition,* ed. Richard R. Lau and David O. Sears (Hillsdale, NJ: Lawrence Erlbaum, 1986).
37. Rahn et al. "A Social-Cognitive Model of Candidate Appraisal."
38. David P. Glass, "Evaluating Presidential Candidates: Who Focuses on Their Personal Attributes?" *Public Opinion Quarterly* 49 (1985): 517–34, and Arthur H. Miller, Martin P. Wattenberg, and Oksana Malanchuk, "Schematic Assessments of Presidential Candidates," *American Political Science Review* 80 (1986): 521–540, find that more educated or more politically sophisticated voters make more use of trait perceptions. Patrick A. Pierce, "Political Sophistication and the Use of Candidate Traits in Candidate Evaluation," *Political Psychology* 14 (1993): 21–35, finds no effect of political sophistication.

5 The Formation of Candidate Character Trait Perceptions

Beauty is in the eyes of the beholder. That well-known proverb certainly applies to the perception of character traits of presidential candidates. Voters differ greatly in their assessments of the personal qualities of candidates. The same candidate may be seen as honest by some voters but dishonest by others. Some voters will be confident that a candidate is a strong leader, while others are sure that he or she is not. Since evaluations of a candidate's personal traits are very subjective, such variation in trait assessments is not surprising. Perceptions of the character traits of the candidates are affected by basic political orientations, such as party identification or ideology, but they are influenced by other attitudes as well, including ones that are shaped by the events and circumstances of the particular election. The candidates and their campaigns have an effect. Some candidates achieve more favorable character evaluations from the voters than do others. Perceptions of candidate character traits also have an idiosyncratic element: voters with seemingly similar basic political attitudes and orientations may nevertheless disagree in their perceptions of the candidates. Although character trait evaluations are subjective assessments, the variation in these perceptions can be explained, at least partly, and that is what we attempt to do in this chapter.

THE EFFECT OF ATTITUDES ON CHARACTER TRAIT PERCEPTIONS

Little research has been done on how voters form their perceptions of candidate character, but based on the general literature on voting behavior, some hypotheses can be constructed. There are several political attitudes or orientations that we would expect to influence how voters perceive the character traits of candidates. Party identification would be at the top of the list. Partisanship is a relatively stable and fundamental orientation that influences many political attitudes, so there is good reason to expect that it would strongly affect something as subjective as the assessment of candidate character traits.[1] Another relatively stable and fundamental political orientation is ideology, which is related to party identification, and more strongly so now than in the past. We would expect ideology to also affect trait perceptions: conservative voters should perceive conservative candidates more favorably in personal terms, for example, because their favorable ideological evaluation of the candidates would color their assessments of the personal qualities of the candidates.[2] The shaping of candidate character trait perceptions by party identification and ideology partly explains how these fundamental orientations affect the vote. Liberal Democrats are more inclined to see the Democratic candidate as superior to the Republican opponent in personal terms, which gives them another good reason to vote for their party's candidate; conservative Republicans are inclined to behave similarly.

Character trait perceptions should be influenced by party identification and ideology, but they also should be affected by short-term attitudes, those that shift from one election to another. For example, evaluations of the president's performance should be a particularly important factor when the incumbent president is running for reelection. If a voter thinks that the president is doing a good job of managing the economy and handling foreign policy, then the voter is likely to conclude that the president is both competent and a strong leader; if the voter thinks that the president is not doing a good job, the likely inference is that the president is an incompetent manager and a weak and ineffective leader. Perceptions of the president's integrity and empathy should be less affected by his performance, but they are not necessarily immune from such effects. A voter who disagrees with the policies proposed by the president may conclude that the president does not care about ordinary people, or even that the president is being deceptive in his policy statements.

Attitudes on specific issues also could affect the perception of candidate character traits. While attitudes on policy issues naturally are related to party identification and ideology, they do not always correspond, and they therefore could have an independent effect on trait perceptions.[3] Many possible examples can be cited. A devout Catholic voter who identifies as a Democrat but disagrees with her party's presidential candidate on abortion, for example, might question the candidate's moral judgment. That same voter might see the Republican candidate as highly moral, based on abortion and other sanctity of life issues. A working-class Republican who thinks that the Republican presidential candidate's tax policies are too generous toward high income individuals may conclude that the candidate does not care enough about the economic situation of the average person. A Jewish Democrat who disagrees with a Democratic president's foreign policy toward the Middle East might judge the president to be a weak leader. Some of the seemingly idiosyncratic features of how individuals perceive the character traits of the candidates could be due to the impact of specific issues that are particularly dear to the individual.

This conceptualization of the formation of candidate character trait perceptions places them far down the funnel of causality, very close to the vote decision.[4] Trait perceptions are affected by attitudes farther up the funnel—party identification, ideology, issue orientations, and assessments of the performance of the president—and in turn, trait perceptions affect the vote. They are intervening variables between these other factors and the vote. Party identification, ideology, and other attitudes affect the vote partly by shaping perceptions of the character traits of the candidates. However, trait perceptions are not merely reflections of these attitudes. They have their own independent effect on the vote, as Chapter 4 documents.

We examine the relationship of various political attitudes with trait perceptions by initially focusing on three presidential elections: 1980, 1996, and 2008, as we did in the previous chapter. These three elections span close to three decades, so we can see whether the effects on trait perceptions have changed over time, and they capture three types of presidential elections: one where an incumbent was defeated, one where an incumbent was reelected, and one that did not involve an incumbent seeking reelection. After the analysis of the impact of various political attitudes on trait perceptions in these three presidential elections, we summarize the basic relationships for all eight elections held from 1980 to 2008 (the analysis of the 2012 election is reserved for a later chapter).

Attitudinal Influences on Trait Perceptions in 1980

The 1980 presidential election featured an unpopular incumbent president attempting to win reelection. Public approval of Jimmy Carter's presidential performance was low, due in large part to a deteriorating economy. His Republican opponent, Ronald Reagan, had an overall advantage on character traits, due to his sizable advantage on leadership. As Chapter 3 outlined, voters were inclined to see Carter as a weak and uninspiring leader, although they did see him as honest and knowledgeable. Perceptions of candidate traits affected the vote, as Chapter 4 showed, so Reagan's advantage on character traits helped him win the election. We complete the analysis by examining the factors that influenced how voters formed their assessments of the candidates in 1980.

Table 5.1 shows the relationship of several political attitudes to the perceptions of Carter's and Reagan's character. The dependent variable in the first column is the overall character trait index, which is the average net score across all of the candidate character trait items asked in that year; it runs from –4.0 (most favorable to the Democratic candidate) to +4.0 (most favorable to the Republican candidate), as explained in Chapter 2.[5] The independent variables are the same ones used in the analysis of the vote in Chapter 4: party identification, ideology, approval of Carter's job performance, and attitudes on social welfare and moral issues. The coefficients in the table are the standardized regression coefficients (beta

Table 5.1 Attitudinal Influences on Trait Perceptions, 1980

Independent variables	Candidate character trait index	Index of Carter's character traits	Index of Reagan's character traits
	Dependent variable		
Party identification	.28*	.13*	.31*
Ideology	.06*	–.02	.11*
Approval of Carter's job performance	.48*	.58*	.21*
Social welfare issues index	.11*	.08*	.10*
Moral issues index	.08*	–.02	.15*
R^2	.55	.45	.35
(N)	(1003)	(1003)	(1003)

*p < .05 (two-tailed test)
Note: The coefficients for the independent variables are standardized regression coefficients (beta weights) from OLS regressions of the specified trait indices. See the text for details on the variables. Positive coefficients indicate that views of candidate character traits that are more favorable to the Republican candidate or less favorable to the Democratic candidate are associated with a more Republican party identification, more conservative ideological and issue orientations, and greater disapproval of Carter's performance.
Source: 1980 American National Election Study. Only major-party voters are included in the analysis.

weights) from ordinary least squares regressions.[6] We report the standardized coefficients because they are most appropriate for comparing the relative effect of each independent variable on the dependent variable. The standardized coefficient specifies the change in the dependent variable, in standard deviation units, for a change of one standard deviation in the independent variable.

Two variables stand out as substantial influences on the overall trait index. First, party identification had a strong effect on the assessment of candidate traits in 1980. Not surprisingly, Republicans were more likely to see Reagan as the better candidate in personal terms, while Democrats were more inclined to view Carter as superior. Second, evaluations of Carter's presidential performance had an even greater effect. The more that the voter approved of Carter's job performance, the more likely the voter was to view Carter as better than Reagan on character traits, even with party identification and other attitudes held constant. Ideology had a limited effect on trait perceptions, with other attitudes taken into account, but ideology was directly related to attitudes on social welfare and moral issues, which did have an effect. The combined effect of ideology and issue orientations rivals that of party identification. Both party identification and ideology also influenced perceptions of Carter's presidential performance, so they had indirect effects on trait perceptions, besides the direct effects evident in Table 5.1. The five attitudes in the equation did a good job of predicting differences in trait perceptions, accounting for 55 percent of the variation, but this shows that trait perceptions were affected by other factors as well.

More insight into the effect of attitudes on trait perceptions comes from an analysis of the two components of the overall trait index: perceptions of Carter's and Reagan's character traits. Columns two and three of Table 5.1 display the analysis of these two variables. As we can see, the effect of evaluations of presidential job performance on the overall trait index is largely a result of effects on the perception of Carter's character traits. Voters who thought that Carter was doing a poor job as president were likely to conclude that Carter was deficient in his personal qualities, which then led them to be likely to see Reagan as superior to Carter on character traits, which is what the overall trait index measures.[7] Evaluations of Carter's job performance had only a small effect on assessments of Reagan's character traits. Further examination of these data, using measures of specific traits, shows that evaluations of Carter's job performance affected the assessment of Carter's character largely by affecting perceptions of Carter's leadership; effects on Carter's integrity were much weaker. Compared to assessments of Carter's character traits, assessments of Reagan's traits were influenced more by party identification and by ideological and issue orientations. Thus, voters made inferences about Carter's character primarily from evaluations of his performance as president. Their judgments of Reagan's character, however, were influenced mostly by their partisanship and ideology.

Attitudinal Influences on Trait Perceptions in 1996

The electoral circumstances in 1996 were quite different. The incumbent president, Bill Clinton, had a high approval rating due in large part to a healthy economy. Nevertheless, his Republican opponent, Bob Dole, had an overall advantage on character traits, as Chapter 3 outlined. Voters judged Dole to be far superior on integrity and a stronger and more effective leader. While voters considered Clinton to be more inspiring and gave him the usual Democratic advantage on empathy, this did not compensate for his disadvantages on integrity and strong leadership. But as Chapter 4 discussed, Clinton was still able to win reelection, partly because of his solid approval rating and partly because voters did not seem to be influenced very much by perceptions of integrity, Clinton's weakest trait. We complete the analysis of 1996 by analyzing the factors that affected trait perceptions in that year.

Table 5.2 presents a very similar analysis to the one reported in Table 5.1. Instead of a single overall measure of approval of Clinton's job performance,

Table 5.2 Attitudinal Influences on Trait Perceptions, 1996

Independent variables	Dependent variable		
	Candidate character trait index	Index of Clinton's character traits	Index of Dole's character traits
Party identification	.35*	.29*	.33*
Ideology	.04	.00	.06
Clinton's handling of the economy	.31*	.38*	.13*
Clinton's handling of national security	.20*	.26*	.08*
Social welfare issues index	.13*	.11*	.12*
Moral issues index	−.01	.00	−.02
R^2	.69	.72	.35
(N)	(762)	(810)	(770)

*p < .05 (two-tailed test)
Note: The coefficients for the independent variables are standardized regression coefficients (beta weights) from OLS regressions of the specified trait indices. See the text for details on the variables. Positive coefficients indicate that views of candidate character traits that are more favorable to the Republican candidate or less favorable to the Democratic candidate are associated with a more Republican party identification, more conservative ideological and issue orientations, and greater disapproval of Clinton's performance.
Source: 1996 American National Election Study. Only major-party voters are included in the analysis.

separate measures of his performance in handling the economy and foreign affairs are used, something that could not be done for 1980 because both measures were not available. As in 1980, overall assessments of the character traits of the candidates were affected most by party identification and by the president's job performance; ideological and issue orientations played a smaller role in the formation of these assessments. Furthermore, the impact of evaluations of Clinton's performance on the overall character trait index came primarily from effects on assessments of Clinton's character, rather than Dole's character. Assessments of Dole's character traits were affected most strongly by party identification, while ideological and issue orientations had relatively weak effects, a somewhat different pattern than we found for Reagan in 1980.

A further analysis that examines individual trait dimensions reveals some differences in effects.[8] The relative assessment of the leadership ability of the two candidates was affected by party identification and evaluations of presidential performance, particularly in handling the economy.

Having a Democratic identification and believing that Clinton did a good job of managing the economy made a voter much more likely to see Clinton as superior to Dole on leadership. Ideology and issue orientations had little effect on perceptions of leadership, however. A similar pattern exists for empathy: party identification and evaluations of Clinton's handling of the economy had a substantial effect, while ideology and issue orientations had little effect. As Chapter 3 points out, leadership and empathy are the two trait dimensions that have a strong connection to the parties, so it is not surprising that party identification has a significant effect on perceptions of these two traits. Party identification had much less effect on the relative assessments of the competence of the candidates; the only important variable here was presidential performance, not a surprising finding for an election in which the incumbent president was running for reelection. Finally perceptions of integrity, the one trait dimension that Clinton was really weak on, were most affected by party identification and evaluations of the president's handling of foreign affairs. Why the latter variable would influence perceptions of the integrity of either candidate is unclear to us.

Attitudinal Influences on Trait Perceptions in 2008

The previous two analyses examine years in which an incumbent president was running for reelection. In both cases, evaluations of the president's job performance had a big effect on assessments of his personal qualities, which in turn influenced overall perceptions of the personal qualities of the two candidates. Voters who thought that the president was doing a good job were led to conclude that he had desirable character traits, especially that he was a strong and effective leader, which then led them to see the president as superior to his opponent in character traits. Voters who felt that the president had done a poor job were more likely to come to opposite conclusions. In 2008, no incumbent president was running for reelection, so voter perceptions of the character traits of the candidates might be shaped by different considerations.

As Chapter 3 recounted, Barack Obama had an overall advantage on character traits in 2008. John McCain failed to gain the normal Republican advantage on leadership, and he did no better than Obama on perceptions of competence and integrity. Obama, however, had the usual Democratic advantage on empathy, and he was viewed as more optimistic. Table 5.3 presents an analysis of the attitudes that influenced trait perceptions in 2008, an analysis that is similar to the ones conducted for 1980 and 1996. One additional variable is in this analysis: a measure of the voter's attitudes toward blacks, which seems potentially important for this election. Black voters are excluded from this analysis; blacks were very favorable toward Obama, and including them in the analysis might distort the effects that the variables had on other voters.

Table 5.3 Attitudinal Influences on Trait Perceptions, 2008

Independent variables	Candidate character trait index	Index of Obama's character traits	Index of McCain's character traits
Party identification	.28*	.22*	.24*
Ideology	.12*	.07*	.12*
Bush's handling of the economy	.13*	.09*	.13*
Bush's handling of national security	.24*	.12*	.28*
Social welfare issues index	.02	.03	.00
Moral issues index	.04*	.11*	−.05
Attitudes toward blacks	.18*	.25*	.05
R^2	.60	.43	.42
(N)	(1218)	(1218)	(1219)

*p < .05 (two-tailed test)

Note: The coefficients for the independent variables are standardized regression coefficients (beta weights) from OLS regressions of the specified trait indices. See the text for details on the variables. Positive coefficients indicate that views of candidate character traits that are more favorable to the Republican candidate or less favorable to the Democrat candidate are associated with a more Republican party identification, more conservative ideological and issue orientations, more favorable assessments of Bush's performance, and more negative attitudes toward blacks.

Source: 2008 American National Election Study. Only non-black major-party voters are included in the analysis.

Party identification was an important influence on trait perceptions in 2008, as it was in 1980 and 1996. Democrats were more likely to think that Obama was the better candidate in personal terms, while Republicans were inclined to believe that McCain was superior. The coefficient for party identification is similar for all three years examined here, ranging from .28 in 1980 and 2008 to .35 in 1996, suggesting that the direct effects of party identification on perceptions of candidate character traits is stable across a variety of presidential elections. We should keep in mind that party identification also has indirect effects on trait perceptions through its effect on other attitudes, especially evaluations of presidential performance.[9]

Evaluations of the incumbent president's performance had a smaller effect on the perception of candidate character traits in 2008 than in 1980 or 1996. The combined effect of the coefficients for the two measures of presidential performance in 2008 is .37, well below the combined effect for 1996 or the effect for the one measure of performance used in 1980.[10] This finding makes sense. Voters should be less likely to use their evaluation of the president's performance to form assessments of the character traits of the candidates when the incumbent president is not one of those candidates. Still, evaluations of Bush's performance had some influence on how the voters perceived Obama and McCain. Voters who thought that Bush had done a poor job as president were more likely to see Obama as better than McCain on character traits, even with party identification controlled for. Of course, the only logical connection between these variables is the party label. Apparently, voters translated their evaluation of the incumbent president into their assessment of the candidates, using the party label to make connections.

Interestingly, issue orientations had little effect on trait perceptions, once party identification and other variables were included in the analysis. Although the coefficients for the social welfare and moral issues indices are smaller in 2008 than they are in earlier years, the coefficient for ideology is stronger than it was in the other two years analyzed. It may be that as issue orientations, ideology, and party identification become more closely related, the effects of issue orientations are captured by party identification and ideology, and they therefore have a smaller independent effect on trait perceptions. Another interesting finding is the strong effect of attitudes toward blacks on trait perceptions. Voters with more negative attitudes towards blacks were more likely to view McCain as better on character traits.

More insight into the formation of assessments of candidate character traits in 2008 comes from an analysis of the formation of the separate assessments of Obama and McCain, which are in columns two and three of Table 5.3. Party identification had a similar effect on assessments of both candidates' character. Evaluations of Bush's presidential performance, on the other hand, had a stronger effect on assessments of McCain's character than Obama's. Even though McCain was not part of—and, in fact, was often at odds with—the Bush administration, voters still inferred his character traits from their views of Bush's performance; this effect exists even though we controlled for party identification, so it is more than just simple partisan bias. Rather, Republicans who thought poorly of Bush's performance—and there were many who felt that way—were less inclined to see McCain in favorable personal terms. Of course, the Obama campaign did its best to tie McCain to the Bush administration, hoping that voters would transfer their personal disenchantment with Bush to McCain, as we discussed in more detail in Chapter 3.

Perceptions of Obama's character traits were influenced by the voter's attitudes toward blacks. Whites with more negative attitudes toward blacks were inclined to see Obama as possessing less positive character traits, and therefore inclined to see McCain as superior to Obama on character. This effect exists even with controls for party identification and ideology. Democrats, for example, who were more negative toward blacks did not evaluate

Obama as highly as other Democratic voters did. As Chapter 4 discussed, some research studies concluded that Obama lost votes in 1980 because of his race.[11] These findings indicate one mechanism for how this effect took place. The effect was limited to perceptions of Obama's character; attitudes toward blacks had little effect on assessments of McCain's character traits.

Attitudinal Influences on Trait Perceptions, 1980–2008

Having examined in depth the attitudinal effects on trait perceptions for three presidential elections, we can take a broader look at these influences across all elections from 1980 to 2008. In analyzing the formation of trait perceptions in these elections, we used just three variables to predict scores on our overall trait index. First, we included approval of the president's job performance, since the research reported above found this variable to have a consistent impact on perceptions of the personal qualities of the candidates, especially in years when the incumbent president was running for reelection. Second, we included party identification, which we also found to have consistent, direct effects on trait perceptions, plus indirect effects through party identification's influence on presidential approval. Third, we included ideology. Although the analysis reported above did not always find a strong relationship between ideology and trait perceptions, it did find that the combined effect of ideology and issue orientations was significant. Since ideology and issue orientations are related, much of the effect of issue orientations on trait perceptions will be captured by ideology. We used just three variables to predict trait perceptions to keep the analysis simple and concise. Essentially, we are comparing the relative impact of party identification, ideological and issue orientations, and evaluations of presidential performance on the overall perceptions of the character traits of the candidates.

The results of the analysis, which are displayed in Figure 5.1, show the standardized regression coefficient for each variable for each year. These coefficients indicate the change in the trait index (in standard deviations) for a change of one standard deviation in the independent variable, with the other variables held constant. For example, the coefficient for presidential approval in 1996 is .56, so an increase of one standard deviation in this variable (which would be about one point on a four-point scale running from strongly approve to strongly disapprove) would produce an increase of over one-half of a standard deviation in the trait index score, which would be close to one point on a scale that goes from −4.0 to +4.0. Thus, for a voter with a given party identification and ideology, the difference between approving and strongly approving of Clinton's performance, or between disapproving and approving, would be associated with a roughly one-point difference in the trait index score—the equivalent, for example, of going from a neutral score of zero to a score of −1.0, which would be moderately favorable to Clinton. Similarly, the coefficient for party identification in 1996 is .33, and when we translate the standard deviations into scores, we find that an

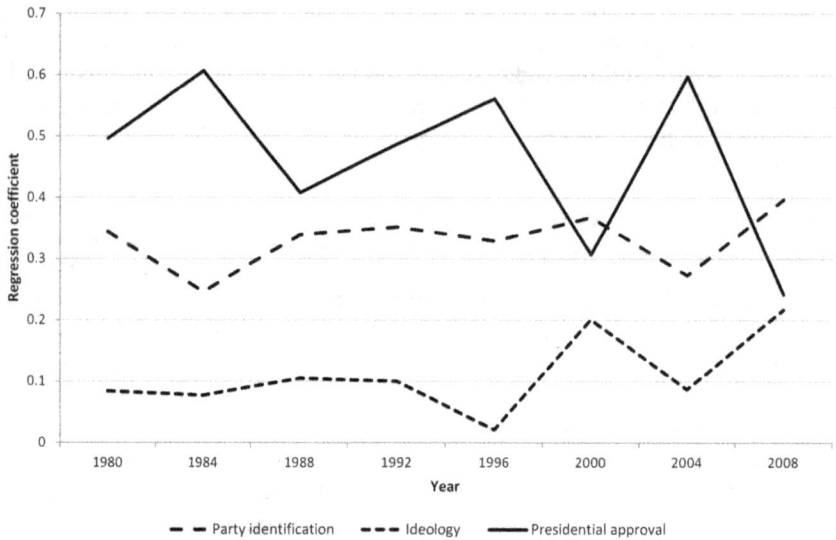

Figure 5.1   Effects of Attitudes on Candidate Character Trait Perceptions, 1980–2008

Note: The coefficients in the chart are standardized OLS regression coefficients that indicate the effec of each of the three variables on the candidate character trait index for the specified year.

increase of two points on the party identification scale (e.g., from a pure Independent to a weak Republican) would produce an increase of about .50 on the trait index (e.g., from zero, or completely neutral, to .50, or slightly favorable to Dole), with the other variables held constant. The coefficient for ideology in 1996 is extremely weak (.02), which shows that once party identification and presidential evaluation are included in the analysis, changes in the voter's ideological orientation had no effect on how the voter perceived the character traits of the candidates.

Several conclusions are evident from these data. First, the effect of presidential approval on character trait perceptions is lower, although still significant, in years when no incumbent president is running for reelection, confirming the conclusion of the analysis of 2008 above. Years with no incumbent president running—1988, 2000, and 2008—have the weakest coefficients for presidential approval. Second, the direct impact of party identification on trait perceptions is fairly stable. The two years with the smallest coefficient for party identification are 1984 and 2004, both years when the coefficient for presidential approval was very high. Party identification quite naturally affects presidential approval, and it thus had an indirect effect on trait perceptions. Thus, in 1984 and 2004, party identification had a somewhat smaller direct effect but a greater indirect effect through its influence on presidential approval. Finally, ideology has less effect on trait perceptions than party identification and presidential approval, but it has been more influential recently, especially in the open-seat years of 2000 and 2008. This suggests that as the two parties have become more ideologically polarized, voters assess the personal qualities of the candidates through an ideological lens more than they did previously.

ELECTION YEAR DIFFERENCES

The previous section shows that within any election year, differences among the voters in their assessments of the character traits of the presidential candidates are related to several basic political attitudes. While these attitudes do not fully explain why voters differ in their trait perceptions, they do account for a substantial portion of the variation. The next question that we investigate is how useful these attitudes are for explaining change in the perceptions of candidate character traits over time. As Chapter 3 outlined, these assessments change greatly. In some years, the Democratic candidate is seen as superior on character traits; in other years, the Republican is assessed more favorably; in still other years, neither candidate has much of an overall advantage. How much of this year-to-year variation is attributable to change in party identification, ideology, or evaluations of presidential performance?

Figure 5.2 charts four variables for 1980 through 2008: party identification, ideology, presidential approval, and the overall candidate character trait index score. The first three variables are centered, so that a score of zero represents a neutral score, namely pure independent for party identification, moderate for ideology, and halfway between approval and disapproval of the president's performance. Each variable is constructed so that positive scores are more favorable to the Republican candidate and negative scores are more favorable to the Democrat. Thus, favorable evaluations of a Republican president receive a positive score, but favorable evaluations of a Democratic president receive a negative score. For party identification and ideology, Republican and conservative identifications receive a positive score, Democratic and liberal identifications a negative score. The candidate character trait index runs from +4.0 to –4.0, with positive scores indicating that the Republican candidate is perceived more favorably than the Democrat.

The candidate character trait index varies considerably across these elections. The Republican candidate had the advantage on character traits in 1980 and 1984, but was disadvantaged in 1988 and 1992. In 1996, the Republican candidate had about as large an advantage as the Democrat did in 2008, but the two intervening elections were ones where neither

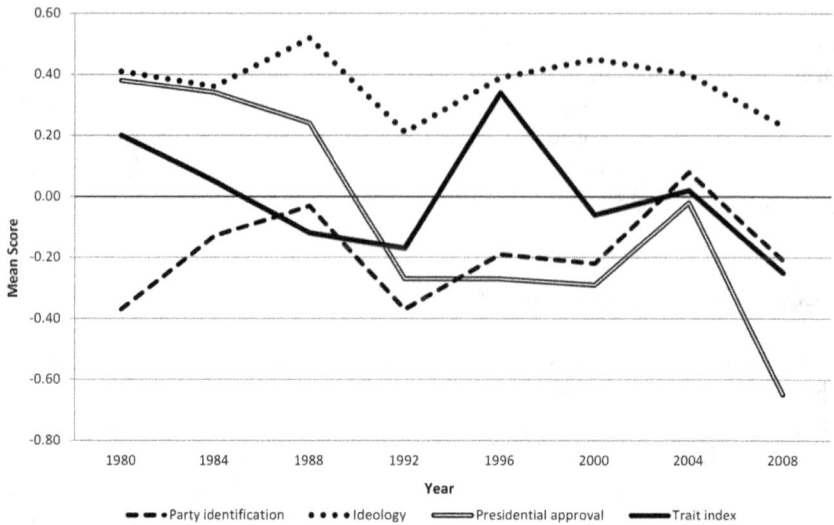

Figure 5.2   Mean Scores for the Candidate Character Trait Index and Related Variables, 1980–2008

Note: The lines show the mean scores for each variable over time for major-party voters.

candidate had any real advantage. This trait index summarizes in a single number the more complex picture that is described in Chapter 3, particularly Table 3.1.

Examining the changes in the other variables plotted in Figure 5.2, we can see that some of the change in the trait index is related to change in the variables that influence trait perceptions, but a considerable amount is not. For example, George H.W. Bush was seen in less favorable personal terms than his 1988 opponent, Michael Dukakis, something that would not be predicted by looking at the other variables in the chart. Presidential approval was quite favorable to the Republicans in 1988, the distribution of party identification had moved close to parity among voters, and ideology had shifted in a more conservative direction. If assessments of the character traits of the candidates were determined simply by these factors, Bush should have been seen as significantly superior to Dukakis. The fact that he was not undoubtedly can be explained by the candidates and circumstances of the election, particularly that Bush was not Reagan. Even more interestingly, Bush was at only a slightly greater disadvantage on character traits in 1992 than he was in 1988, even though presidential approval, party identification, and ideology all shifted sharply in a Democratic direction. Again, the explanation lies partly in the candidates and circumstances of the individual elections. Bill Clinton was judged poorly on integrity in 1992, as discussed in Chapter 3, which prevented him from earning a greater advantage on character traits. Had Clinton been perceived as equal to Duka-kis on integrity, he would have been far more advantaged overall. Another element is that Bush was hurt more by his low approval rating in 1992 than he was helped by Reagan's high approval rating in 1988, since the link between presidential approval and character trait assessment is stronger when the incumbent president is running.

Perhaps the most deviant year in the chart is 1996, when Dole had the greatest advantage that any candidate had on character traits, a far greater advantage than one would predict from looking at the mean scores for party identification and presidential approval, two variables that our previous analysis found to be good predictors of trait assess-ments at the individual level. The distributions of both of these variables were quite favorable to the Democrats in 1996, but Clinton neverthe-less lost to Dole on trait assessments. Again the explanation has to do with the candidates in the election. Clinton had even worse integrity scores in 1996 than he did in 1992, while Dole did very well on char-acter traits compared to other Republican candidates in the years that we examine.

In 2000, Bush and Gore were about even in the voters' overall assessment of their character traits. However, both party identification and evaluations of presidential performance were quite favorable to the Democrats in that year. On that basis, we would expect Gore to have a clear advantage on character traits. While Gore did not do as badly on character perceptions as many pundits thought, a point discussed in Chapter 3, he did not do as well as he should have, given the distribution of basic political attitudes in the electorate. In this sense, some of the criticisms leveled by commentators about the Gore campaign and the candidate's debate performances were on the mark.

One point should be emphasized. Our analysis concentrates on the over-all trait index. We think that is appropriate because what should count in the voter's mind is whether one candidate is better than the other. If a voter perceives a candidate in favorable terms, that does not incline the voter to choose that candidate if the voter sees the opponent in equally favorable terms. Therefore, a presidential candidate could be perceived very favorably, but if his or her opponent is assessed just as favorably, then neither candidate will have an advantage. Conversely, a candidate could be perceived not so favorably, but if his or her opponent is assessed even more unfavorably, then the first candidate will have an advantage on character traits. It is important to keep in mind the fact that perceptions of both candidates must be consid-ered, a point that helps in the interpretation of shifts in the trait index score that are displayed in Figure 5.2. For example, we pointed out that Bush did not have an advantage on character traits in 1988, even though the distribu-tion of basic attitudes would suggest that he should have had one. Bush's fail-ure to secure an advantage was partly due to his weakness on leadership, as perceived by the voters, but it was also due in part to the positive evaluations that Dukakis received from the voters. The pundits and commentators in 1988 may havethought that Dukakis failed to impress the voters in personal terms, but the data show that Dukakis was perceived very favorably on empathy, integrity, and competence, and he did decently on leadership for a Democrat. Similarly, the Republican advantage on character traits in 1996 was due partly to Clinton's low rating on integrity, but also to the fact that Dole did very well on leadership, integrity, and competence.

CONCLUSION

Perceptions of the character traits of presidential candidates are not objective, dispassionate assessments by the voters. They are subjective, biased judgments. Voters see the candidates through a lens that is tinted by their partisan and ideological leanings. Trait perceptions also are influenced by assessments of the performance of the president, particularly when the incumbent president is running for reelection, but even in years when this is not so. While these attitudes affect trait perceptions, they do not determine them. Character trait perceptions are more than simple reflections of party identification, ideology, and presidential performance evaluations. Some presidential candidates are better able than others to elicit favorable assessments from voters of the other party. Most significantly, the variation in these perceptions from one election to the next is only partly explained by changes in these political attitudes. Factors that are unique to the election, such as the nature of the candidates and their campaigns, also seem to play a significant role.[12]

While our findings suggest that candidates and campaigns are important, our conclusions are based on a small number of elections. The data are suggestive, but hardly definitive. Furthermore, we lack the data to test hypotheses about specific features of candidates and campaigns that influence the perceptions of the character traits of the presidential candidates. Such research is beyond the scope of this study, although it points to some worthwhile avenues of inquiry. What we can say with confidence is that there is an independent role for the candidates and their campaigns, along with campaign events and circumstances, in the formation of trait perceptions. It is difficult to say two or three years before the election, before the nominees are even known, whether one candidate will have an advantage on trait perceptions. Such an advantage, if one materializes, will be determined during the election year, perhaps even well into the fall campaign, and it will be affected by how the campaigns unfold and how the candidates present themselves.[13] Furthermore, if one candidate is able to obtain a significant advantage on character traits, that will increase his or her electoral appeal, since trait perceptions influence voters, as Chapter 4 demonstrated. Being seen as the better candidate in personal terms does not guarantee victory, but it certainly helps.

NOTES

1. Larry M. Bartels, "The Impact of Candidate Traits in American Presidential Elections," in *Leaders' Personalities and the Outcomes of Democratic Elections,* ed. Anthony King (Oxford: Oxford University Press, 2002); Kathryn M. Doherty and James G. Gimple, "Candidate Character vs. the Economy in the 1992 Election," *Political Behavior* 19 (1997): 177–196; Whitt H. Kilburn, "Does the Candidate Really Matter?" *American Politics Research* 33 (2005): 335–356; Wendy M. Rahn, John H. Aldrich, Eugene Borgida, and John L. Sullivan, "A Social-Cognitive Model of Candidate Appraisal," in *Information and Democratic Processes,* ed. John A. Ferejohn and James H. Kuklinkski (Urbana: University of Illinois Press, 1990).
2. Bartels, "The Impact of Candidate Traits;" Doherty and Gimpel, "Candidate Character vs. the Economy;" Rahn et al., "A Social-Cognitive Model of Candidate Appraisal."
3. For a discussion of how attitudes on particular issues can cause voters to defect from their normal partisan preference, see D. Sunshine Hillygus and Todd G. Shields, *The Persuadable Voter* (Princeton, NJ: Princeton University Press, 2008). We extend their argument to the perception of candidate character traits. Ronald B. Rapoport, Kelly L. Metcalf, and Jon A. Hartman, "Candidate Traits and Voter Inferences: An Experimental Study," *Journal of Politics* 51 (1989): 917–932, report the results of an experimental study that indicates that individuals infer candidate character traits from issue positions.
4. Our conceptualization of the causal order of the variables follows the one outlined by Warren E. Miller and J. Merrill Shanks, *The New American Voter* (Cambridge, MA: Harvard University Press, 1996), 189–211.
5. No measure of empathy was asked in 1980, so the character trait index does not capture this dimension for that year. Since the Democratic candidate normally does better on empathy, the absence of this trait dimension means that the trait index probably exaggerates Reagan's overall advantage on character traits. However, it probably does not affect the correlations of other variables with the index.
6. For a discussion of standardized regression coefficients, see Jerry M. Wooldridge, *Introductory Econometrics: A Modern Approach* (Cincinnati, OH: South-Western College Publishing, 2000), 181–182; and Lawrence S. Meyers, Glenn Gamst, and A. J. Guarino, *Applied Multivariate Research: Design and Interpretation* (Thousand Oaks, CA: Sage Publishing, 2006), 167–169.
7. Steven Greene, "The Role of Character Assessments in Presidential Approval," *American Politics Research* 29 (2001): 196–210, argues that perceptions of the president's character traits can influence approval of the president's performance. We believe that it makes more theoretical sense to see trait perceptions as affected by evaluations of presidential performance, and this seems consistent with the conceptualization commonly used in the field. If trait perceptions do affect presidential approval, then the effect that trait perceptions have on the vote would be greater than what we estimate, since trait perceptions would have indirect effects on the vote through effects on evaluations of presidential performance.
8. For the analysis that these conclusions are based on, see David B. Holian and Charles Prysby, "Determinants of Voter Perceptions of Candidate Personal Traits, 1992–2004" (paper presented at the annual meeting of the Midwest Political Science Association, Chicago, IL, April 3–5, 2008).
9. As partisan polarization in the nation has increased, the relationship between party identification and approval of the president's job performance has

tightened. See Alan I. Abramowitz, *The Disappearing Center* (New Haven, CT: Yale University Press, 2010), 45–46.

10. Adding the coefficients to get the total effect shows what the change in the trait index would be if both measures of performance each increased by one standard deviation.

11. Jonathan Knuckey, "Racial Resentment and Vote Choice in the 2008 U.S. Presidential Election," *Politics & Policy* 39 (2011): 559–582; Michael S. Lewis-Beck, Charles Tien, and Richard Nadeau, "Obama's Missed Landslide: A Racial Cost?" *PS: Political Science and Politics* 43 (2010): 69–76; Spencer Piston, "How Explicit Racial Prejudice Hurt Obama in the 2008 Election," *Political Behavior* 32 (2010): 431–451.

12. For example, Lynda Lee Kaid and Mike Chanslor, "Changing Candidate Images: The Effects of Political Advertising," in *Candidate Images in Presidential Elections,* ed. Kenneth L. Hacker (Westport, CT: Praeger, 1995) found that political advertisements affected the images that voters had of the candidates.

13. James A. McCann, "Changing Electoral Contexts and Changing Candidate Images During the 1984 Presidential Campaign," *American Politics Quarterly* 18 (1990): 123–40, traced changes in voter perceptions of the 1984 presidential candidates over the course of the entire election year, and he found significant changes in perceptions as the electoral context changed.

6 Candidate Character Traits in the 2012 Presidential Election

The character traits of the two presidential candidates played an important role in 2012, both in the minds of the voters and in the campaign strategies of the two candidates and their campaigns. Early in 2012, Republicans felt that they could make Barack Obama a one-term president. The president's approval rating was below 50 percent in Gallup polls in January and February, the national economy was stalled in a weak recovery from the Great Recession of 2008–2009, and the Affordable Care Act, President Obama's most prominent legislative accomplishment, was failing to win the support of a majority of Americans.[1] Many pundits and political scientists agreed that these circumstances could well lead to a Republican victory in November.[2] According to a number of commentators, Obama's best hope for victory was to shift the election spotlight away from his first-term performance over to criticisms of the Republican candidate, a strategy that inevitably would lead to a highly negative campaign. When Mitt Romney captured the Republican nomination, many political observers thought that he would be vulnerable to such attacks. Some Republicans feared that Romney's personal weaknesses, at least as unfavorably portrayed by the Democrats, could result in the GOP losing a presidential election they thought they should win. As the analysis in this chapter will show, these speculations or predictions were quite accurate: Romney was perceived much less favorably than Obama in personal terms, and voters were significantly influenced by their perceptions of the character traits of the two presidential candidates, two factors that contributed to Obama's reelection victory.

Romney's personal weaknesses were outlined at the beginning of Chapter 1. Perhaps the most prominent criticism of his character traits was that he lacked warmth and likeability. Commentators unflatteringly described him as a robot, an android, and a tin man.[3] A commonly expressed view was that Romney often seemed socially awkward when he was not able to stick to a carefully scripted set of remarks, frequently making statements that did not fit the situation. One well-publicized example occurred during a July 2012 trip to Europe, a trip that was supposed to enhance and favorably display his diplomatic skills. In London, Romney responded to an easy question from the press about his perceptions of British preparations for the upcoming Olympics not by complimenting the country for its efforts, but by questioning whether London was prepared to host the summer games and whether the British people would "come together and celebrate the Olympic moment."[4] Romney's faux pas evoked immediate rebukes from British leaders, which were highlighted in the news. Even American conservative commentators found it difficult to explain Romney's gaffe: Charles Krauthammer assessed Romney's statements as "unbelievable . . . beyond human understanding . . . incomprehensible."[5]

While Romney was particularly taken to task for his lack of warmth, President Obama also was criticized for being too cold and aloof. Both of the presidential candidates were characterized by Mark Shields as lacking in humor and humility, especially when compared to Presidents Ronald Reagan and George W. Bush, both of whom were able to deflect criticism with self-deprecating humor.[6] Maureen Dowd described Obama as an introvert who could be "thin-skinned and insecure at times."[7] Nevertheless, the consensus among commentators was that Obama was the more likable of the two candidates. Kathleen Parker, while lamenting the fact that likability mattered so much to voters, concluded that Obama was counting on his ability to win votes from "admirers who will overlook his flaws simply because they like him."[8] Even Republicans reluctantly acknowledged that Romney lacked warmth; for example, House Speaker John Boehner publically conceded that voters "probably aren't going to fall in love with Mitt Romney."[9]

The emphasis on Obama being more likable, in the sense of being a warmer human being who would be more fun to spend time with, may be misplaced. As we showed earlier in this book, most voters do not seem influenced very much by their perceptions of the personal warmth or likability of the candidates, even though pundits often claim that they are. The data for 2012 are consistent with the results for previous elections. When asked what they liked and disliked about each candidate, voters in 2012 made few references to personal warmth.[10] Instead, they usually cited aspects of leadership, competence, integrity, and empathy—the character traits that we have identified as most important over the past several decades. If Obama received an electoral boost from being more likable, it was at best a small boost. Lack of warmth was the least of Romney's personal problems.

A more serious concern for Romney was the widespread view among political analysts that he possessed little empathy. His background as a wealthy and successful businessman played into this characterization. Of course, Romney hoped that his business background would be a positive quality by allowing him to argue that he was highly qualified to manage the economy. Instead, during the contest for the Republican nomination, Romney's opponents criticized him for his actions as a venture capitalist, attacking him for making large sums of money even when his private equity firm, Bain Capital, was putting people out of work by selling off parts of enterprises or closing businesses. One Republican opponent, Texas Governor Rick Perry, described Romney as a "vulture capitalist," while another,

Newt Gingrich, dismissed Romney's business success as "a bunch of rich people figuring out clever ways to loot a company."[11] While these criticisms did not prevent Romney from securing the Republican nomination, they laid a foundation for Democratic attacks later in the year, attacks that surely seemed more credible because even Republicans had echoed them.

Romney unintentionally contributed to the perception that he did not understand the economic situation of the average family. Attempting to show that his family bought American, rather than foreign, automobiles, he proudly pointed out that his wife owned two Cadillacs.[12] Trying to give advice to young people who were having trouble finding a suitable job, he suggested that they start their own business by borrowing money from their parents, using an example of a friend who borrowed $20,000 from his parents.[13] Undoubtedly, the most damaging single statement that Romney made in 2012 was when he told a group of supporters that 47 percent of the people in the country would not vote for him because they depended on government handouts, adding that he would "never convince them that they should take personal responsibility and care for their lives."[14] Although the statement was made at a private meeting, it was surreptitiously recorded, later made public, and given considerable media exposure. Reactions to the statement were heavily negative, chastising Romney for suggesting that people who received such things as social security checks or veterans' benefits were mooching off the government. Media reports of simple details about the Romney family, such as the fact that one of his homes had an elevator for his autos, only added to the perception of Romney as someone so wealthy that he had little understanding of how most people lived.

Compounding his problems, Romney also was characterized as someone who too frequently shifted his positions in an effort to tell voters what they wanted to hear. Again, Romney contributed to this characterization by his statements and actions. Most notably, as Massachusetts governor from 2003 to 2006, he supported a state health plan that in many ways served as a blueprint for President Obama's Affordable Care Act. But as a presidential candidate in 2012, Romney attacked Obamacare and said that he would work to repeal it as soon as he took office.[15] Moreover, during the October presidential debates, when Obamacare seemed more popular than it was earlier in the year, Romney argued that while he would repeal the ACA, he would keep many of its good features, leading to questions about his trustworthiness.[16] As governor, Romney also had taken moderately liberal positions on abortion and gun control, but as a presidential candidate, he stated that he now was staunchly conservative on both issues. After proposing a tax plan in early 2012 that was criticized for being too beneficial to upper-income individuals, Romney claimed in the fall that his plan would not change the share of taxes paid by high income people, a claim that was viewed with considerable skepticism.[17]

Perhaps because of his perceived flip-flopping on issues, Romney was not seen as a strong leader by many pundits. As we pointed out in earlier chapters, a *Newsweek* cover story in August painted Romney as much weaker than previous Republican candidates, even George H. W. Bush, who was the subject of a similar *Newsweek* cover story in 1987.[18] The article, which was written by a liberal journalist, was criticized by many commentators as unfair, but even if unfair, it nevertheless reflected how a number of media commentators described Romney. It was unclear what he really stood for. He made several well-publicized faux pas, such as the "47 percent" comment that was discussed above. Another statement that may have been damaging occurred in early September, immediately after an attack on the U.S. consulate in Benghazi, Libya, resulted in the deaths of four Americans. Romney attacked the president for sympathizing with those who waged the attacks instead of condemning them. He attempted to press that point in the second presidential debate, but Obama responded that on the day following the attack he did condemn it, calling the event an act of terror and stating that we would hunt down the people responsible for the crime. When Romney attempted to dispute the president's claim, the debate moderator broke in and confirmed that Obama was correct.[19] Many pundits thought that the incident left Romney appearing as someone who was trying to misconstrue a national tragedy in order to gain a political advantage, hardly the picture of a strong leader.

In sum, media commentators and analysts generally agreed that Romney had several character-related weaknesses: he communicated little appreciation of and concern for the economic problems of ordinary people; he changed his mind on so many issues that he seemed to lack strong convictions on anything; he failed to impress voters as a strong leader; and he lacked warmth and likability. However, the assessments of the character traits of the candidates by the pundits do not necessarily reflect how the candidates are seen by the voters, as we have demonstrated previously in this book. To determine how the voters truly perceived the presidential candidates in personal terms, we need to examine the available survey data on the American electorate in 2012, which is what we do in the remainder of this chapter.

PERCEPTIONS OF THE CANDIDATES BY THE VOTERS

We examine the data for the 2012 presidential election in this chapter, rather than in Chapter 4, where the data for 1980–2008 are analyzed, because the 2012 ANES survey asked the questions about the character traits of the candidates in a somewhat different format than in the previous years. As we explained in Chapter 2, the ANES provided the respondents in 2012 with five choices for each trait question: they could say that a trait characterized the candidate extremely well, very well, moderately well, not very well, or not well at all. From 1980 to 2004, respondents had just four choices: two positive ones and two negative ones; the middle position, moderately well, was not provided to respondents in those years. In 2008, one-half of the sample was asked the questions with the old, four-category response set, and one-half the questions with the new, five-category response set. Therefore, the responses from 2012 are not exactly comparable to those for earlier years, but a reasonable approximation can be made.

For 2012, we scored the extremely well and very well responses as +2 and +1, respectively, and the not very well and not well at all as –1 and –2, respectively, with the middle category receiving a score of 0. The same method was used for the one-half of the 2008 sample that received the new version of the trait questions. The data for 1980–2004 (and the 2008 half sample that received the old version of the trait questions) also are scored as +2 to –2, the difference being that there was no middle category offered to respondents. For both scoring systems, a positive mean score indicates a surplus of positive responses over negative ones, while a negative mean score indicates the opposite. Essentially, we count the "moderately well" category for the new questions as neutral, exactly halfway between positive and negative. That would imply that those who selected the middle category would have divided evenly between positive and negative responses, if forced to do so. Of course, this may not always be true. In some cases, the people who chose "moderately well" might have disproportionately selected a more positive response if that middle position had not been available; in other cases, those who selected the more neutral middle position might have disproportionately selected one of the negative choices if presented with the old, four-category response set. Our analysis of the 2008 data, which employed both the old and new question formats, indicates that there is no consistent pattern between responses to the old and new question formats.[20] Therefore, precise comparisons to earlier years are difficult, but this method does allow for some reasonable comparisons to be made across the years, and it is the best approach given the data that are available.

Table 6.1 displays the responses to the six candidate character trait questions that were asked about both presidential candidates in 2012. Romney did as well as Obama on only one of the four trait dimensions, leadership, where the two candidates were essentially tied in voter evaluations. This probably counts as a loss for Romney, since Republicans usually have an advantage on this trait. As Table 3.1 (Chapter 3) shows, only one Republican presidential candidate was not seen by the voters as a stronger leader than his Democratic opponent: George H. W. Bush was almost even with Michael Dukakis on leadership in 1988 and behind Bill Clinton in 1992. Moreover, Romney's lack of any advantage on leadership was not due to Obama being rated highly by the voters; about 39 percent rated Obama positively and 39 percent negatively on this trait, with 22 percent choosing the more neutral response of "moderately well." Obama did no better on leadership than Gore in 2000 or Kerry in 2004, two Democratic candidates who had problems projecting an image of a strong leader, and he was perceived less favorably in 2012 than he was in 2008. Nevertheless, Obama still came out even with Romney.

Table 6.1   Voter Perceptions of the Character Traits of Obama and Romney

Character trait	Percent who say that the trait characterizes the candidate				Mean score
	Extremely or very well	Moderately well	Not very well/ Not at all	Total	
Obama					
Strong leader	38.8	21.9	39.2	100%	-.10
Knowledgeable	53.9	22.3	23.8	100%	.45
Intelligent	66.2	19.0	14.8	100%	.78
Honest	43.3	19.5	37.2	100%	.00
Moral	47.2	19.9	32.9	100%	.17
Cares about people	43.6	18.0	38.4	100%	.01
Romney					
Strong leader	36.0	25.8	38.2	100%	-.09
Knowledgeable	43.4	27.5	29.1	100%	.17
Intelligent	55.2	23.9	20.9	100%	.46
Honest	30.4	22.7	46.8	100%	-.35
Moral	43.0	22.0	35.0	100%	.10
Cares about people	22.9	20.8	56.4	100%	-.66

Note: The percentages are based on the responses from major party voters only. To simplify the table, the percentages for the two most positive categories (extremely and very well) are combined, as are the two most negative categories. The mean scores are calculated using all five categories, scored from +2 (extremely well) to –2 (not at all). The Ns vary for each item, but they are approximately 4,000 in each case.
Source: American National Election Studies 2012 survey.

As Chapter 3 explained, Democratic presidential candidates normally possess an advantage on empathy, so the fact that Obama was perceived more favorably than Romney was on this trait dimension is what we would expect. However, the size of Obama's advantage was enormous: only 23 percent of the voters felt that the phrase "he cares about people" fit Romney extremely or very well, compared to 44 percent for Obama. Over 56 percent of the voters said that the phrase did not fit Romney. These data support the conclusions of several political pundits who argued that Romney lost in part because of his large empathy gap.[21]

The emphasis that journalists and commentators placed on the empathy gap between Romney and Obama was an accurate description of how voters perceived the candidates on this dimension. It also was one of the few years in which the media emphasized empathy as an important factor, even though in every election that we have analyzed, the Democratic candidate has held an advantage on empathy and has gained votes from that advantage. Regardless, in most years, the media ignored, dismissed, or downplayed this factor. In both 2000 and 2004, for example, pundits rarely talked about an empathy advantage for Gore or Kerry, even though both candidates were perceived more favorably than their opponent, George W. Bush, on this trait dimension. In fact, many pundits in 2000 stressed the benefits that would accrue to Bush in running as a "compassionate conservative," despite the fact that the public still considered Gore to be the more empathetic candidate. Commentators and analysts also focused on Bush's leadership advantage, on his integrity advantage in 2000, and on his warmth and charm. Based on this selective use of character traits, the pundits concluded that voters saw Bush as superior to his opponents on character, when the reality was that he had no appreciable overall advantage in either 2000 or 2004, once perceptions of empathy were included in the calculations.

The emphasis by media pundits on empathy in 2012 could be because Romney was seen as much worse in this area than the typical Republican nominee. The fact that this issue was raised by other Republican candidates during the nomination contest also may have encouraged journalists to focus on it. Romney's personal wealth, which at $200 million or more was far larger than that of any other presidential candidate in the past few decades, may have contributed to this emphasis as well. Moreover, some of Romney's own statements, most notably the "47 percent" remark, drew attention to questions of empathy. Finally, in some previous elections, many analysts seem to have concluded (erroneously) that the Republican candidate was doing just fine on empathy because he was the warmer, more down-to-earth candidate, unlike his aloof, elitist Democratic opponent, and therefore did not focus on that trait. That was the case in 2000 and 2004, for example. In 2012, journalists and commentators could not make that argument because Romney was seen as cold and aloof. Whatever the reasons, the media emphasis on empathy in 2012 was appropriate, accurate, and a welcome change from the coverage in previous elections.

Obama also had an overall advantage on integrity. Voters rated Obama as significantly more honest than Romney, although the two candidates were viewed rather evenly on morality. Romney's integrity deficit does not seem to be a case of voters thinking of him as personally unethical or dishonest. This interpretation seems confirmed by his relatively good showing on the question about morality and by the fact that there were few questions raised during the campaign about unethical, immoral, or illegal behavior on his part. Rather, Romney's integrity problem most likely stemmed from his shifting positions on issues. When voters said that they did not find Romney very honest—47 percent gave him a low mark on this trait—they most likely meant that he was too willing to take positions that he personally did not believe in just to please the voters. Whether Romney was truly an insincere flip-flopper or someone who honestly changed his views is impossible to say, but he did provide evidence for the argument that he shifted positions for political convenience.

Finally, Obama had a clear advantage on competence: Romney was seen by the voters as less knowledgeable and less intelligent than Obama. This seems somewhat surprising, since Romney did not receive much criticism for being uninformed, certainly not the way George W. Bush did in 2000, for example. Of course, Obama generally was considered to be well-informed, and he was the incumbent president, so it may have been difficult for any Republican challenger to match Obama on competence. Moreover, Romney had held just one elected office, that of Massachusetts governor for one four-year term. Additionally, his perceived flip-flopping on issues and his well-publicized gaffes may have contributed to a perception that he did not always thoroughly think things through. Finally, the simple fact of winning the presidential nomination of a major party probably demonstrates to many voters that the candidate must be competent, but the Republican field in 2012 was widely viewed as weak, so perhaps Romney's nomination victory did not boost perceptions of his competence as much as would typically have been the case. Still, Romney was perceived favorably on knowledge and intelligence, just not as favorably as Obama.

In sum, Romney was perceived as only equal to Obama on leadership, worse on both competence and integrity, and much worse on empathy. In the 32-year span that we analyze in this study, no other presidential candidate, Democrat or Republican, has failed to secure an advantage on at least one of the four trait dimensions. If the Democratic strategy was to compensate for Obama's potential weakness regarding the state of the economy by convincing voters that he had the superior presidential character, the strategy was successful. Furthermore, these data were collected largely after the first presidential debate, which Romney won by a wide margin: 87 percent of the interviews took place after October 3. Romney's performance in that debate, combined with Obama's lackluster effort, reduced the advantage that Obama had on character trait perceptions.[22] What matters, of course, is how the candidates were perceived on election day (or earlier, in the case of early voters), and the data reported here are timely. If the ANES interviews had been conducted mostly in September, there might be uncertainty about whether they reflected perceptions that were close to the time of the vote, but fortunately that was not the case. No momentous campaign events occurred after the first debate, so we can be confident that the perceptions reported here reflect how voters felt when they were casting their ballots.[23]

A further evaluation of how poorly Romney did on character traits can be made by comparing 2012 to earlier presidential elections. As was discussed earlier, precise comparisons cannot be made, due to differences in question wording, but we can obtain a good general assessment of Romney's performance, compared to that of previous presidential candidates, by using the mean scores, calculated as we outlined above. Figure 6.1 displays the net mean scores for the four trait dimensions that we have identified as important: leadership, competence, integrity, and empathy. The specific questions used are the ones about providing strong leadership, being knowledgeable, being honest, and caring about people. The net mean score for each trait is the score for the Republican candidate minus the score for the Democratic candidate. A positive mean score indicates that the Republican candidate was perceived more favorably, and a negative score just the opposite.

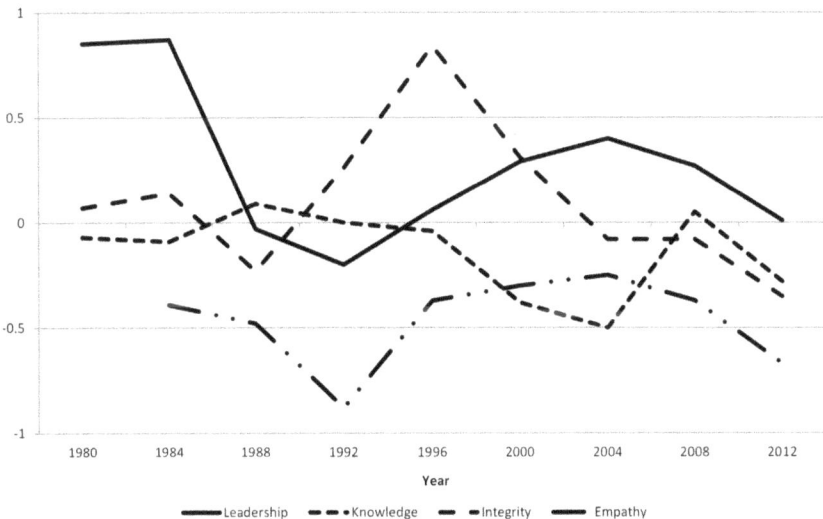

Figure 6.1   Net Mean Trait Scores for Presidential Candidates, 1980–2012

The patterns in the chart are quite clear. Romney did poorly across the board, compared to other Republican candidates. In most years, the mean score for leadership was positive, indicating a Republican advantage, but it was almost exactly zero in 2012. Compounding Romney's problems, the mean scores for the other three traits were negative in 2012. The only times that a Republican candidate, or any candidate for that matter, had such a disadvantage on knowledge were in 2000 and 2004, when Bush was seen as considerably inferior to his Democratic opponents, Gore and Kerry. Only one candidate of either party had a greater disadvantage than Romney on honesty: Clinton in 1996 (although Clinton in 1992 and Gore in 2000 did almost as badly). Republicans routinely do worse on empathy, but only the elder Bush in 1992 had a greater disadvantage on caring about people than did Romney in 2012. Relative to his opponent, Romney clearly was worse off than any other presidential candidate in the past 32 years.

What is particularly revealing is the fact that Romney was significantly disadvantaged in trait perceptions even though Obama was not perceived very favorably. In most of the earlier years, when one presidential candidate had a disadvantage on a trait dimension, it simply meant that he was seen less favorably than his opponent, even though he was still viewed in positive terms. For example, in 1992, President Bush was seen as a weaker leader than Clinton (the net mean score for leadership was -.20 for that year), but in absolute terms, Bush was seen somewhat positively; it simply was the case that Clinton was seen more favorably. Similarly, Gore was seen as significantly worse than Bush on honesty in 2000, but in absolute terms, Gore was assessed rather positively, just not as positively as his opponent, who had a very high score that year. In 2012, however, Romney did poorly not just in relative terms, but in absolute assessments. Figure 6.2 shows the mean scores for Republican candidates for the four traits from 1980 through 2012. As we can see, Romney is the only Republican to receive a negative score on leadership, meaning that negative responses outweighed positive ones. For knowledge, Romney was assessed positively, but only marginally so. His mean score of .17 was slightly lower than Bush's score in 2004, which was the previous low mark. Romney was also the only Republican to receive a negative score on honesty. In fact, his negative score was about the same as that received by Clinton in 1996. Finally, Romney set an all-time low for a Republican candidate on empathy: his mean score of -.66 was considerably worse that the -.43 that Bush received in 1992.

As we suggested earlier, some caution should be exercised in comparing the 2012 data to those from earlier years, due to the change in question wording. However, even making allowances for this fact does not alter the basic conclusions about voter perceptions of Romney. First of all, we can compare the 2012 results to the 2008 results using the new version of the

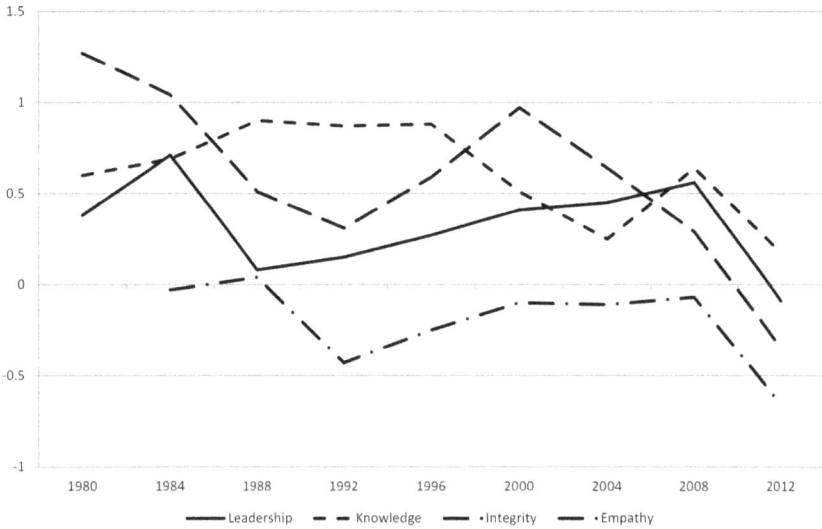

Figure 6.2 Mean Trait Scores for Republican Candidates, 1980–2012

trait questions, which was asked of one-half of the sample in 2008 (the 2008 data in Figures 6.1 and 6.2 use the responses to the old versions of the trait questions to maintain comparability to previous years). What we find is that Romney did much worse than John McCain, especially on leadership, integrity, and knowledge. McCain was viewed in rather positive terms in 2008 on knowledge, and he received moderately positive ratings on leadership and integrity, although he did not do better than Obama on any of these traits. In contrast, Romney was assessed negatively on leadership, very negatively on empathy, and only moderately positively on knowledge. Even on empathy, where McCain did poorly, Romney did even worse. Since these comparisons are made using the same question wording, we can be quite confident about these conclusions. A comparison of the results from the old and new trait questions in 2008 indicates that the new question wording yields slightly lower mean scores, about .20 lower on average. That suggests that Romney would not have done quite as badly in absolute terms as our data show if the old trait questions had been employed in 2012, although he still would have done just as poorly relative to Obama. Even if we adjust the 2012 scores for this difference in question wording, Romney still comes off poorly in absolute terms, compared to previous Republican candidates. It appears that voters truly held less favorable overall assessments of his character traits than they did for previous Republican candidates.

Obama's advantage on character traits was almost entirely a function of Romney's poor performance in this area. The president actually was seen in very lukewarm terms by the voters in 2012, especially compared to how he was assessed in 2008. Again, we can make more precise comparisons between 2008 and 2012 because we have data from the same new, five-category trait questions for both years. In 2012, Obama had a slightly negative mean score for leadership and mean scores that were almost exactly zero for both honesty and empathy; in 2008, his scores for all three of these traits were quite positive: .26 for leadership, .22 for honesty, and .26 for empathy. Not only was Obama viewed much less favorably in 2012 than in 2008, but some of his character trait evaluations in 2012 also compare unfavorably to those received by other Democratic candidates. For example, Kerry was belittled by Republicans in 2004 as a weak and indecisive leader, but Obama's score for leadership was only slightly better than Kerry's. Voter assessments of Obama's honest in 2012 were below those received by every Democratic candidate in the past three decades, except for Clinton. If Romney simply had been able to be perceived as favorably on leadership and integrity as McCain had been in 2008, he would have been significantly ahead of Obama on these two traits, and if he had done as well as McCain on knowledge, he would have been even with Obama on that trait.

THE EFFECT OF CANDIDATE CHARACTER TRAIT PERCEPTIONS ON THE VOTE

Obama was perceived more favorably than Romney on character traits by the voters, but this would confer an electoral advantage on Obama only to the extent that these perceptions influenced the behavior of the voters. The analysis in Chapter 4 shows that perceptions of the character traits of the presidential candidates affected the vote for every election from 1980 through 2008, so it would be surprising if that were not also true in 2012. We analyzed the influence of character trait perceptions on the 2012 vote using the same method employed in Chapter 4 for previous elections: we ran logistic regression analyses, using both the overall character trait index and measures of individual trait perceptions, along with other variables that normally influence the vote, including party identification, ideology, assessments of the president's handling of the economy and national security, and orientations on social welfare and moral issues.[24] As we did for 2008, we excluded black voters from the analysis, since they voted almost entirely for Obama, and we included a measure of attitudes toward blacks in the analysis.[25] The analysis results are presented in Table 6.2.

In the first column of the table, we analyze all voters and use the overall trait index. The results show that perceptions of the character traits of the candidates had a substantial effect on the vote, even with all of the other

Table 6.2 Logistic Regression of Presidential Vote, 2012

Independent variable	All voters	Democrats	Independents	Republicans
Party identification	.505***	.361		.299
	(.062)	(.234)		(.231)
Ideology	-.186	-.386	-.010	.006
	(.099)	(.147)	(.293)	(.164)
Evaluation of Obama's handling of the economy	.705***	.862***	.241	.824***
	(.108)	(.170)	(.318)	(.177)
Evaluation of Obama's handling of foreign affairs	.135	.107	.108	.205
	(.099)	(.157)	(.289)	(.164)
Social welfare issues index	.522***	.570***	.610*	.434**
	(.094)	(.154)	(.278)	(.165)
Moral issues index	.687***	.871***	1.083***	.264
	(.122)	(.199)	(.303)	(.207)
Index of attitudes toward blacks	.196**	.307**	.043	.164
	(.076)	(.123)	(.193)	(.130)
Candidate trait index	1.313***			
	(.113)			
Leadership		.211	.680**	.357*
		(.157)	(.271)	(.162)
Knowledge		.361**	.407	.271
		(.156)	(.271)	(.182)

(Continued)

Table 6.2 (Continued)

Independent variable	All voters	Democrats	Independents	Republicans
Empathy		.448***	.606**	.157
		(.130)	(.233)	(.146)
Honesty		.167	.197	.467**
		(.149)	(.254)	(.160)
	Nagel. R^2 = .91	Nagel. R^2 = .68	Nagel. R^2 = .78	Nagel. R^2 = .65
	% cases corr.	% cases corr.	% cases corr.	% cases corr.
	predict. = 95.2	predict. = 95.7	predict. = 90.0	predict. = 96.0

*** p < .001, ** p < .01, * p < .05 (one-tailed tests).

Note: Blacks and minor party voters are excluded from the analysis. Entries are logistic regression coefficients, with standard errors in parentheses. The dependent variable is the presidential vote.

See the text for details on the independent variables. Positive coefficients indicate that the likelihood of voting for Obama is increased by having a Democratic identification, a liberal ideological orientation, approval of Obama's handling of the economy and of foreign affairs, conservative orientations on the two issue indices, a positive view of blacks, and positive views of Obama's traits relative to Romney's.

Source: 2012 American National Election Study.

variables controlled for. The effect is somewhat smaller than what we found for 2008 (see Table 4.3): the logistic regression coefficient for the trait index is 1.31 for 2012, compared to 1.58 in 2008. This is consistent with the observation in Chapter 4 that candidate character trait perceptions have a greater impact in elections that do not involve an incumbent president running for reelection. The presidential vote also was affected by party identification, evaluations of Obama's handling of the economy, attitudes on issues, and attitudes toward blacks. As in 2008, ideology did not have a significant effect on the vote, once all of the other variables are included in the analysis. However, ideology did have significant indirect effects through its influence on other variables in the equation, such as party identification, assessment of Obama's performance, and attitudes on issues.

Since the logistic regression coefficient does not provide a simple estimate of how much the vote was affected by trait perceptions, we calculated predicted probabilities of voting for Romney, given different scores on the trait index, for average Democrats, independents, and Republicans, just as we did for previous elections.[26] These predicted probabilities are shown in Figure 6.3. Independents were much more influenced than were Democrats or Republicans, a pattern present for almost every election that we have analyzed. An average independent who rated the two candidates even overall on character traits (i.e., a trait index score of zero) had about a 64 percent

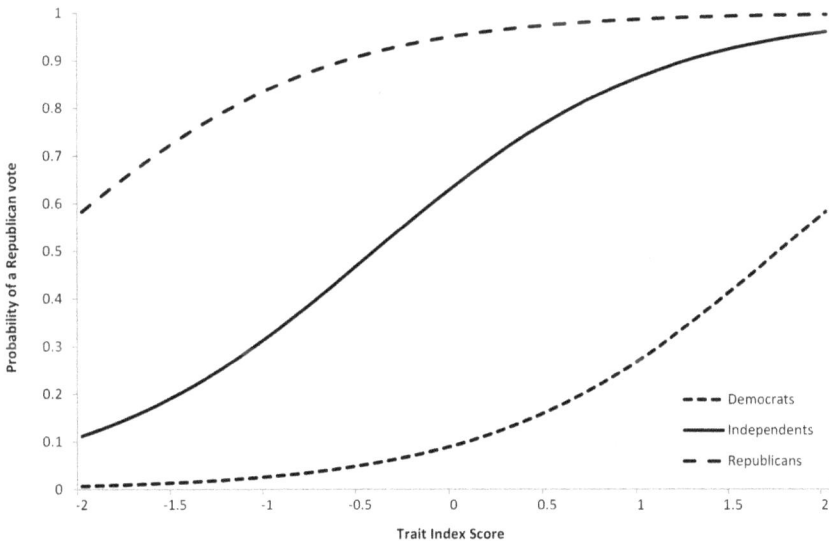

Figure 6.3 Predicted Probability of a Republican Vote for Different Trait Index Scores

probability of voting for Romney, and one who saw Romney as moderately better than Obama (e.g., a trait index score of 1.0) had about an 86 percent likelihood of voting Republican. However, an average independent who saw Obama as moderately better on character traits (e.g., a trait index score of –1.0) had only a 32 percent likelihood of voting for Romney. Unfortunately for Romney, independents tended to judge him less favorably: the average trait index score for all independents was -.13, and only 36 percent perceived him more favorably than Obama. The result was that Romney received less than half of the independent vote, when he needed to receive a solid majority to compensate for the fact that there were more Democratic than Republican voters in 2012.

Democrats and Republicans were less affected by their perceptions of the character traits of the candidates. Democrats were highly likely to see Obama as superior to Romney, but even if they did not, their likelihood of voting for Obama did not decline a great deal. An average Democrat who saw Romney as moderately better than Obama on character traits (e.g., a trait index score of 1.0) still had close to a 75 percent probability of voting Democratic, and an average Democrat who rated the two candidate even overall on character traits was over 90 percent likely to vote for Obama. Republicans were even less affected. An average Republican who thought that the two candidates were even overall on traits was 95 percent likely to vote for Romney, and this only declined to about 84 percent for those who thought that Romney was moderately inferior to Obama (e.g., a trait index score of –1.0). Even so, Romney lost some votes from Republicans who did not think favorably of his character traits. Nearly 10 percent of Republican voters saw Obama as better than Romney on character traits. By comparison, only 6 percent of Democratic voters thought that Romney was superior to Obama.

In Chapter 4, we considered the possibility that perceptions of the character traits of the presidential candidates might be just rationalizations of the decision to vote for a candidate, rather than factors that affected that decision, and we provided both theoretical reasons and empirical evidence to support the conclusion that trait perceptions truly affected the vote. We repeated the same analysis in that chapter for 2012, and we obtained very similar results.[27] Some vote rationalization is present, but direct effects of trait perceptions on the vote are present as well. That makes sense, given the pattern of trait perceptions and the division of the vote. If trait perceptions were simply rationalizations of the vote, then Romney should not have been perceived of as substantially worse than Obama in personal terms. Romney's share of the popular vote was only about 4 percentage points less than Obama's, hardly enough of a difference to produce large differences in assessments of their character traits.

Further insight into the effect of candidate character trait perceptions on the presidential vote in 2012 comes from columns two through four in Table 6.2, which show the results of separate logistic regression analyses of the vote for Democrats, independents, and Republicans. These analyses use four separate trait measures—leadership, knowledge, empathy, and honesty—rather than the overall trait index, because the analysis in Chapter 4 showed that different traits tended to be important to different partisan groups. In 2012, independents were most affected by their perceptions of the leadership and empathy of the two candidates; the two trait dimensions that overall have been the most important ones over the past several decades. Democrats, on the other hand, were not influenced very much by their assessments of the leadership abilities of the candidates; they were most affected by their perceptions of how empathetic and knowledgeable the candidates were. Republicans were just the opposite of Democrats; they were significantly influenced by evaluations of the leadership ability and the integrity of the two candidates, but they were not affected very much by perceptions of empathy or knowledge.

The 2012 patterns are similar to those for earlier years in several ways. Leadership and empathy again emerge as the two most important trait dimensions. Independents, who usually are particularly influenced by trait perceptions, were most affected by perceptions of leadership and empathy in 2012. Democrats were most affected by perceptions of empathy, and Republicans were strongly affected by perceptions of leadership, although not as much as by perceptions of integrity. Integrity did not matter much to Democrats or independents, which seems to fit the pattern of a declining concern for this character trait after the 1990s, as discussed in Chapter 4. The fact that integrity mattered to Republicans, but not to others, is interesting. If, as we suggested earlier, questions of Romney's integrity largely reflected whether people thought that he was inclined to take positions that did not reflect his true convictions, then it might seem that all voters, not just Republicans, who felt that he was insincere would be less likely to vote for him, but that is not the case. Perhaps the explanation is that for many Republicans, thinking that Romney was not sincere in his beliefs meant that they did not regard him as truly conservative, which made him less ideologically appealing. But for independents and Democrats, thinking that Romney was not truly conservative may not have made Romney less appealing; in fact, it might even have had the opposite effect. Knowledge did not matter much to Republicans and independents, which is consistent with the lesser importance of this trait that was discussed in Chapter 4, but it did matter to Democrats, an unexpected finding that we cannot explain.

FACTORS THAT INFLUENCED PERCEPTIONS OF CANDIDATE CHARACTER TRAITS

Voter perceptions of the character traits of presidential candidate are influenced by a number of factors. As we discussed in Chapter 5, party identification plays a key role. Democrats are inclined to view their candidate more favorably; Republicans behave the same way. Ideology, which is strongly associated with party identification, also has an effect; liberals evaluate the candidates quite differently than do conservatives. Besides these fundamental political orientations, attitudes that vary from one election to the next also play a key role. In particular, assessments of the performance of the incumbent president affect perceptions of the character traits of the candidates, especially when an incumbent president is running for reelection. Voters who think that the president is doing a good job of managing the economy and handling foreign affairs and national security are more likely to conclude that the president is a competent and strong leader. Those who feel that the president's performance is weak are more likely to conclude that he lacks the character traits of a good president.

Our analysis of how perceptions of the character traits of the presidential candidates are related to other attitudes shows that the same patterns that characterized earlier years were present in 2012 as well. As we did for other elections in Chapter 5, we ran regression analyses of trait perceptions, using a number of attitudes as independent variables: party identification, ideology, evaluations of the president's handling of the economy and foreign affairs, attitudes on social welfare and moral issues.[28] As in 2008, we included a measure of attitudes toward blacks, and we excluded black voters from the analysis. Blacks voted almost entirely for Obama, so there is little to be gained by examining the factors that affected their perceptions of him. We first analyzed overall trait perceptions (using the trait index), then examined perceptions of leadership and empathy, which were the two most important traits in 2012, as they typically are. Since the measures of trait perceptions are continuous variables, we used ordinary least squares (OLS) regression. The results of this analysis are in Table 6.3. The coefficients in the table are standardized regression coefficients. As we explained in the previous chapter, the standardized (beta) coefficients are best for comparing the relative effect of the independent variables because they show how much of one standard deviation the dependent variable changes as a result of a change of one standard deviation in the independent variable.

The most important factor influencing how the voters perceived the candidates is the evaluation of Obama's performance as president. The more favorably the voter evaluated Obama's handling of the economy and foreign affairs, the more favorably the voter assessed Obama's character traits relative to Romney's. Voters who were unhappy with the performance of the president tended to conclude that he was not a particularly competent and effective leader. Even perceptions of empathy were affected by evaluations of Obama's performance. The mixed evaluations that Obama received in 2012 are one reason why Obama was seen in less positive terms in 2012 than he was in 2008. A majority of the voters disapproved of Obama's handling

Table 6.3   Regression Analysis of Perceptions of Candidate Character Traits, 2012

Independent variable	Trait index	Leadership	Empathy
Party identification	.207***	.166***	.238***
Ideology	.068***	.056***	.067***
Evaluation of Obama's handling of the economy	.300***	.328***	.277***
Evaluation of Obama's handling of foreign affairs	.268***	.264***	.257***
Social welfare issues index	.133***	.143***	.095***
Moral issues index	.067***	.036***	.074***
Index of attitudes toward blacks	.016*	−.010	.022*
Adjusted R^2	.82	.73	.77

***p <. 001, **p < .01, *p < .05 (one-tailed tests).
Note: Blacks and minor party voters are excluded from the analysis. Entries are standardized regression (beta) coefficients. The dependent variable in the first column is the overall candidate character trait index. The dependent variable in the second and third columns is the net score for leadership and for empathy, respectively. See the text for details on the independent and dependent variables.
Source: 2012 American National Election Study.

of the economy, although he did better on managing foreign affairs, where 54 percent approved of his performance. If voters had evaluated Obama's presidential performance more favorably, that would have translated into more positive assessments of his character traits relative to Romney's.

Party identification also significantly influenced how voters perceived the candidates in 2012, just as it did for previous elections, as shown in Chapter 5. The standardized coefficient for party identification is somewhat smaller than what it is for the two measures of presidential performance, so the direct effect of party identification is somewhat less than it is for the performance measures. However, we should keep in mind that evaluations of presidential performance are influenced by party identification, so there are indirect effects of party identification on trait perceptions that are not captured by the coefficient. If we take into account the strong impact that party identification has on evaluations of the president's performance, then the partisan bias in the assessment of candidate character traits becomes much greater. Ideology also had a statistically significant effect on the perception of character traits, but it was small in magnitude; the beta coefficient for the effect of ideology on the overall trait index is just .068, and it is no higher for effects on leadership and empathy. Of course, ideology affects party identification and other variables in the analysis, so some indirect effects exist.

Interestingly, attitudes toward blacks had a relatively modest impact on assessments of the character traits of the presidential candidates. Voters who had more negative attitudes toward blacks were only slightly more likely to view Obama more unfavorably, relative to Romney. Some analyses of the 2008 election concluded that Obama lost votes because of his race, which would suggest that voters in 2012 would be influenced by their racial attitudes as well.[29] The fact that these attitudes had so little effect on assessments of the character traits of the candidates, once other attitudes are included in the analysis, suggests that Obama's race did not influence how voters perceived him in 2012. Table 6.2 does show that for Democrats, but not for independents or Republicans, attitudes toward blacks affected the vote; white Democrats who had more negative orientations toward blacks were slightly more likely to defect in their vote, even when other variables were included in the analysis. However, that effect could be due to policy issues, such as opposition to affirmative action, which would affect the vote regardless of the race of the Democratic candidate.

CONCLUSION

Obama was perceived much more favorably than Romney in personal terms. He was seen as equal to Romney on assessments of leadership, which is a victory for a Democratic candidate, and he was viewed significantly more positively on the other three dimensions of character traits: competence, integrity, and empathy. While Democrats routinely do better on empathy, Obama's advantage here was extraordinary large. His advantage on character traits derived largely from Romney's poor evaluations. Voters had mixed assessments of Obama's character traits, but they were quite negative when it came to Romney, who did worse on character traits, both in absolute terms and relative to his opponent, than any other Republican candidate in the 32 years that we analyze in this book.

Perceptions of the character traits of the presidential candidates influenced the vote, as they have in every other election that we investigated. As usual, independents were more strongly affected by these perceptions. They wound up voting for Obama by about 53 to 47 percent, according to the ANES data, even though their attitudes on other issues seemed more favorable to Romney. Defection rates among both Democrats and Republicans were low, but those who did vote for the candidate of the other party were the ones who did not think so highly of the personal qualities of the candidate of their party, at least compared to the opponent. Had Romney been perceived as favorably as Obama on character traits, he would have gained votes from independents, reduced Republican defections somewhat, and increased Democratic defections a bit. Whether this would have added up to a victory we cannot say. There were other factors that contributed to an Obama victory. His party had been in the White House for just one term, and first-term presidents whose parties have been in power for just four years rarely fail to win reelection: Jimmy Carter in 1980 was the only such president in over 100 years to be defeated.[30] The economy was improving, albeit at a slower-than-desired pace, and unemployment dropped to under 8.0 percent by the fall.[31] Furthermore, while a majority of the voters disapproved of how Obama was managing the economy, most also placed much of the blame for the poor economy on George W. Bush.[32] Only a minority of voters thought that the economy would be better under Romney—although if Romney had been seen as a stronger, more empathetic, and more honest leader, perhaps voters would have had more confidence in his ability to improve the economy. While the above factors might have been enough to produce a Democratic victory anyway, Obama's advantage on character traits at the very least added to his narrow popular vote margin.

Perceptions of the character traits of the presidential candidates in 2012 were shaped strongly by party identification, as we would expect and as the data from previous elections suggest. Democrats were far more likely to view Obama as clearly superior to Romney in personal qualities; Republicans were just the opposite. However, trait perceptions were not simply determined by partisanship. Romney did far worse on character trait assessments than would be predicted from party identification alone. More voters identified as Democrats than Republicans, but if the supporters of each party had been equally positive about their candidate (and equally negative about the candidate of the opposing party), and if independents were neutral in their evaluations, then Romney would have come off only slightly worse than Obama on character traits. Instead, Obama had a sizable advantage.

Evaluations of Obama's performance as president also had a strong effect on these assessments. Voters who thought that Obama was doing a poor job of managing the economy or handling foreign affairs were less likely to see him as better than Romney on character traits. This factor helps to explain why some Democrats were not so favorable, or why some Republicans were not so unfavorable, in their assessments of Obama's personal qualities, relative to Romney's. Democrats who thought that Obama had mismanaged the economy were likely to translate those evaluations into less favorable assessments of the president's character traits, for example. However, evaluations of Obama's performance were mixed: slightly less than one-half of the voters approved of his handling of the economy, and slightly more than one-half did so for foreign affairs. Thus, this factor does not explain why Romney did so much worse than Obama on character trait assessments.

In sum, if assessments of the character traits of the candidates in 2012 were determined solely by party identification and evaluations of Obama's performance as president, we would expect that Obama would have received only a small advantage on personal qualities. This leads us to conclude that the campaign and the candidates mattered. We lack the data to determine exactly what aspects of the candidates and the campaigns produced this outcome. It may be that many of the perceptions of Romney were shaped early in 2012, when he was fighting for the Republican nomination. On the other hand, it could be that the behavior of the candidates and their campaigns during the summer and fall played a significant role in forming these perceptions.[33] The investigation of the shaping of these character trait perceptions in 2012 is another research project, one beyond the scope of this book. Regardless, it does seem that the conclusions of a December 2012 *Boston Globe* analysis of the election are insightful: "One of the gravest errors . . . was the Romney team failure . . . to sell voters on the candidate's personal qualities and leadership gifts."[34]

NOTES

1. For the approval of Obama's job performance in January and February Gallup polls, see "Presidential Approval Ratings—Barack Obama," http://www.gallup.com/poll/116479/barack-obama-presidential-job-approval.aspx (accessed January 30, 2014). For support for the Affordable Care Act in early 2012, see "Americans Divided on Repeal of 2010 Healthcare Law," http://www.gallup.com/poll/152969/Americans-Divided-Repeal-2010-Healthcare-Law.aspx (accessed January 30, 2014).
2. Nate Silver, one of the most respected political forecasters, rated Obama as a slight underdog for reelection in his analysis one year before the election; see Nate Silver, "Is Obama Toast? Handicapping the 2012 Election," *New York Times,* November 11, 2011, national edition, Sunday magazine section. For the forecasts of a number of political scientists made in the summer of 2012, see the symposium in *PS: Political Science and Politics* 45 (2012), 610–674. Several of the forecasts in this symposium predicted that Obama would receive less than 50 percent of the popular vote.
3. Maureen Dowd, "Odyssey of a Statue Candidate," *New York Times,* August 2, 2012, national edition; Timothy Eagan, "Romney the Unknowable," *New York Times,* August 16, 2010, national edition; Kathleen Parker, "If Only the Machine Could See the Real People" *Greensboro News and Record,* September 18, 2012.
4. Michael Tomasky, "A Mouse in the White House? Mitt Has Bowed to Reporters and Cowered from the Right. He's a Candidate with a Serious Wimp Problem," *Newsweek,* August 6, 2012, 24.
5. Quoted in Maureen Dowd, "Mitt's Olympic Meddle," *New York Times,* July 29, 2012, national edition, Sunday Review.
6. Mark Shields, "Campaign 2012 Deficits—Humility and Humor," Creators Syndicate, October 18, 2012, http://www.creators.com/liberal/campaign-2012-deficits-humility-and-humor.html (accessed September 19, 2013).
7. Maureen Dowd, "Likability Index," *New York Times,* August 12, 2012, national edition, Sunday Review.
8. Kathleen Parker "They Like Me, They Like Me Not, They Like Me . . . ," *Greensboro News and Record,* May 17, 2012.

9. Quoted in Maureen Dowd, "Likability Index."
10. The text of the responses to the like/dislike questions about the candidates are included in the 2012 ANES data file. We coded all responses to character traits for these questions and found that only 7 percent of the dislikes of the personal qualities of Romney referred to his lack of warmth, charm, or general likability. Most of the dislikes of his character traits identified either lack of integrity or lack of empathy as the problem. Respondents rarely cited warmth as a reason for liking Obama either: fewer than of all of the likes about Obama that cited a character trait, fewer than 8 percent identified warmth or something similar as a reason for voting for him.
11. Michael John Burton, "The Republican Primary Season: Strategic Positioning in the GOP Field," in *Campaigning for President 2012,* ed. Dennis W. Johnson (New York: Routledge, 2014), 49; NBC News, "Meet the Press transcript for Jan. 15, 2012," http://www.nbcnews.com/id/46004652/ns/meet_the_press-transcripts/t/meet-press-transcript-jan/#.UuwNV_ldV0Y (accessed January 30, 2014).
12. Felicia Sonmez, "Mitt Romney: Wife Ann drives 'a couple of Cadillacs'," *Washington Post* Blogs, http://www.washingtonpost.com/blogs/election-2012/post/mitt-romney-wife-ann-drives-a-couple-of-cadillacs/2012/02/24/gIQAMBz6XR_blog.html (accessed January 30, 2014).
13. Felicia Sonmez, "Romney to college students: Pursue your dreams, even if you have to borrow to do so," *Washington Post* Blogs, http://www.washingtonpost.com/blogs/post-politics/post/romney-to-college-students-pursue-your-dreams-even-if-you-have-to-borrow-to-do-so/2012/04/27/gIQAFGM8lT_blog.html (accessed January 30, 2014).
14. Dan Balz, *Collision 2012: Obama vs. Romney and the Future of Elections in America* (New York: Viking, 2013), 6.
15. David Morgan, "Mitt Romney Health Care Plan Would Make Consumers Pay for Basic Services," Reuters, http://www.huffingtonpost.com/2012/10/02/romney-health-care-plan_n_1931711.html (accessed February 3, 2014).
16. Transcript of the first presidential debate, October 3, 2012, http://www.npr.org/2012/10/03/162258551/transcript-first-obama-romney-presidential-debate (accessed February 3, 2014).
17. Jackie Calmes, "Test for Obama as Deficit Remains Above $1 Trillion." *New York Times,* September 25, 2012, national edition; Donald Marron, "The problem with analyzing Romney's tax plan: it's more of an outline than a plan," *Forbes,* August 8, 2012, http://www.forbes.com/sites/beltway/2012/08/08/the-problem-with-analyzing-romneys-tax-plan-its-more-of-an-outline-than-a-plan (accessed January 28, 2014); Ron Scherer, "On eve of first debate, Romney floats tax proposal that hits the rich." *Christian Science Monitor,* October 2, 2012, http://www.csmonitor.com/USA/DC-Decoder/2012/1002/On-eve-of-first-debate-Romney-floats-tax-proposal-that-hits-the-rich-video (accessed January 28, 2014).
18. Tomasky, "A Mouse in the White House?"
19. Chris McGreal, "Obama deflects Romney challenge on Benghazi attack during Hofsra debate," *The Guardian,* October 17, 2012, http://www.theguardian.com/world/2012/oct/17/romney-obama-benghazi-defeated- debate (accessed January 28, 2014).
20. Charles Prysby and David Holian, "Studying Voter Perceptions of the Character Traits of Presidential Candidates: Methodological Questions and Problems" (paper presented at the annual meeting of the Southern Political Science Association, New Orleans, LA, January 5–8, 2011).
21. Chris Cilliza and Aaron Blake, "Barack Obama's Empathy Edge," posted to "The Fix," *Washington Post,* April 10, 2012, http://www.washingtonpost.

com/blogs/th-fix/barack-obama's-empathy-edge.html (accessed September 18, 2013); Scott Wilson and Philip Rucker, "The Strategy that Paved a Winning Path," *Washington Post,* November 7, 2012.

22. Jeffrey M. Jones, "Romney Narrows Vote Gap After Historic Debate Win," Gallup Poll Report, October 8, 2012, http://www.gallup.com/poll/157907/romney-narrows-vote-gap-historic-debate-win.aspx (accessed February 4, 2014).

23. A week prior to election day, a powerful tropical storm, Superstorm Sandy, hit the Northeast coast. Most analysts felt that the event benefitted Obama by allowing him to effectively project an image of strong presidential leadership. Thus, Obama may have been perceived in slightly more favorable personal terms on election day than he was throughout most of October.

24. Party identification was measured on a seven-point scale ranging from strongly Democratic to strongly Republican. Ideology also was measured on a seven-point scale ranging from very liberal to very conservative. There were a number of voters who did not place themselves on the seven-point ideology scale but who did classify themselves as liberal, moderate, or conservative with further prompting; these voters were classified as slightly liberal, moderate, and slightly conservative, respectively.

Two measures of retrospective evaluations of presidential performance were used in the analysis: approval of Obama's handling of the economy, and approval of his handling of foreign affairs. Each of these items is a four-point scale ranging from strongly approve to strongly disapprove.

An index of social welfare issues was constructed from responses to four questions: (a) whether government services and spending should be increased or decreased; (b) whether the federal government should see that everyone had a job and a good standard of living; (c) what level of government involvement in health care was desirable; and (d) whether or not the government should try to reduce economic inequality. All four components were measured on a scale from 1 to 7, with 7 being the most conservative score. The index is the mean score on the component items for respondents who had at least three valid responses.

An index of moral issues was formed from the following two components: (a) a question about the circumstances in which abortion should be allowed; and (b) an index of gay rights, formed from four separate questions. Both components were measured on a scale running from 1 to 4, with 4 the most conservative score; the index is the mean score on the two component items.

25. We created a measure of attitudes toward blacks from three questions: (a) whether blacks should work their way up without any special favors, as other minorities did; (b) whether blacks face special conditions that make it difficult to work their way up; and (c) whether blacks have received less than they deserve. The index runs from 1 to 5, with 5 being the most negative score.

26. Specifically, the average Democrat has a score of 1.86 (out of 7) on party identification, 3.20 (out of 7) on ideology, 1.82 (out of 4) on Obama's handling of the economy, 1.63 (out of 4) on Obama's handling of foreign policy, 3.61 (out of 7) on the social welfare issues index, 2.70 (out of 5) on the attitude toward blacks index, and 1.75 (out of 4) on the moral issues index. The corresponding scores for average independents and Republicans, respectively, are: party identification, 4.00 and 6.15; ideology, 4.25 and 5.40; Obama's handling of the economy, 3.06 and 3.75; Obama's handling of foreign policy, 2.66 and 3.52; the social welfare issues index, 4.51 and 5.50; the attitude toward blacks index, 3.40 and 3.87; and the moral issues index,

2.25 and 2.72. In all cases, the average Democrat holds the most liberal score, the average Republican the most conservative, with the average independent in between.

27. We investigated the question of causal direction by positing two alternative models, using party identification, ideology, candidate character trait perceptions, and the presidential vote as the variables. In the first model, which we term the direct effects model, perceptions of the character traits of the candidates is affected by party identification and ideology, and these perceptions in turn affect the vote, but there is no effect of the vote on the perceptions. In the second model, which we term the vote rationalization model, the vote is affected by party identification and ideology, and it then affects character trait perceptions, but trait perceptions do not influence the vote.

To determine if the direct effects model is accurate, we examined the relationships that party identification and ideology have with the vote, with and without trait perceptions in the analysis. If the direct effects model is accurate, then we would expect to see the coefficients for party identification and ideology diminish when trait perceptions are included in the equation, given that part of their effect on the vote is through their effects on trait perceptions. But if there are no direct effects, just vote rationalization, then the coefficients for party identification and ideology should not decrease. The analysis results show that these coefficients do decline substantially when the index of trait perceptions is included in the equation, supporting the conclusion that there are direct effects of trait perceptions on the vote.

To determine if the vote rationalization model is accurate, we examined the relationship s that party identification and ideology have with trait perceptions, with and without the vote in the analysis. If there is no vote rationalization, then the coefficients for the effect of party identification and ideology on the trait index should not change when the vote is included in the equation; if trait perceptions are completely rationalizations of the vote, then the coefficients for party identification and ideology should disappear. The analysis results show that the coefficients do not disappear, but they do decline, indicating that there is some vote rationalization, but that direct effects also exist. See Charles Prysby and David B. Holian, "Candidate Character Traits in the 2012 Presidential Election" (paper presented at the annual meeting of the American Political Science Association, Chicago, August 29–September 1, 2013) for details on the analysis.

28. See notes 24 and 25 for details on the variables in the analysis.

29. Jonathan Knuckey, "Racial Resentment and Vote Choice in the 2008 U.S. Presidential Election," *Politics & Policy* 39 (2011): 559–582; Michael S. Lewis-Beck, Charles Tien, and Richard Nadeau, "Obama's Missed Landslide: A Racial Cost?" *PS: Political Science and Politics* 43 (2010): 69–76; Spencer Piston, "How Explicit Racial Prejudice Hurt Obama in the 2008 Election," *Political Behavior* 32 (2010): 431–451.

30. James E. Campbell, "A First Party-Term Incumbent Survives: The Fundamentals of 2012," in *Barack Obama and the New America,* ed. Larry J. Sabato (Lanham, MD: Rowman and Littlefield, 2013), 66–67.

31. For comparisons of the economic conditions in 2012 with those for previous presidential elections involving an incumbent president see James E. Campbell, "A First Party-Term Incumbent Survives: The Fundamentals of 2012," in *Barack Obama and the New America,* ed. Larry J. Sabato (Lanham, MD: Rowman and Littlefield, 2013), 65; and Charles L. Prysby, "Explaining the Presidential Vote," in *Winning the Presidency 2012,* ed. William J. Crotty (Boulder, CO: Paradigm Publishers, 2013), 119.

32. In the ANES survey, 47 percent of the voters said that they blamed former president Bush a great deal or a lot for the condition of the economy, while only 32 percent said that they blamed President Obama that much.
33. For an argument that the campaign mattered in 2012, see Marc J. Hetherington, "The Election: How the Campaign Mattered," in *The Elections of 2012*, ed. Michael Nelson (Thousand Oaks, CA: CQ Press, 2013), 47–72.
34. Michael Kranish, "The Story Behind Mitt Romney's Loss in the Presidential Campaign to President Obama," *Boston Globe*, December 22, 2012.

7 Media Consumption, Character Trait Perceptions, and Voting

Voter perceptions of candidate character traits exert substantial effects on the vote. That is clear from the analyses in earlier chapters. However, our research to this point has treated such effects as constant across all voters when, in fact, trait perceptions may well be more central to the vote choice for certain types of voters. In particular, differences in media consumption may lead to differences among voters in their reliance on candidate character traits. In this chapter, we consider such variation over the course of an era in which people's media usage patterns have undergone extraordinary changes. As recently as 1996, 60 percent of Americans reported relying on newspapers as one of their primary sources of election news; this figure fell to 27 percent during the 2012 general election campaign.[1] In contrast, Internet usage has risen steadily over the past two decades and surpassed newspapers in 2012 as a primary source. Forty-seven percent of Americans reported reliance on the Internet during the most recent general election. This trails only the 67 percent of respondents who chose television as a primary source, a figure that held steady from four years earlier.

Such variation in usage raises the question of whether one learns different lessons from campaign coverage depending on the source, and whether these lessons affect voters as they consider their choices. Many scholars argue that the pseudo intimacy that the visual nature of television coverage promotes between voters and candidates evokes emotional reactions from audiences in ways that newspaper or radio reports simply cannot.[2] Because of these effects, the argument goes, television personalizes candidates and politics by emphasizing candidate character in a variety of politically relevant settings, such as reports about campaign events, campaign advertising, and presidential debates.[3] On the other hand, voters who rely heavily on newspaper coverage may be relatively less dependent on their perceptions of candidate character traits than those who do not follow the campaign in this manner. Newspaper campaign stories tend to be longer and more detailed, making them potentially more policy oriented than analogous television reports, which usually do not extend beyond a few minutes of any given evening news program. Regardless of content, the transcript of the average television news report is substantially shorter than the average newspaper story, which necessarily means that the former contains far less information than the latter.[4] As to the Internet's effect, there is little consensus, scholarly or otherwise, as to whether web content represents something quite distinct from its old media counterparts, or whether the Internet and its potential effects merely embody "old wine in new bottles."[5] In this chapter, we ask whether and to what extent voters who consume high levels of various types of media respond differently to candidate character traits in contemplating their votes.

TELEVISION CONSUMPTION AND CHARACTER TRAITS

The argument that television personalizes voting behavior has been made frequently by scholars and pundits. The claim rests on the fact that television coverage of presidential campaigns differs from newspaper coverage in important ways that influence how strongly perceptions of candidate character affect the vote. Television's evolving role in covering the nation's politics has contributed to the emergence of the candidate as the focus of presidential campaigns.[6] This is in part because televised political coverage is more image oriented than newspaper coverage, so voters who rely on television relative to newspapers are more likely to receive information relevant to candidate personality.[7] Because television relies on images to communicate political information, the medium's preferred method is to organize its stories around more easily relatable personality frames rather than distant and sterile institutions.[8]

While voters can draw inferences about a candidate's personal traits from other media, television is more likely to promote such inferences, given its visual representation of a candidate's movements, physical appearance, and other non-verbal idiosyncrasies.[9] The very nature of television, evident as far back as the seminal Kennedy-Nixon debates, suggests that viewers with access to candidate images and the resulting visual cues experience political information differently.[10] First, visuals allow viewers to develop a rapport with candidates, a familiarity that encourages viewers to assess the personal qualities of politicians much as they would evaluate the traits of a new acquaintance.[11] Second, to the extent that television is more likely to convey information—both implicitly and explicitly—related to personal traits, television viewers are more likely to have considerations related to image and personality foremost in their minds. Under these conditions, it is reasonable to expect these viewers to rely more heavily on these considerations when deciding among candidates.

While theory leads us to expect that television-reliant voters will be more influenced by their perceptions of candidate traits, to this point, tests of this hypothesis have been limited and contradictory. A 1987 analysis examined ANES data from 1952 to 1980 and found that candidate image-related responses to the open-ended candidate like-dislike questions were more strongly related to the vote among television viewers than newspaper readers after 1960.[12] This analysis suggests that the greater reliance on candidate character traits among television viewers supported the personalization hypothesis, especially in light of the fact that candidate perceptions explained an increasing amount of variance in the vote decision relative to party identification and, strikingly, voter perceptions of the parties, which were also measured using the party like-dislike questions.

A more recent study, on the other hand, came to a different conclusion even though it also used the ANES data and relied on the open-ended like-dislike questions to uncover voter attitudes about the candidates.[13] This analysis of elections from 1952 through 2004 was concerned primarily with whether voting behavior became more personalized over time as reliance by voters on television for political coverage increased. The author found that traits were not significantly more important predictors of the vote in 2004 than they were in the 1950s. More importantly for our study, this analysis also found that in none of the individual election years were voters who watched television programs about the campaign more likely to be influenced by their personal trait perceptions than were those who did not watch such programs.[14]

As for campaign coverage in newspapers, there is no doubt that voters garner plenty of information about candidate personality from this medium. The mere reporting of news related to candidate-centered campaigns guarantees this. Furthermore, while newspapers clearly provide more coverage, the mix of personality- and issue-based content does not differ a great deal from that which television provides.[15] However, the question regarding newspaper coverage is whether the quantity of information available relative to television allows for facts about and analysis of policy proposals to compete with the increasingly dramatized clash between two highly visible and remarked on personalities. Evidence here is contradictory as well. On the one hand, some studies argue that the information processing that goes along with reading the quantity of information offered in newspapers promotes greater learning about issues.[16] On the other hand, some scholarship suggests that this effect disappears once one accounts for the fact that those who choose newspapers as a primary source of political news are already knowledgeable about politics.[17]

While we will consider how newspaper consumption is related to reliance on candidate trait perceptions, our main concern is the personalization hypothesis. Given the limited research into this question, along with the contradictory results of the two major attempts to test this hypothesis, further study is appropriate. Despite the inconsistent findings, we hypothesize that because television primes personal qualities more strongly than do print media, television-reliant voters will more strongly base their vote on perceptions of candidate personal traits. As we have discussed above, the theoretical arguments in support of this hypothesis seem convincing, even if the empirical evidence is rather thin. We test this hypothesis by using 1984 through 2008 ANES data. This slightly truncated time period is dictated by the availability of comparable data. We begin in 1984, as opposed to 1980, because more detailed questions about media consumption first appeared in this year.[18] We end in 2008 because of the change in the way that the ANES worded the trait questions, which we have discussed in earlier chapters.[19]

We pool the data for these seven presidential elections. We do this for two reasons. First, we are not concerned with analyzing variation in the impact of trait perceptions from one election to the next. While it might be interesting to examine each year separately in order to explore variations in the relationships across the years, we lack the data to engage in a fruitful theoretical analysis of such patterns, so we focus on the overall relationships. Since the primary concern of this investigation is to determine whether television personalizes the candidates in a way that impacts the degree to which people rely on their perceptions of the candidates' character traits, the focus on the general relationship is more appropriate. Pooling the data smooths out the variation in the results across the years, which yields a clearer picture of the overall general relationship between the key variables.

A second reason for pooling the data is to obtain large sample sizes for the various subgroups in our analysis. For example, in some election years, categorizing respondents into high, medium, and low television news consumers would leave us with sample sizes small enough to call into question the stability of our estimates. Furthermore, breaking down these groups into those of varying education levels, as we do later in this chapter, would make estimation virtually impossible in a number of years. With our pooled dataset, no such problems exist. To account for the fact that the ANES sample size varies from election to election, the data are weighted so that each year contributes equally to the entire sample. We also restrict our analysis to major-party voters because, with the exception of 1980 and 1996, the ANES did not ask trait questions about third party candidates.

As in previous chapters, the independent variable of particular interest is the respondents' relative evaluation of the two presidential candidates on the trait questions asked in any given year. This variable is scaled so that it ranges from +4 (most favorable to the Republican candidate) to –4 (most favorable to the Democrat). A zero on the trait index indicates that the respondent has an evenly balanced mix of trait perceptions. We examine the impact of the overall trait index on the vote rather than examine the impact of each individual trait for two reasons. First, our aim is in determining whether television viewing leads voters to rely more on candidate character traits in general, not on any specific trait. Second, the impact of specific traits varies from one election to the next, and while the question of why the media prime certain traits in particular years and not others is interesting, it is beyond the scope of this study.

We combine two measures of the extent to which respondents followed campaign news on television. The first is the number of days per week that the voter watched an evening network news show; the second is the amount of attention the voter paid to campaign news on television. We used the resulting measure to divide voters into three groups based on the extent of their consumption of television campaign coverage.[20] About 30 percent of the voters were classified in the high television exposure group, 30 percent in the low exposure group, and 40 percent in the middle group. We divided television viewing into high, medium, and low categories, rather than just dichotomizing the variable, because of the possibility that the effects of television viewing are not linear. Previous research into the effects of media consumption on other aspects of political attitudes or behavior has sometimes found nonlinear patterns, so we examine this possibility with our data.[21]

The logical place to begin is to determine what influence trait perceptions have on the presidential vote in general. The relevant analysis is in the first column of Table 7.1, which shows the results for a logistic regression of the vote on party identification, ideology, evaluations of the president's handling of the economy and foreign policy, and the index of candidate trait perceptions. All of the independent variables are coded such that increasing values are associated with a higher likelihood of voting for the Republican presidential candidate.[22] We also include dummy variables for each election year, treating 1984 as the base or excluded category against which the coefficients for the other years can be compared. The coefficient for the candidate trait evaluation variable is strong and statistically significant, which supports the hypothesis that evaluations of the character traits of the candidates affect the vote decision.[23] As we have demonstrated in cross-sectional analyses in previous chapters, the more favorably that a voter rates one candidate over the other on character traits, the more likely the voter is to vote for that candidate, all else equal.

This is an unsurprising confirmation of the cross-sectional analyses we have discussed in earlier chapters and serves merely as a starting point for this analysis. The specific question we are interested in is whether the effect of trait perceptions on the vote varies with the level of exposure to television news coverage of the election. More precisely, do voters who watch a lot of television choose their presidential candidate more on the basis of character traits? We test this hypothesis by running the same logistic regression that we estimated in the first column of Table 7.1 separately for low, medium, and high television news viewers.[24] The results are in the final three columns of Table 7.1. For all three groups, evaluation of candidate character traits has a substantial and statistically significant effect on the vote. However, the effect is stronger for those who have a high level of television news consumption. The difference between the coefficients for the high and the medium groups is statistically significant at the .01 level.[25] The difference between the medium and the low exposure groups is much smaller and is not statistically significant.[26] These results indicate that the effects of increased television viewing are not linear; instead, they take effect only after a threshold level is reached.

Logistic regression coefficients can be difficult to interpret directly. To aid in their substantive interpretation, Figure 7.1 displays the predicted probability of a Republican vote for each of the television usage groups for a range of trait evaluation scores, with the other variables set at their means.[27] Although the full range of the trait index is +4 to −4, predicted probabilities are shown only for scores between +2 and −2. Trait index scores outside this range are held almost exclusively by strong partisans, who almost always vote for their party's candidate. Figure 7.1 reinforces the conclusion that high

Table 7.1 Pooled Logistic Regressions of the Presidential Vote Overall and by Television News Viewing, 1984–2008

Independent variables	All voters	Level of television news viewing		
		Low	Medium	High
Party identification	.622** (.028)	.651** (.052)	.590** (.040)	.667** (.061)
Ideological orientation	.252** (.038)	.279** (.067)	.260** (.057)	.195* (.089)
Evaluation of president's handling of the economy	.282** (.054)	.408** (.101)	.285** (.077)	.079 (.121)
Evaluation of president's handling of foreign policy	.206** (.049)	.133 (.092)	.140* (.069)	.415** (.111)
1988	−.589** (.171)	−.234 (.496)	−.562* (.238)	−.977* (.402)
1992	−1.247** (.192)	−.982** (.361)	−1.339** (.281)	−1.750** (.454)
1996	−2.133** (.196)	−1.801** (.326)	−1.977** (.278)	−3.438** (.513)
2000	−.687** (.178)	−.636* (.281)	−.515 (.275)	−1.324** (.455)
2004	−1.219** (.175)	−1.351** (.299)	−1.018** (.253)	−1.468** (.434)
2008	−.623** (.190)	−.418 (.333)	−.570* (.267)	−1.208* (.487)
Evaluation of candidate character traits	1.832** (.063)	1.594** (.111)	1.728** (.089)	2.475** (.165)
N	7558	2084	3105	2270
Chi-square	7412.65	1912.13	2886.81	2527.63
−2 log likelihood	3061.94	976.86	1417.96	612.02
Nagelkerke R^2	.83	.80	.81	.89
% correctly predicted	92.5	91.1	91.3	95.2

*p < .05; **p < .01 (two-tailed tests)

Note: Cell entries are logistic regression coefficients, with standard errors in parentheses. The dependent variable is the presidential vote. Only major-party voters are included in the analysis. See the text for details on the independent variables and on the pooled dataset.

levels of television news consumption intensify the impact of candidate trait evaluations on the vote. There is a greater change in the probability of voting Republican as the voter's score on the trait index changes for the high television viewing group than for the other two groups. For example, consider the effect of a change in trait perceptions from –1, which is moderately favorable to the Democratic candidate, to +1, which is moderately favorable to the Republican candidate. These two scores represent about the 30th and the 70th percentiles on the trait index variable, respectively. Such a change for a voter who is a high consumer of television news and average on other variables would result in an increase in the likelihood of voting Republican from 6 percent to 90 percent, a change of 84 points. The same change for a low consumer of television news would result in an increase in the likelihood of voting Republican from 17 percent to 83 percent, a change of 66 points. The ratio of the percentage point change for the high television viewing group to the low group is 1.27 (i.e., 84/66). Using this as a measure of the difference in impact, the effect of trait perceptions on the vote for high television viewers is 27 percent greater than the effect for low television viewers.

Although these findings appear to support the hypothesis that increased exposure to television news coverage makes voters more likely to vote on the basis of candidate character traits, we should consider the possibility that our findings are the result of the effects of some confounding variable. The

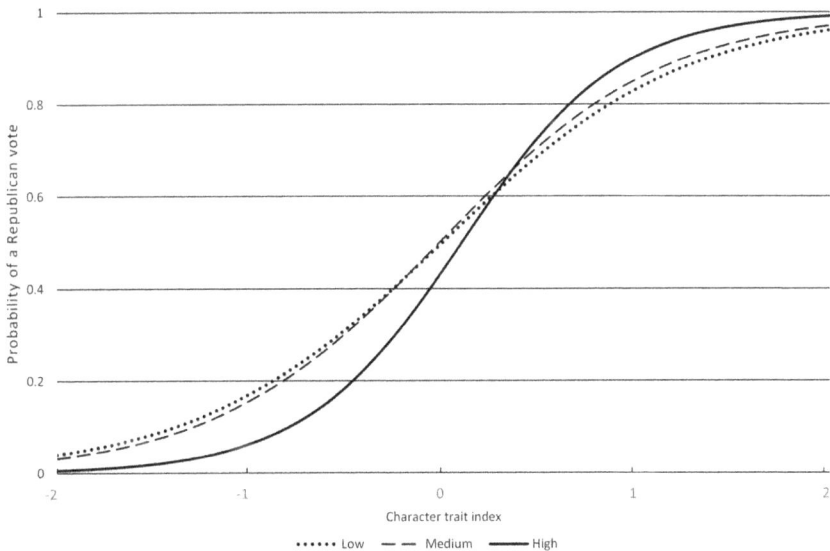

Figure 7.1 Predicted Probability of Voting Republican by Evaluation of Candidate Character Traits and Level of Television News Consumption

Note: The lines represent voters with high, medium, and low levels of consumption of television news at varying levels of the candidate trait index. All other variables in the equation are set at the mean levels for each television usage group.

two most likely suspects are age and education, two variables that could well be related to both television consumption and reliance on character traits. Younger voters might be more likely to receive their news from television, and they might be more likely to vote on the basis of candidate personality because they have not yet formed strong partisan and ideological attachments. Highly educated voters might be less likely than poorly educated voters to rely on television for news, and they might be less likely to vote on the basis of character traits because they have more knowledge about issues. To rule out the possibility that the results shown in Table 7.1 are spurious relationships, we repeated the analysis for specific groups of voters, defined by education or age.

Table 7.2 presents the analysis for two groups of voters defined by education (those with a high school education or less and those with at least a four-year college degree) and two groups defined by age (those 35 years of age and younger and those aged 50 and over). To save space, we report only the coefficients for the candidate trait index, but the logistic regressions include all of the variables listed in Table 7.1, and there are no surprises in terms of how the control variables, such as party identification, affect the vote choice. For each group, the difference in the coefficients between the high television consumption group and both of the other groups is both substantial and statistically significant. Thus, the findings reported earlier are not the result of the confounding effects of education or age, increasing our confidence that voters who consume more television news put more weight on the character traits of the candidates.

Table 7.2   Effect of Television News Viewing for Selected Groups of Voters, 1984–2008

	Level of television news viewing		
Voter groups	Low	Medium	High
Education			
High school or less	1.426* (.148)	1.719* (.140)	2.390* (.239)
College degree or more	1.876* (.284)	1.549* (.177)	3.073* (.445)
Age			
35 and under	1.781* (.185)	1.885* (.141)	2.741* (.438)
50 and over	1.832* (.276)	1.679* (.140)	2.569* (.236)

*p < .01 (two-tailed tests)
Notes: Cell entries are logistic regression coefficients, with standard errors in parentheses. The dependent variable is the presidential vote. Only major-party voters are included in the analysis. See the text for details on the independent variables and on the pooled dataset.

Next, we present the same analysis for newspaper readership in order to test the possibility that reliance on any form of media campaign coverage leads to a greater reliance on the candidates' personal qualities. Our measure of newspaper reliance is built in the same way as our television variable, using the number of days per week that the voter read a daily newspaper and the amount of attention that the voter paid to campaign news in the papers, and dividing the resulting index into low-, middle- and high-usage groups. Once again, the index runs from 1 (zero days, no attention) to 5 (seven days and a great deal of attention). Our approach to the analysis is the same as the one for television news: we predict the vote for president using the same variables, including the candidate trait index, for each level of newspaper readership. These results are reported in Table 7.3.

In striking contrast to the results for television viewership, the effect of the candidate trait index varies little across the three levels of newspaper usage. The effect of candidate traits is statistically significant for all three groups individually and the magnitude of the effect is slightly greater for the group that reports the lowest amount of newspaper readership. In other words, avid newspaper readers were slightly less influenced by their character trait perceptions than those in the other two groups, however these differences are slight and do not rise to the level of statistical significance.[28] Whereas heavy consumers of television news take greater account of candidate character, there are no such differences across varying levels of newspaper readership. While the substantive impact of the character trait index across these groups would be better appreciated in a graph of the predicted probabilities of voting Republican, as displayed in Figure 7.1 for television use, we do not include the comparable graph for levels of newspaper readership because the three lines are barely distinguishable. In any case, the foregoing analysis demonstrates support for the personalization hypothesis among television-reliant voters.[29]

THE INTERNET AND CHARACTER TRAITS

Of course the media landscape has changed a great deal over the last three decades. Newspapers have struggled to survive in the digital age; broadcast outlets have proliferated; the audience for news has fragmented given the ability to choose from more and increasingly partisan and ideological outlets.[30] A related change has been the rise of the Internet as a major source of political news. The medium can be used in a variety of ways: as a platform for traditional media to reach a wider—and younger—audience; as an alternative to and safeguard against the traditional media's evaporating control of what constitutes news; and as a virtual home—and echo chamber—for politically interested citizens seeking out those with similar ideological orientations. This diversity of functions has made questions regarding the political content and potential influence of new media as difficult to answer as they are compelling.

Table 7.3 Logistic Regressions of the Presidential Vote by Level of Newspaper Use, 1984–2008

Independent variables	Level of newspaper use		
	Low	Medium	High
Party identification	.652**	.601**	.635**
	(.050)	(.043)	(.053)
Ideological orientation	.352**	.126*	.326**
	(.072)	(.060)	(.074)
Evaluation of president's handling of the economy	.281**	.213*	.400**
	(.095)	(.087)	(.104)
Evaluation of president's handling of foreign policy	−.002	.254**	.356**
	(.087)	(.078)	(.096)
1988	−.283	−.489	−.894**
	(.370)	(.258)	(.306)
1992	−.777*	−1.377**	−1.594**
	(.386)	(.305)	(.363)
1996	−1.629**	−2.226**	−2.310**
	(.390)	(.297)	(.379)
2000	−.869*	−.535	−.575
	(.359)	(.275)	(.341)
2004	−.791*	−1.050**	−1.969**
	(.337)	(.297)	(.350)
2008	−.756*	−.506	−.219
	(.360)	(.300)	(.381)
Evaluation of candidate character traits	1.868**	1.831**	1.802**
	(.112)	(.108)	(.133)
N	2350	2583	2514
Chi-square	2295.56	2406.29	2622.32
−2 log likelihood	962.16	1173.56	857.45
Nagelkerke R^2	.83	.81	.86
% correctly predicted	92.9	90.6	94.2

*p < .05; **p < .01 (two-tailed tests)
Note: Cell entries are logistic regression coefficients, with standard errors in parentheses. The dependent variable is the presidential vote. Only major-party voters are included in the analysis. See the text for details on the independent variables and on the pooled dataset.

On the one hand, the absence of the time and space constraints that limit broadcast and print reports, as well as less devotion to traditional journalistic conventions, give the Internet the potential to provide content that is quite distinct from that delivered by mainstream outlets.[31] One of the major constraints on the traditional news media is their reliance on authoritative government sources, a professional norm that allows for balance and, at least the appearance of objectively reporting the daily political combat among Democrats and Republicans, conservatives and liberals.[32] Among the shortcomings of this reliance are stories that hew closely to the perspectives of the powerful, including government officials, regardless of whether actual facts support these perspectives. In the worst case scenario, such as national crises during which authoritative sources are often loath to criticize the government, this can lead to news narrowly reported from only one perspective.[33] To the extent that Internet content can be lengthier and less beholden to official sources, it has the potential to provide more in-depth, substantive political coverage from a wider variety of viewpoints. If this were the case, we might expect Internet-reliant citizens to pay less attention to personalities and more to issues.

However, there are also good reasons to expect political content on the Internet to be little different from traditional media coverage. This is principally due to the reality that a substantial percentage of political coverage available on the Internet is both reported and made available by traditional outlets that have expanded their reach into the digital world.[34] It is also the case that a large dose of the information and discussion provided by the partisan and ideological blogosphere links to traditional content, albeit often to provide acerbic critiques of mainstream media content. Furthermore, while the Internet can be the source of the kind of diversity of information necessary for a democratic citizenry, the reality is that this potential flies in the face of the biases that affect how people pay attention to and retain information. Rather than opening dialogue across partisan and ideological divides, the Internet seems to have provided a technologically advanced way to filter in the information and ideas with which we already agree and filter out those we disdain.[35] Under these circumstances, candidate personal traits would be even more central to the vote decision, given the large amount of traditional content that focuses on candidate personalities. Of course, if Internet-reliant voters are more likely to receive ideologically homogenous information, this might have the effect of turning character judgments into mere reflections of ideology, thus lessening their impact.

We now turn to a test of whether Internet-reliant voters are more or less influenced by their perceptions of candidate character traits than are less digitally savvy citizens. Our analysis is cross-sectional, based only on the 2012 election, which provides measures comparable to those we have already used to analyze television and newspaper use and a large enough sample size to make reasonable statistical inferences. Our goals for this analysis are exploratory in nature and our findings are meant to be merely suggestive.

While we admit that the media use measures we have relied on to this point are rather blunt given their self-reported nature and the variety of possibilities encompassed by "read[ing] news in a print newspaper" or "watch[ing] national news on TV," a similar question about Internet usage is even more subject to such a shortcoming given that seeking out news in this manner can range from reading an article in the on-line editions of the *New York Times* or *Wall Street Journal,* to commenting on a candidate or issue on a partisan blog, to watching a candidate's speech or advertisement on YouTube.

In this spirit, we again estimate a series of logistic regressions of the presidential vote on partisan and ideological identification, retrospective evaluations of presidential performance, social and moral issue indices, and the candidate trait index, all coded such that increasing values lead to a higher probability of a vote for Mitt Romney. These results are displayed in Table 7.4, the first column of which reproduces the results from Table 6.2 for all major-party voters, except black voters, who we exclude from the analysis. The remainder of the table categorizes voters by their Internet use based on the number of days per week that the respondent watched, read, or listened to news, and the amount of attention the respondent paid to national politics via this medium. We used the resulting measure to divide voters into three roughly equal groups based on the extent of their Internet use for political news.

Whereas the influence of candidate traits on the vote increased with consumption of television news, Internet usage exhibits the opposite pattern. As Internet usage increases, the influence of candidate traits decreases, although the measure is still highly statistically and substantively significant for each group individually. The coefficient for the candidate trait index among high Internet users differs significantly from that for the low Internet users. This coefficient also differs from the medium group. There is no significant difference between the medium and low groups.

Again, coefficients generated from logistic regression are difficult to interpret directly. Therefore, we display the predicted probability of a Republican vote for each of the three Internet use groups across a range of trait evaluation scores, with the other variables held at the mean levels of each group. We again only look at predicted probabilities for trait scores between +2 and –2 and present the results in Figure 7.2. The change in the probability of voting Republican is greater for the low and medium groups than the high Internet use group. If we restrict our analysis to trait evaluations between –1 (moderately favorable to Obama) and +1 (moderately favorable to Romney) for the low and high usage groups, we see that the increase in the probability of a Romney vote among the low group, as evaluations of Romney's character improve relative to Obama's, is 62 percentage points. The comparable increase among the high Internet group is 50 points. The ratio of this change for the low Internet group versus the high Internet group is 1.24 (i.e., 62/50). Thus, the effect of trait perceptions on the vote among low Internet users is 24 percent greater than the effect among high Internet users.

Table 7.4 Logistic Regressions of the Presidential Vote Overall and by Internet Use, 2012

Independent variables	All voters	Level of Internet use		
		Low	Medium	High
Party identification	.505***	.554***	.523***	.505***
	(.062)	(.083)	(.129)	(.112)
Ideological orientation	–.186	–.462***	.098	.030
	(.099)	(.160)	(.214)	(.178)
Evaluation of Obama's handling of the economy	.705***	.418**	.932***	.673***
	(.108)	(.204)	(.119)	(.189)
Evaluation of Obama's handling of foreign policy	.135	–.073	.293	.276*
	(.099)	(.198)	(.193)	(.164)
Social welfare issues index	.522***	.427***	1.158***	.122
	(.094)	(.496)	(.208)	(.168)
Moral issues index	.687***	.613***	1.115**	.549***
	(.192)	(.219)	(.257)	(.210)
Index of attitudes toward blacks	.196**	.095	.560***	.186
	(.196)	(.144)	(.163)	(.132)
Candidate trait index	1.313***	1.647**	1.497***	1.135***
	(.063)	(.213)	(.247)	(.176)
Nagelkerke R^2	.91	.80	.81	.89
% correctly predicted	95.2	91.1	91.3	95.2

*p < .05; **p < .01; ***p < .001 (two-tailed tests)
Note: Cell entries are logistic regression coefficients, with standard errors in parentheses. The dependent variable is the presidential vote. Only major-party voters are included in the analysis. See the text for details on the independent variables.

Of course, since we argued that age and education were potentially confounding factors as one considers the relationship between reliance on television and the influence of candidate trait perceptions, the same can be said for Internet use. Internet usage is far higher among younger voters, who may well also be more dependent on trait assessments than older, more partisan and ideological voters. Education is a less likely suspect, given that we have seen little evidence in previous chapters that less educated voters are consistently more reliant on trait perceptions, but education is clearly related to Internet use. Therefore, as we did as part of our analysis of television above, we repeat the logistic regressions presented in Table 7.4 for older and younger voters, and for less educated and highly educated ones. These results are presented in Table 7.5.

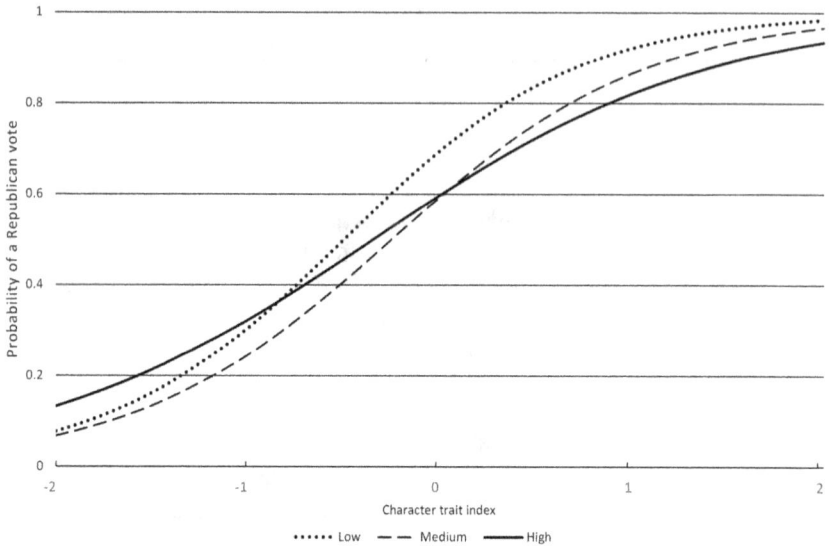

Figure 7.2   Predicted Probability of Voting Republican by Evaluation of Candidate Character Traits and Level of Internet Content Consumption

Note: The lines represent voters with high, medium, and low levels of consumption of Internet content at varying levels of the candidate trait index. All other variables in the equation are set at the mean levels for each Internet usage group.

To preserve space, we display only the logistic regression coefficients for the candidate trait index. These results present quite a contrast with our analysis of television viewership by age and education, which resulted in little evidence of spurious relationships. For voters with only a high school degree or less, increased Internet usage is associated with greater reliance on trait perceptions, although the difference is slight. The difference between the coefficients for the high and low Internet users are not statistically significant and, as we shall see below, the change in the predicted probabilities of a Republican vote are small across the range of candidate trait perceptions. For the college educated, on the other hand, those in the high Internet use group were less reliant on character trait perceptions. While the relatively large standard error for the low Internet use group prevents the difference between the coefficients for the high and low groups from being statistically significant, and therefore makes any conclusions based on these data necessarily circumspect, the predicted probabilities suggest the possibility of a substantial difference in the influence of character traits depending on Internet usage.

Figure 7.3 displays the percentage change in the probability of a vote for Romney for the low, medium, and high Internet groups as we vary the candidate trait index from −1 to +1. Among the less educated, indicated by the first three bars in the figure, differences are slight across Internet usage groups.

Table 7.5   Effect of Internet Use for Selected Groups of Voters, 2012

Voter groups	Level of Internet use		
	Low	Medium	High
Education			
High school or less	1.429* (.334)	1.697* (.577)	1.706* (.370)
College degree or more	3.377* (1.212)	1.578* (.543)	1.012* (.363)
Age			
35 and under	5.251* (2.662)	†	1.207* (.438)
50 and over	1.756* (.305)	1.579* (.394)	1.539* (.276)

*p < .01 (two-tailed tests)

Note: Cell entries are logistic regression coefficients, with standard errors in parentheses. The dependent variable is the presidential vote. Only major-party voters are included in the analysis. See the text for details on the independent variables.

† Categorizing younger voters into low, medium, and high Internet usage groups worked out in such a way that the logistic regression for the low group was perfectly determined, making estimation impossible. Therefore, we divide young voters in half based on their Internet use and create only low and high Internet use groups.

However, for those with a college degree or more, the differences are larger. For the low Internet users among more educated voters, moving from moderately preferring Obama's character to moderately preferring Romney's increases the probability of a Romney vote by 70 percentage points. Doing the same thing for the high Internet users increases the probability by less than 50 points.

The results for age are similarly intriguing. As with variation in educational attainment, the youngest and oldest voters also incorporate candidate character traits quite differently depending on their level of Internet usage. As Table 7.5 shows, the coefficient for the trait index among young voters who are least reliant on the Internet is five times as large as that for the most reliant group.[36] For voters 50 and older, no pattern exists. We again turn to the patterns in the predicted probabilities, which are displayed in Figure 7.4.

The increase in the probability of a Romney vote for younger voters who use the Internet least is over 90 percentage points as one moves from moderately favorable to Obama to moderately favorable to Romney. The equivalent change among young, high Internet users is 51 points. On the other hand, the bars representing older voters are essentially flat. The increase in the probability of a Romney vote is about 60 points for older voters at all

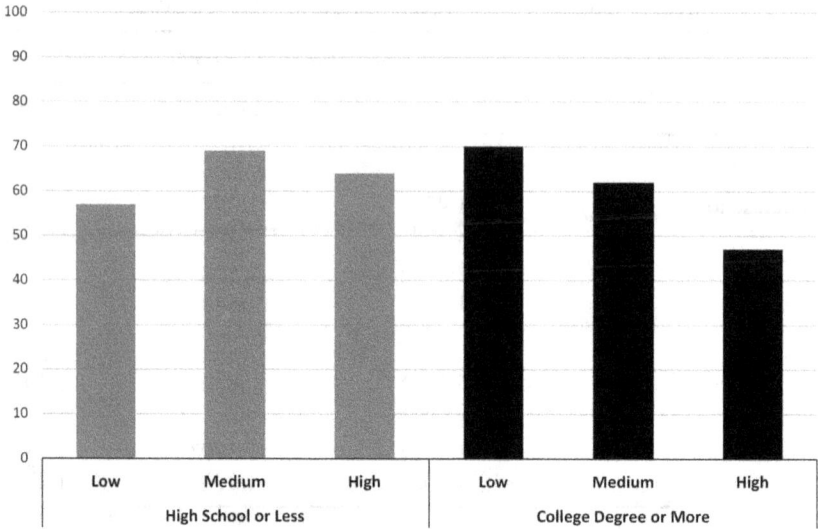

Figure 7.3   Change in the Predicted Probability of Voting Republican by Evaluation of Candidate Character Traits and Level of Internet News Consumption for the Least and Most Educated Voters

Note: Bars represent the change in the probability of a Republican vote as the average member of each group moves from –1 to 1 on the character trait index. The groups are defined by the level of Internet consumption and education level. For example, the change in the likelihood of a Republican vote for the average college-educated high Internet user would be about 47 percentage points.

levels of Internet use. While we must be careful interpreting these results, it is worth speculating as to what might explain them.

The overall pattern we see in Table 7.4 suggests that for all voters, the effect of candidate character traits on the vote is less for those in the upper third of Internet use than it is for those in the lower two-thirds. This is opposite the pattern we saw for television (Table 7.1) and makes some sense given the differences between receiving political information from television versus the Internet. Television is a more passive medium. For example, some scholarly literature suggests that the passive reception of televised content makes learning about issues less likely than the act of reading, which allows for the ability to process content more slowly.[37] Whereas the Internet combines aspects of both television and newspapers, we believe that using the Internet is in two important ways more like reading a newspaper: first, there is the ability to move at one's own pace, and second there is the opportunity to seek out certain types of information while ignoring other types.[38] Therefore, one conclusion we might draw from our overall analysis of Internet use as presented in Table 7.1 is that seeking political information on the Internet serves a beneficial purpose if one assumes that greater reliance on issues, retrospective evaluations, and partisanship, and relatively less reliance on

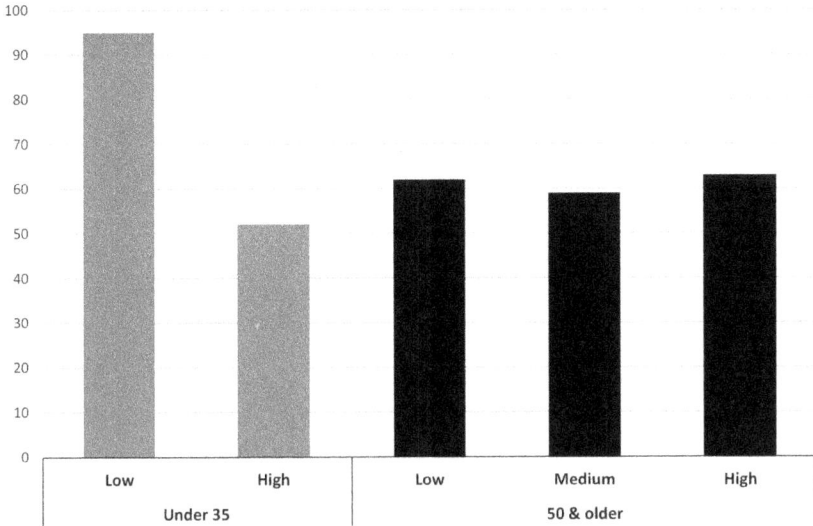

Figure 7.4 Change in the Predicted Probability of Voting Republican by Evaluation of Candidate Character Traits and Level of Internet News Consumption for Younger and Older Voters

Note: Bars represent the change in the probability of a Republican vote as the average member of each group moves from –1 to 1 on the character trait index. The groups are defined by the level of Internet consumption and age. For example, the change in the likelihood of a Republican vote for the average younger high Internet user would be about 52 percentage points. Because of an anomaly in the data, we could not estimate equations for young voters who used the Internet the least. This logistic regression was perfectly determined, making estimation impossible. Therefore, we divide all young voters into just two groups: low and high Internet use.

candidate character traits makes for a more informed vote decision. Understood in this light, heavy Internet users are also more informed voters, making the Internet's great potential to serve democratic ends more likely to be a reality.[39]

The results presented in Table 7.5, however, suggest a more circumspect interpretation. Among the least educated voters—in other words, the voters most likely to benefit from the near instantaneous availability of political information—heavy Internet use exerts little effect on the use of character traits in voting. In fact, the small differences in the candidate trait coefficients across groups argue for the opposite interpretation: for the less educated, high Internet users are more affected by their trait perceptions. Conversely, it is the college graduates who strongly mirror the overall results: high Internet use decreases reliance on traits. Given the nature of our data, we can only speculate. However, heavy Internet users among the more educated may well be motivated to seek out information that reinforces what is already a more ideologically sophisticated worldview than the less educated possess. And, in fact, our Internet usage measure is more highly correlated with general interest in politics for the college educated than it is for those with a high school education or less. Voters with low education levels are likely to seek out less sophisticated information, which quite likely contains more emphasis on character traits rather than issues.

The relationship between age and Internet use is also interesting, although here we have to be even more cautious in our interpretation given the data constraints that prevented us from analyzing the effect of character traits on the presidential vote for low, medium, and high levels of Internet use among younger voters. Thus, Table 7.5 divides these voters into high- and low-use categories only. Among older voters, Internet reliance does not affect the importance of candidate character trait perceptions to the vote decision. For younger voters, however, Internet usage has quite a large effect. Younger voters who do not rely heavily on the Internet, and who are also less interested in politics generally than high Internet users, are strongly affected by their character trait perceptions. For high Internet users, the coefficient for the candidate character trait variable is statistically significant, but the substantive effect of the trait measure, as displayed in Figure 7.3, is much less pronounced. Again, however, we hesitate to argue that this results from the policy oriented content provided by the Internet given the alternate explanations. First, for motivated younger, more Internet savvy, more politically engaged voters, character judgments may reflect stronger partisan or ideological attachments. Second, younger voters low in Internet use are likely to be especially susceptible to the effects of their perceptions of candidate character because what campaign information they are getting comes from television, which we have already argued personalizes the vote decision. Unfortunately for the newspaper industry, far fewer younger voters rely on newspapers today, leaving television as the most likely source of campaign news.[40]

CONCLUSION

The literature on media and politics suggests that it makes a difference from which source voters obtain their campaign-related information. A frequent argument is that television tends to personalize politics, emphasizing candidates and personal traits, while de-emphasizing policy. Although such claims are frequently made, there has been little empirical research to test the hypothesis that increased consumption of television news leads voters to rely more on candidate personal traits in making their vote decision. Moreover, the two attempts by political scientists to investigate this question come to opposite conclusions about the legitimacy of the personalization hypothesis. Our analysis attempts to settle this dispute using better measures of media consumption. We find that voters who are heavy consumers of television news do place more emphasis on candidate character traits. We also find that this effect is not linear. The increased emphasis on character traits appears only after a threshold level of television news consumption is reached. There is little difference between voters with moderate levels of television news consumption and those with low levels. Furthermore, we find that there is also little difference in the influence of character traits across varying levels of newspaper readership.

Finally, while our conclusions regarding Internet usage are of necessity speculative, we find that overall, greater Internet usage means less reliance on candidate traits, a finding opposite that for television. We also find that more educated and younger voters become especially less influenced by their perceptions of character traits at high levels of Internet usage. While these findings could be interpreted as a data point in favor of the idea that Internet content encourages issue voting relative to voting based on personality, we find it to be more likely that strong partisans and ideologues are more motivated to use the Internet to seek out political information. However, our data do not allow us to rule either possibility in or out.

We conclude by cautioning against exaggerating the findings of this study. While high levels of television news consumption do increase voter reliance on candidate character traits, and low levels of Internet usage do the opposite, it would be incorrect to characterize those who frequently watch television news and those who do not avail themselves of Internet content as concerned primarily with candidate personality and other voters as not affected by such concerns. Character traits matter to both groups of voters; they just matter somewhat more to certain types of voters. Furthermore, the voters we have identified as particularly taking account of their perceptions of the candidates' character traits also are strongly influenced by partisanship, ideology, and evaluations of government performance; they do not vote simply on the basis of candidate character. The effects of varying levels of media consumption are not that drastic, but they do exist.

NOTES

1. Media usage figures are from various Pew Research Center surveys as reported in Diana Owen, "The Campaign and the Media," in *The American Elections of 2012,* eds. Janet M. Box-Steffensmeier and Steven E. Schier (New York: Routledge, 2013), 40.
2. Roderick P. Hart, *Seducing America* (Thousand Oaks, CA: Sage Publications, 1999); Diana C. Mutz, "Effects of 'In-Your-Face' Television Discourse on Perceptions of a Legitimate Opposition," *American Political Science Review* 101 (2007): 621–635.
3. See e.g., Doris A. Graber, "Seeing is Remembering: How Visuals Contribute to Learning from Television News," *Journal of Communication* 40 (1990): 134–155; Doris A. Graber, *Processing Politics: Learning from Television in the Internet Age* (Chicago: University of Chicago Press, 2001); Stephen Ansolabehere and Shanto Iyengar, *Going Negative: How Political Advertisements Shrink and Polarize the Electorate* (New York: Free Press, 1995); James N. Druckman, "The Power of Television Images: The First Kennedy-Nixon Debate Revisited," *Journal of Politics* 65 (2003): 559–571; Susan A. Hellweg,

Michael Pfau, and Steven R. Brydon, *Televised Presidential Debates,* (New York: Praeger, 1992); Kurt Lang and Gladys Engel Lang, *Television and Politics* (New Brunswick, NJ: Transaction Publishers, 2002); Michael Pfau, Jaeho Cho, and Kirsten Chong, "Communication Forms in U.S. Presidential Campaigns: Influences on Candidate Perceptions and the Democratic Process," *Harvard International Journal of Press/Politics* 6 (2001): 88–105; Darrell M. West, *Air Wars,* 5th ed. (Washington, DC: CQ Press, 2010); W. Lance Bennett, *News: The Politics of Illusion,* 9th ed. (Boston: Longman, 2012).

4. W. Russell Neumann, Marion R. Just, and Ann R. Crigler, *Common Knowledge: News and the Construction of Political Meaning* (Chicago: University of Chicago Press, 1992), 10; Jeffery J. Mondak, *Nothing to Read: Newspapers and Elections in a Social Experiment* (Ann Arbor: University of Michigan Press, 1995), 77–78.

5. Danny Hayes, "The News Anew? Political Coverage in a Transformed Media Age," in Travis N. Ridout, ed., *New Directions in Media and Politics* (New York: Routledge, 2013), 194.

6. Martin P. Wattenberg, *The Rise of Candidate-Centered Politics* (Cambridge, MA: Harvard University Press, 1991).

7. Graber, *Processing Politics*; Keeter, "The Illusion of Intimacy"; Lang and Lang, *Television and Politics.*

8. Ian McAllister, "The Personalization of Politics," in *The Oxford Handbook of Political Behavior,* eds. Russell J. Dalton and Hans-Dieter Klingemann (Oxford: Oxford University Press, 579).

9. McAllister, "The Personalization of Politics," 582; Shawn W. Rosenberg, Shawn W., Lisa Bohan, Patrick McCafferty, and Kevin Harris, "The Image and the Vote: The Effect of Candidate Presentation on Voter Preference," *American Journal of Political Science* 30 (1986): 108–127.

10. James N. Druckman, "The Power of Television Images: The First Kennedy-Nixon Debate Revisited," *Journal of Politics* 65 (2003): 559–571.

11. Hart, *Seducing America,* 24; McAllister, "The Personalization of Politics," 579.

12. Scott Keeter, "The Illusion of Intimacy: Television and the Role of Candidate Personal Qualities in Voter Choice," *Public Opinion Quarterly* 51 (1987): 344–358. Keeter relied on the question that asked respondents which source of political information they used the most, so his measure captures the relative reliance on television versus other sources (usually newspapers) for news about politics. The ANES did not include more detailed items on media consumption (e.g., "How many days in the past week did you watch the national news on TV?") until 1984, so Keeter's measure yields a simple dichotomy.

13. Danny Hayes, "Has Television Personalized Voting Behavior?" *Political Behavior* 31 (2005): 231–260.

14. Because Hayes analyzed elections beginning in 1952, his measure of television consumption is blunt, as more detailed items on media consumption were not asked until 1984. He relied on the question, "Did you watch any programs about the campaign on television?", which prompted a simple yes or no response.

15. James N. Druckman, "Media Matter: How Newspapers and Television News Cover Campaigns and Influence Voters," *Political Communication,* 22 (2005): 463–481.

16. John P. Robinson and Dennis K. Davis, "Television News and the Informed Public: An Information-Processing Approach," *Journal of Communication* 40 (1990): 106–119; David Weaver and Dan Drew, "Voter Learning and Interest in the 2000 Presidential Election: Did the Media Matter?" *Journalism and Mass Communication Quarterly* 78 (2001): 787–798.

17. Vincent Price and John Zaller, "Who Gets The News? Alternative Measures of News Reception and Their Implications for Research," *Public Opinion Quarterly* 57 (1993): 133–164.
18. In 1984, the ANES included for the first time a question about the number of days per week respondents watched the national network news and read a daily newspaper. We incorporate these variables into our measures of media consumption.
19. In 2008, we include only the half of all respondents who received the same version of the closed trait items questions used in previous years. The ANES dropped this version of the trait question wording in 2012.
20. Respondents were asked how many days in the past week they watched network television news and how much attention they paid to campaign news on television: a great deal, quite a bit, some, very little, or none. Our index of reliance on television news is the mean score for these two variables. The first variable was converted to a five-point scale to make it equivalent to the second. Thus the index runs from 1 to 5. For example, a respondent who watched television news every day and who paid a great deal of attention to presidential campaign news on television would receive a score of 5. Someone who did not watch television at all and paid no attention to television campaign news would receive a score of 1. Other combinations would be somewhere between these two extremes. Note that since the question about the number of days a respondent watched television news or read a newspaper asked about the "last week," some error is introduced into our measure to the extent that the last week was atypical for the respondent.
21. See, e.g., John Zaller, *The Nature and Origins of Mass Opinion,* (Cambridge: Cambridge University Press, 1992).
22. As in analyses in previous chapters, party identification is measured on a seven-point scale, from strong Democrat to strong Republican. Ideology is also measured on a seven-point scale, ranging from very liberal to very conservative. A substantial number of voters did not place themselves on the seven-point ideology scale but did classify themselves as liberal, moderate, or conservative with further prompting; these voters are classified as slightly liberal, moderate, and slightly conservative, respectively. Evaluations of the president's handling of both the economy and foreign affairs are measured on a four-point scale running from strongly disapprove to strongly approve, and these variables are coded so that a pro-Republican response is given a high score in each year.
23. Additionally the pseudo R^2 and proportion of cases correctly predicted are improved over what we obtain from a logistic regression of the vote using all of the variables except the trait index. Adding the trait index to the analysis raises the Cox & Snell R^2 from .54 to .63 and increases the percentage of cases correctly predicted from 88.0 to 92.5.
24. An alternative approach would be to use an interactive term that combined television news consumption and candidate character trait evaluation. We prefer to use a conditional modeling approach because it allows the coefficients for the other variables to vary, which is a more realistic assumption. For example, those who watch little television news might rely more on their party identification or their ideological orientation in their voting than those who watch a great deal of television news. Using a single regression equation with an interactive term assumes that the coefficients for the other variables in the model are the same for all respondents, unless one includes a great many interactive terms, which makes the model overly complicated.
25. The level of significance of the difference of the coefficients is calculated by the following formula: $Z = (b_1 - b_2)/(se_1 + se_2)^{2}$, +where b_i and se_i are the

logistic regression coefficient and its standard error for group i, and Z is the Z-score for a standardized normal distribution. See Robert Brame, Raymond Paternoster, Paul Mazerolle, and Alex Piquero, "Testing for the Equality of Maximum-Likelihood Regression Coefficients Between Two Independent Equations," *Journal of Quantitative Criminology* 14 (1998): 245–261, for a discussion of tests of the significance of the difference between two MLE coefficients.

26. To verify that pooling the data does not distort the findings, we repeated the analysis reported in Table 7.1 separately for each year. The overall pattern across the seven elections is very similar to the pattern present in the pooled data analysis. While the extent of difference between high television viewers and those with medium or low levels of television exposure varies across the years, the average difference in the logistic regression coefficients between the high and medium television viewers is very similar in magnitude to the difference present in Table 7.1. Also, the average difference between the logistic regression coefficients for the medium and low television groups is small, just as it is in Table 7.1.

27. In calculating the predicted probabilities, the other variables in the equation were set to the mean scores of each grouping, although these means do not vary a great deal from the low to the high television users. Thus, Figure 7.1 displays the change in the probability of voting Republican for voters who identify as independent, ideological moderates, and who have average evaluations of the performance of the president's handling of the economy and foreign affairs.

28. The significance of the difference between the largest (the low group) and the smallest (the high group) coefficients is $p = .14$.

29. Besides voters' absolute reliance on television and newspapers, we also investigated the relative mix of voters' consumption of these media. To operationalize this measure, we subtracted our index of newspaper readership from the index of television viewership. We then divided the result into three categories: relatively dependent on television for news, relatively balanced on both sources for news, and relatively dependent on newspapers for news. The measure of relative consumption differs from the measure of absolute consumption because a voter with considerable television consumption could also have heavy newspaper consumption, and thus would be classified as relatively balanced; similarly, a voter with only moderate television consumption could have no exposure to newspapers, and thus would be classified as relatively highly dependent on television. The absolute level of television news consumption and the relative reliance on television news are correlated. Those with high relative reliance are more likely to be high in absolute consumption. However, the relationship is not that strong, so these are distinct variables. (The correlation coefficient for the association between the trichotomous measures employed in this analysis is .43, and Kendall's tau-b is .37.) We ran the same analysis reported in Tables 7.1 and 7.2 for these three groups: those heavily television reliant relative to newspapers; those who consumed a balanced mix of both media; and those heavily newspaper reliant relative to television. Similar to the results presented in Table 7.1, we found that high television users were most influenced by their perceptions of character traits. The coefficient for this variable was significantly different from both the coefficient for the balanced mix of sources and the coefficient for respondents who reported high levels of newspaper use and low levels of television use. The coefficients for the latter two groups did not differ significantly. These results suggest that relative reliance on television is also

meaningful and reinforces our claims regarding television reliance and the personalization hypothesis.

30. Natalie Jomini Stroud, *Niche News: The Politics of News Choice* (New York: Oxford University Press, 2011).

31. See Hayes, "The News Anew?", 198–201, for an excellent discussion of the similarities and differences between old and new media.

32. Timothy Cook, *Governing With the News,* 2nd ed. (Chicago: University of Chicago Press, 2005).

33. See, Bennett, *News: The Politics of Illusion,* 15, 21–22, for his introduction to the concept of indexing; See, W. Lance Bennett, Regina G. Lawrence, and Steven Livingston, *When the Press Fails* (Chicago: University of Chicago Press, 2008), especially Chapter 3 for a discussion of how a dependent political press's news coverage changed in response to shifting elite discourse about the Abu Ghraib scandal.

34. Richard Davis, "Interplay: Political Blogging and Journalism," in *iPolitics: Citizens, Elections, and Governing in the New Media Era,* ed. Richard L. Fox and Jennifer M. Ramos (New York: Cambridge University Press, 2011).

35. Cass R. Sunstein, *Republic.com 2.0,* (Princeton, NJ: Princeton University Press, 2007); Cass R. Sunstein, *Going to Extremes: How Like Minds Unite and Divide,* (Oxford, UK: Oxford University Press, 2009); Farhad Manjoo, *True Enough: Learning to Live in a Post-Fact Society,* (Hoboken, NJ: John Wiley and Sons, 2008).

36. Because of an anomaly in the data, we could not estimate equations for low, medium, and high Internet users among young voters. The logistic regression for the low Internet use group was perfectly determined, making estimation impossible. Therefore, we divide young voters in half according to their Internet use and create only low and high categories.

37. Robinson and Davis, "Television News and the Informed Public"; Weaver and Drew, "Voter Learning and Interest in the 2000 Presidential Election."

38. Of course, technological advances in the streaming of digital information along with the fast increasing use of televisions as receivers of Internet content may, one day soon, blur or eliminate the differences we find.

39. See Max McCombs, R. Lance Holbert, Spiro Kiousis, and Wayne Wanta, *The News and Public Opinion: Media Effects on Civic Life* (Cambridge, UK: Polity Press, 2011) for a discussion of this potential.

40. Over half of all younger respondents fall in the bottom third of our newspaper reliance index. Conversely, over half of all voters 50 and older are in the top third.

8 May the Best Person Win

Presidential elections are contests between the two major parties, but they are more than just that. Presidential elections are contests between two candidates who differ not only in their party affiliations and policy preferences, but also in their personal qualities. The character traits of the presidential candidates always receive considerable attention during the election campaign. Media commentators frequently interpret the election in terms of the personal appeal of each candidate. The presidential candidates often emphasize their desirable character traits, along with the opponent's supposed shortcomings. Voters respond to this information by perceiving character traits of the candidates and using these perceptions to determine their vote choice. All this makes voter perceptions of the character traits of presidential candidates an important topic to investigate thoroughly. Surprisingly, political scientists have not done so. The only book on this topic was published in the mid-1970s. Relative to the work on other aspects of voting behavior, only a small number of journal articles on this topic have appeared. These studies have advanced our knowledge of this topic, and our study builds on this foundation laid by earlier work. However, most of the existing studies are narrowly focused, as one would expect from scholarly journal articles, and several aspects of this topic have not been studied. Our aim in this book has been to provide a broad and comprehensive treatment of the role that voter perceptions of candidate character traits play in presidential elections, relying on three decades of survey data on the American electorate. Furthermore, we believe that the discussion of this topic by media pundits is often misleading, so we have tried to show when interpretations in the popular media are unsupported by survey data on voter perceptions and attitudes. The findings of this study can be distilled down to five basic sets of conclusions, which we summarize below.

VOTERS ASSESS THE CHARACTER OF
PRESIDENTIAL CANDIDATES

Voters readily form perceptions of the character traits of presidential candidates, and the traits that they see as relevant can be conceptualized as falling along four basic dimensions: leadership, competence, integrity, and empathy. In Chapter 2, we define these dimensions in some depth, identifying the components of each. This conceptualization matches that developed by other political scientists, and our analysis of the data indicates that it describes the structure of trait perceptions quite well. While these four trait dimensions are interrelated, they are distinct dimensions. Candidates often are evaluated quite differently on these four dimensions by the voters. Bill Clinton, for example, was seen by the voters as high in empathy but low in integrity in both 1992 and 1996. Similarly, George W. Bush was judged to be a strong leader in 2000 and 2004, but in both years he was seen as weak in knowledge and intelligence, two key aspects of the competence dimension.

Another potential character trait dimension, warmth or personal likability, is frequently cited by media pundits as crucial, but our analysis of survey data for presidential elections from 1980 on shows that most voters do not consider personal warmth to be an important character trait. A related trait, elitism, also is often mentioned by pundits as important; presidential candidates who are too elitist supposedly are unable to relate to the common person and therefore suffer at the polls as a result. We find little evidence to support this contention either. We find that voters focus more on traits that are relevant to being a good president than many pundits give voters credit for, even if the voters assess these traits in a very subjective manner. Voters do not, as some commentators suggest, behave as though they are voting for their high school class president.

Voters are concerned about the empathy of presidential candidates. This character trait dimension has been ignored by many media pundits and even some scholarly studies. Unlike the other trait dimensions, empathy appears to have a strong underlying policy component, rather than being a judgment solely about an individual's personal compassion. Voters seem to assess empathy largely in terms of the policies proposed and the groups that are favored by the candidates. Candidates who champion policies that ostensibly benefit business and upper-income groups usually rank low on empathy in the eyes of the voters. Candidates who support government action to help those who are economically less well-off score higher. These judgments usually have a strong partisan component. Democratic candidates are presumed to care more about the average person, so they are seen as more empathetic. Simply professing to care about people in personal terms does not earn a candidate a high empathy rating. Nor does simply being a down-to-earth person with a common touch. Some media commentators have concluded in past elections that a presidential candidate who seemed to have that quality was perceived by the voters as the one who could relate to their problems. This was the view that some pundits had of G. W. Bush, especially compared to his supposedly elitist opponents in 2000 and 2004, Al Gore and John Kerry. The data do not support this conclusion, however. In both elections, the candidate thought to be cold and aloof was seen by the voters as more empathetic. Although the mass media failed to recognize the nature and significance of empathy sufficiently in the past, that changed in the most recent presidential contests, and many journalists wrote and talked about it in 2012. Their observations and interpretations were accurate: Mitt Romney did very poorly on empathy, providing President Barack Obama with a great advantage on this character trait.

On a more general note, our analysis of the data shows that media pundits frequently are mistaken about how the candidates are perceived by the voters in personal terms. They sometimes believe that one candidate has a sizable advantage on character traits, when the available survey data show that this is not the case. This often comes from concluding that the candidate who is leading in the pre-election polls must be the candidate who the voters think more highly of in personal terms. Sometimes it comes from extrapolating overall character judgments from performance on one dimension, assuming, for example, that because voters think one candidate is the stronger leader, they must think that candidate to be superior in overall personal terms to his or her opponent. Commentators sometimes even incorrectly estimate how specific traits are assessed by the voters, believing, for example, that the voters find one candidate to be weak on a particular trait, at least compared to his or her opponent, when in fact no such disadvantage exists, or if it does exist, it is far weaker than what is claimed to be the case. For example, Gore was described by the media in 2000 as someone who was quite willing to bend the truth to make himself look good, yet the survey data show that voters rated him only slightly behind Bush in integrity. Similarly, Michael Dukakis was portrayed as a weak leader by the media in 1988, but ANES respondents rated him no weaker than George H. W. Bush on leadership. Thus, we need to rely on survey data to obtain an accurate picture of how candidate character traits are perceived by the voters. What might seem likely from observing the candidates, the claims of their campaigns, and then anticipating how voters will respond to these influences may not be true. Of course, sometimes the popular characterizations of the candidates accurately describe how the voters see them: Clinton was judged by the voters to be weak on integrity in 1992 and 1996, the younger Bush was seen as lacking in knowledge in 2000 and 2004, and Romney was seen as not understanding the problems faced by ordinary Americans in 2012, just as most commentators thought in each case.

CANDIDATE CHARACTER TRAITS MATTER TO VOTERS

Voters do not just perceive character traits of presidential candidates. They use these trait perceptions in deciding which candidate they will vote for. Some scholars have dismissed character trait perceptions as rationalizations of the vote, not attitudes that truly affect the vote, and that may be one reason why character trait perceptions have not received more study. However, our analysis indicates that these perceptions are not mere rationalizations of the vote. Some vote rationalization occurs, but it also is clear that substantial direct effects of trait perceptions on the vote exist. These empirical findings make theoretical sense. Given the amount of attention that both media commentators and political actors give to character traits during a campaign, along with the ease with which voters are able to form perceptions of the candidates, it would be surprising if assessments of character traits did not affect the vote.

While these perceptions influence the vote, they do not determine it. Being seen as the better presidential candidate in personal terms is an advantage, but it does not ensure victory. Pundits often conclude that the losing candidate must be seen in less favorable personal terms, which is one reason why political commentators sometimes have a mistaken image of how the voters assess the candidates. However, presidential candidates have won despite being at a disadvantage on character traits. Clinton won reelection in 1996 even though the voters thought more highly of Bob Dole's personal traits, and the senior Bush won in 1988 even though Dukakis was seen as slightly better on character traits. In some elections, however, character traits have contributed significantly to a candidate's victory. In 2012, for example, Obama had a sizable advantage over Romney on character traits, which clearly helped him narrowly win reelection. Even being just even with the opponent on character traits may contribute to a candidate winning election. The younger Bush was only even with both of his Democratic opponents on overall perceptions of character traits in 2000 and 2004. Bush's advantage on leadership was balanced by Gore's and Kerry's advantages on competence and empathy. However, had Bush been seen by the voters as worse than his opponents on character traits, he might have failed to win the narrow elections that he did. In that sense, voter perceptions of the character traits of the candidates always influence the outcome of a presidential election.

Leadership and empathy tend to be the most important traits to voters. The Republican candidate usually has an advantage on leadership, although there have been exceptions during the time period we examine. Empathy has been owned by Democrats without exception, largely because they are seen by most voters as the party that favors economic policies that benefit average citizens. Competence tends to be the least important trait to voters, although perceptions of a candidate's competence may affect perceptions of leadership, giving competence an indirect effect on the vote. Integrity seems to have been less important to voters in recent elections than in the 1980s or 1990s, a possible result of twice electing Clinton, who was considered to be a successful president by a majority of Americans, even though many harbored doubts about his integrity. Neither party appears to have a natural advantage on competence or integrity. While Clinton received extremely low marks for integrity, other Democrats did fine on this trait. Bush did poorly on competence in both 2000 and 2004, but voters perceived most other Republicans as knowledgeable and intelligent.

While leadership and empathy tend to be the most important traits to voters, the impact of each trait on voting varies across elections. Leadership has been more important in some years than in others. The same is true for empathy. The importance of integrity to the voters also has changed across elections. Variation in the importance that voters attach to individual traits helps explain election outcomes. A candidate benefits when the traits that he is most advantaged on are the ones that voters care the most about and when the traits that he is disadvantaged on are the ones of least concern to the voters. For example, voters did not rely much on their perceptions of integrity in choosing between the presidential candidates in 1996, but they seemed very responsive to perceptions of empathy. This worked to the benefit of Clinton, since he was seen as better than Dole on empathy, but much worse on integrity. The variation in the importance of particular traits across elections points to the need to be cautious about generalizing about trait effects from the analysis of a single election. Just because a particular trait, such as integrity, is important to voters in one election does not mean that it usually is. All of this leads to the question of why certain traits are more important to the voters in some elections rather than in others, a question that is beyond the scope of this study, but one worthy of future investigation.

Perceptions of candidate character traits do not influence all voters equally. Independents are much more affected than strong partisans. Independents, of course, tend to have a mix of political attitudes that do not push them strongly in either partisan direction. Therefore, if they see one presidential candidate as superior to the other on character traits, this can determine their vote. Strong partisans are far less affected. Even in those rare instances when strong Democrats or strong Republicans see the candidate of the other party as better in personal terms, they are still reluctant to vote for that candidate; strong partisans simply have too many other reasons to support their party's candidate. However, when partisans do defect in their presidential vote, which is more likely in the case of weak partisans, perceptions of the character traits of the candidates usually make a strong contribution to this decision.

Perhaps in contradiction to conventional wisdom, there is little evidence that voters who are less educated or less politically sophisticated are more likely to cast their ballot on the basis of candidate character traits. Those who are more educated, more politically aware, and more politically sophisticated rely on trait perceptions in their vote decision just as much as those who are less educated or politically aware. Of course, it may be that more educated or more politically sophisticated voters form their trait perceptions on the basis of more information and a richer political schema, but it is not the case that these voters eschew character traits and vote instead on the basis of public policy issues.

CANDIDATE CHARACTER TRAIT PERCEPTIONS
VARY ACROSS ELECTIONS

The way in which voters perceive the personal traits of the presidential candidates does not merely track who wins and who loses. If this were true, the victorious George H. W. Bush and Bill Clinton would have been held in much higher esteem by voters relative to their opponents in 1988 and 1996, but this was far from the case. Furthermore, while fundamental political attitudes such as party identification and ideological orientation are important influences on trait perceptions, they do not determine them. This is clear from the fact that the assessments of the character traits of the presidential candidates often shift considerably from one election to the next, even though little change has taken place in the basic political orientations of the electorate. Thus, voter perceptions of the character traits of the presidential candidates should not be dismissed as nothing more than reflections of underlying partisan and ideological bias.

The overall advantage that one party's candidate has on trait perceptions changes from one election to the next. In some years the Democratic nominee's character is more highly regarded; in other years, the Republican's character is; other years are a wash. For example, in 2004, the two candidates were rated about even overall on character traits; eight years later, Romney was seen as much worse than Obama. The same candidate can be perceived differently from one election to the next. Obama was assessed by the voters less favorably in 2012 than he was in 2008; fortunately for him, Romney was seen much less favorably than McCain was in 2008, so Obama still retained a sizable advantage on character traits despite the decline in the favorability of perceptions of his character. Clearly, the candidates, campaigns, and election circumstances affect how the voters assess character traits.

Sometimes the advantage as revealed by the data does not match the conventional wisdom generated by the pundits' accounts of the race. In particular, a number of Democratic candidates over the course of this study have been derided as aloof, elitist, know-it-alls whose personalities cost them votes, and possibly even the election. Yet our analysis suggests that voters—unlike the media—put little stock in personal warmth as an important qualification for the presidency. Furthermore, media commentators may correctly estimate how the candidates are seen on one dimension of character traits, but then erroneously conclude that one candidate's advantage on that dimension makes him or her the better candidate across all dimensions. Thus while, for example, the leadership abilities of Gore and Kerry were not viewed especially favorably by voters, as the pundits claimed, both Democratic candidates had advantages on empathy and competence, which resulted in their performing no worse on the overall candidate trait index than their common Republican opponent, George W. Bush.

Not only does the overall character trait index vary across elections, but so do perceptions of the individual traits that form the index in any given year. The Democratic candidate is always seen as more empathetic, but the size of that advantage has varied from Clinton's and Obama's sizable advantages in 1996 and 2008, respectively, to Gore's much narrower lead in 2000. The Republican candidate often enjoys a substantial advantage regarding which candidate is likely to be the stronger leader, but there have been exceptions. Moreover, Democrats tend to do better on other aspects of the leadership dimension, such as being inspiring and optimistic. There are no overall partisan advantages on integrity or competence, but in individual years we have seen sizable candidate effects that have led to large gaps in perceptions of these traits. The integrity-challenged Clinton and the younger Bush's perceived shortcomings regarding knowledge and intelligence, two components of competence, come to mind in this regard.

CANDIDATE CHARACTER TRAIT PERCEPTIONS ARE AFFECTED BY POLITICAL ATTITUDES

The perceptions that voters have of candidate character traits vary considerably across elections, but within each election, these perceptions are strongly influenced by several basic political attitudes. Party identification and ideology shape the subjective judgments that voters make about the candidates. Partisan ideologues are more likely than any other type of voter to see their party's candidate as superior across the range of character traits, which provides them with yet another reason to pull the lever for that person. Nevertheless, partisanship does not determine trait perceptions. In any election, some partisans see the candidate of the opposite party as better on character than their party's candidate. About 10 percent of Republicans felt that way about Obama and Romney in 2012, for example. Similar percentages of the supporters of one of the parties holding such discordant views of the candidates are found in other years.

Retrospective assessments of the president's handling of his job also are important influences on trait perceptions, especially when the incumbent is on the ballot. Voters who think that the president has performed poorly in office are less likely to favorably assess his character, especially regarding leadership and competence. This effect holds true even when the voter's party identification and ideological orientation is taken into account, and it helps to explain why some partisans do not view their party's candidate as better on character traits. In 1992, for example, Republicans who disapproved of Bush's performance as president were less likely to see him in favorable personal terms, especially regarding leadership. Even when the term-limited sitting president is not on the ballot, his successor will enjoy an advantage or bear the burden of public perceptions of the incumbent. In 2008, voters' performance evaluations of President Bush influenced their assessments of John McCain's character. Given that the outgoing president was politically toxic at the time, these unfavorable retrospective evaluations of Bush's handling of the economy and national security imposed a penalty on McCain, despite the fact that McCain's and Bush's fraught relationship distanced them from each other about as far as a president and a presidential candidate of the same party could be.

Issue positions can also affect judgments of candidate character, particularly on issues salient to the voter and in the more exceptional cases when these positions do not accord with party identification and ideology. For example, support for or opposition to social safety net programs may particularly influence perceptions of empathy, which in turn affect the overall trait assessment of a candidate. Long-standing differences in the images of the two parties on social welfare issues help to explain why Democratic presidential candidates begin the election with an advantage on empathy. Similarly, the candidates' stands on any number of specific issues, from war and peace to guns and capital punishment may influence voter perceptions of qualities associated with leadership. The effect that issues have on perceptions of character traits for any individual voter may be complex, given individual differences in how voters stand on these issues. A voter who is strongly anti-abortion might judge a candidate who takes that position to be high in morality, but the same response is unlikely to be found in a voter who has the opposite view on abortion, for example.

Finally, because evaluations of a candidate's personal traits are, ultimately, quite subjective, factors unique to a given election are important. Voters learn about each candidate's background and experience. They evaluate a candidate's demeanor in such settings as debate performances and interviews. The campaign in general and the competing advertising strategies in particular inform character-based judgments given that modern, highly personalized campaigns are quick to point out their candidate's abundant personal strengths, while contrasting these with the vast, potentially dangerous personal shortcomings of their opponent. These candidate-specific factors are significant. If they were not, there would not be such variation across elections in the perceptions of the character of the candidates. Unfortunately, it is not easy to identify the relevant factors and to predict how they will play out in an election, suggesting another area for future research.

MEDIA CONSUMPTION MAY AFFECT HOW VOTERS USE CHARACTER TRAITS

Perceptions of candidate character traits exert a strong overall influence on the vote in presidential elections. However, our analysis leads us to conclude that the type of media voters consume can affect the degree to which they rely on their candidate character trait evaluations. We find evidence to support the hypothesis that the personalized and dramatized nature of television campaign coverage leads to greater reliance on candidate character traits. The heaviest consumers of television campaign news are more affected by their perceptions of candidate character. Low and moderate television viewers differ only slightly in the degree to which they vote based on personal traits, so some threshold level needs to be reached before this effect develops. Moreover, this finding does not depend on age or education. On the other hand, no differences in reliance on character traits exist for the fast-dwindling number of voters who consume newspaper coverage of the campaign. There is little variation in the degree to which voters rely on trait perceptions across all levels of print consumption, which suggests that while heavy newspaper readership does not encourage reliance on traits, neither does it stimulate issue voting relative to voting based on personality assessments.

While television encourages personality-driven voting, increased Internet usage leads to less reliance on character traits as a factor in the vote decision. Also in contrast to our findings for television, the nature of this effect depends on age and education. Only small differences exist in respondents' reliance on character traits at varying levels of Internet usage for older and less educated voters. Conversely, younger and more educated voters are far less likely to rely on their trait perceptions as their Internet use increases. One way to interpret these findings is to claim that the Internet has accomplished what newspapers have not by encouraging voting that is less likely to be personality driven. The less sanguine interpretation is that more partisan, more ideological voters are drawn to the Internet not necessarily to learn about the issues that distinguish the candidates, but to enter the echo chamber populated by fellow partisans.

IMPLICATIONS FOR FUTURE RESEARCH

Although we have analyzed survey data for many elections and have investigated a variety of topics, many questions remain unanswered, so we conclude with some suggestions for future research on this topic. One question that we have involves the effect of the high levels of partisan polarization that now characterize the American political system: are candidate character trait perceptions likely to have less influence on the vote than in the past? It seems plausible that this could be the case. In a more polarized electorate, fewer voters are up for grabs. Fewer partisans can be convinced to defect and vote for the candidate of the other party because that candidate has the superior presidential character. Illustrating this point, defection rates in the last three presidential elections were low; 90 percent or more of Democrats and Republicans stayed loyal to their party in each election. Of course, in these elections, independents were fairly evenly divided in their vote, and they are the voters who are most influenced by their perceptions of the character traits of the presidential candidates. Moreover, even though defection rates were low, some partisans were convinced to vote for the opposing party's candidate, and perceptions of the character traits of the candidates influenced these decisions. In a close election, the effects on independents and the small number of partisans who are persuadable can be decisive. It could be argued that such was the case in 2012. Given the ambiguity of the data on this point, it seems worthwhile to examine the role of candidate character traits in future presidential elections.

Another question that we have is whether it will be more difficult in future elections for any presidential candidate to be seen in the quite positive personal terms that Ronald Reagan realized, or even, to a lesser extent, that losing candidates such as Dukakis and Dole managed. Neither Obama nor Romney was assessed very favorably in 2012, although Romney came out substantially worse. Perhaps that outcome resulted from factors unique to the candidates and circumstances of that election. However, it might reflect more fundamental changes in American politics, particularly the increase in partisan polarization, the decline of civility in political discourse, the fragmentation of the media in general, and the increased partisan and ideological tone of certain outlets in particular. All of this may produce an electorate that is more negative toward the other party, or perhaps toward both parties, and one that receives more hostile information about one, if not both, of the two major-party candidates. If presidential candidates have little hope of being seen in positive personal terms by the supporters of the other party, then even if candidates are assessed quite favorably by the supporters of their party, the best they will be able to do is receive mixed evaluations. If this is the case, it would have implications for presidential campaigns, potentially shifting them even more in the direction of mobilizing supporters as opposed to persuading the shrinking number of persuadable voters. Moreover, this would also have consequences for the ability of the new president to govern, as the possibility of achieving high levels of public approval for a sustained amount of time beyond rather brief rally effects diminishes. We hesitate to read too much into the 2012 election, but it does seem to be a possibility that future research could examine.

A third question is how new patterns of media consumption will affect how voters perceive the character traits of the presidential candidates and how they will use these perceptions in their vote decision. Just as pundits and campaign professionals grapple with understanding the effects of new media on elections, so must scholars. The rise of television clearly focused popular attention on candidates as the focal points of presidential campaigns. The Internet has the potential to permit people to actively access more substantive, issue-based information about the candidates, as opposed to remaining passive receptors of image-based advertising and broadcast news reports. However, it seems increasingly apparent that the way in which people use the Internet—to confirm pre-existing biases rather than avail themselves of contrary points of view—may well frustrate the medium's latent benefits. While we have found evidence to suggest that certain types of heavy Internet users rely less on their perceptions of character traits in deciding their votes, our survey data give us little purchase as to why this is. Laboratory experiments or surveys that embed within them experimental methods seem to be fruitful avenues for future research on the Internet and the personalization hypothesis.

A final question for future research is what factors associated with an election influence the importance of each trait dimension in the voters' minds and affect how the candidates are assessed by the voters on character traits. Why, for example, are voters more influenced by perceptions of the leadership ability of the candidates in some elections than in others? Why do some candidates receive more favorable character assessments than do others? The data that we examine in this study are inadequate to answer these questions, as we pointed out in earlier chapters. At best, we are able to suggest some possibilities. Nevertheless, these are important questions, and the answers could tell us a great deal about electoral politics. The variation across elections in how candidates are perceived undoubtedly is the result of a number of factors: the characteristics of the candidates themselves; the nature of the campaigns that are waged; the way that the media cover the campaign, and the recent events and circumstances in the country that voters see as relevant. Understanding the effects of these factors should be both interesting and informative.

Bibliography

Abramowitz, Alan I. *The Disappearing Center.* New Haven, CT: Yale University Press, 2010.

Abramson, Paul R., John H. Aldrich, and David W. Rohde. *Change and Continuity in the 1980 Elections.* Washington, DC: Congressional Quarterly Press, 1982.

Abramson, Paul R., John H. Aldrich, and David W. Rohde. *Change and Continuity in the 1988 Elections.* Washington, DC: CQ Press, 1989.

Abramson, Paul R., John H. Aldrich, and David W. Rohde. *Change and Continuity in the 1996 Elections.* Washington, DC: Congressional Quarterly Press, 1998.

Abramson, Paul R., John H. Aldrich, and David W. Rohde. *Change and Continuity in the 2008 and 2010 Elections.* Washington, DC: Congressional Quarterly Press, 2012.

Alvarez, R. Michael. *Information and Elections.* Ann Arbor: University of Michigan Press, 1997.

Ansolabehere, Stephen, and Shanto Iyengar. *Going Negative: How Political Advertisements Shrink and Polarize the Electorate.* New York: Free Press, 1995.

Arterton, F. Christopher. "Campaign '92: Strategies and Tactics." In *The Election of 1992,* edited by Gerald M. Pomper, 74–109. Chatham, NJ: Chatham House Publishers, 1993.

Baker, Ross K. "The Outlook for the Carter Administration." In *The Election of 1976,* edited by Gerald M. Pomper, 115–146. New York: David McKay Company, 1977.

Balz, Dan. *Collision 2012: Obama vs. Romney and the Future of Elections in America.* New York: Viking, 2013.

Barber, James David. *The Presidential Character.* Englewood Cliffs, NJ: Prentice-Hall, 1972.

Barilleaux, Ryan J., and Randall E. Adkins. "The Nominations: Process and Patterns." In *The Elections of 1992,* edited by Michael Nelson, 21–56. Washington, DC: CQ Press, 1993.

Bartels, Larry M. "Partisanship and Voting Behavior, 1952–1996." *American Journal of Political Science* 44 (2000): 35–50.

Bartels, Larry M. "The Impact of Candidate Traits in American Presidential Elections." In *Leaders' Personalities and the Outcomes of Democratic Elections,* edited by Anthony King, 44–69. Oxford: Oxford University Press, 2002.

Bennett, W. Lance. *News: The Politics of Illusion,* 9th edition. Boston: Longman, 2012.

Bennett, W. Lance, Regina G. Lawrence, and Steven Livingston. *When the Press Fails.* Chicago: University of Chicago Press, 2008.

Bishin, Benjamin G., Daniel Stevens, and Christian Wilson. "Character Counts: Honesty and Fairness in Election 2000." *Public Opinion Quarterly* 70 (2006): 235–248.

Box-Steffensmeier, Janet M., and Steven E. Schier, eds. *The American Elections of 2008.* Lanham, MD: Rowman and Littlefield, 2009.

Brame, Robert, Raymond Paternoster, Paul Mazerolle, and Alex Piquero. "Testing for the Equality of Maximum-Likelihood Regression Coefficients Between Two Independent Equations." *Journal of Quantitative Criminology* 14 (1998): 245–261.

Brands, H. W. *TR: The Last Romantic.* New York: Basic Books, 1997.

Burnham, Walter Dean. "Bill Clinton: Riding the Tiger." In *The Election of 1996,* edited by Gerald M. Pomper, 1–20. Chatham, NJ: Chatham House Publishers, 1997.

Burton, Michael John. "The Republican Primary Season: Strategic Positioning in the GOP Field." In *Campaigning for President 2012,* edited by Dennis W. Johnson, 43–55. New York: Routledge, 2014.

Campbell, Angus, Philip E. Converse, Warren E. Miller, and Donald E. Stokes. *The American Voter.* New York: John Wiley, 1960.

Campbell, James E. "Candidate Image Evaluations: Influence and Rationalization in Presidential Primaries." *American Politics Quarterly* 11 (1983): 293–313.

Campbell, James E. "A First Party-Term Incumbent Survives: The Fundamentals of 2012." In *Barack Obama and the New America,* edited by Larry J. Sabato, 59–74. Lanham, MD: Rowman and Littlefield, 2013.

Cappella, Joseph, and Kathleen Hall Jamieson. *Spiral of Cynicism: The Press and the Public Good.* New York: Oxford University Press, 1997.

Carmines, Edward G., and James A. Stimson. "The Two Faces of Issue Voting." *American Political Science Review* 74 (1980): 78–91.

Ceaser, James, and Andrew Busch. *Upside Down and Inside Out: The 1992 Elections and American Politics.* Lanham, MD: Rowman and Littlefield Publishers, 1993.

Ceaser, James W., and Andrew E. Busch. *Losing to Win: The 1996 Elections and American Politics.* Lanham, MD: Rowman and Littlefield Publishers, 1993.

Ceaser, James W., and Andrew E. Busch. *The Perfect Tie: The True Story of the 2000 Presidential Election.* New York: Rowman & Littlefield Publishers, 2001.

Ceaser, James W., and Andrew E. Busch, *Red Over Blue: The 2004 Elections and American Politics.* Lanham, MD: Rowman & Littlefield Publishers, 2005.

Ceaser, James W., and Andrew E. Busch. *The Perfect Tie: The True Story of the 2000 Presidential Election.* Lanham, MD: Rowman and Littlefield, 2001.

Ceaser, James W., Andrew E. Busch, and John J. Pitney, Jr. *Epic Journey: The 2008 Elections and American Politics.* Lanham, MD: Rowman and Littlefield, 2009.

Conley, Patricia. "The Presidential Race of 2004: Strategy, Outcome, and Mandate." In *A Defining Moment: The Presidential Election of 2004,* edited by William J. Crotty, 108–135. Armonk, NY: M. E. Sharpe, 2005.

Conover, Pamela J. "Political Cues and the Perception of Candidates." *American Politics Quarterly* 9 (1981): 427–448.

Cook, Timothy. *Governing With the News,* 2nd edition. Chicago: University of Chicago Press, 2005.

Crotty, William J., ed. *Winning the Presidency 2008.* Boulder, CO: Paradigm Publishers, 2009.

Dallek, Robert. *Nixon and Kissinger.* New York: HarperCollins Publishers, 2007.

Davis, Richard. "Interplay: Political Blogging and Journalism." In *iPolitics: Citizens, Elections, and Governing in the New Media Era,* edited by Richard L. Fox and Jennifer M. Ramos, 76–102. New York: Cambridge University Press, 2011.

Doherty, Kathryn M., and James G. Gimple. "Candidate Character vs. the Economy in the 1992 Election." *Political Behavior* 19 (1997): 177–196.

Downie, Leonard, Jr., and Robert G. Kaiser. *The News About the News: American Journalism in Peril.* New York: Vintage Books, 2002.

Druckman, James N. "The Power of Television Images: The First Kennedy-Nixon Debate Revisited." *Journal of Politics* 65 (2003): 559–571.

Druckman, James N. "Media Matters: How Newspapers and Television News Cover Campaigns and Influence Voters." *Political Communication,* 22 (2005): 463–481.

Farrah, Barbara G., and Ethel Klein. "Public Opinion Trends." In *The Election of 1988,* edited by Gerald M. Pomper, 103–128. Chatham, NJ: Chatham House Publishers, 1989.

Fiorina, Morris P. *Retrospective Voting in American National Elections.* New Haven, CT: Yale University Press, 1981.

Frankovic, Kathleen A. "Public Opinion Trends." In *The Election of 1980,* edited by Gerald M. Pomper, 97–118. Chatham, NJ: Chatham House Publishers, 1981.

Funk, Carolyn L. "The Impact of Scandal on Candidate Evaluations: An Experimental Test of the Role of Candidate Traits." *Political Behavior* 18 (1996): 1–24.

Funk, Carolyn L. "Understanding Trait Inferences in Candidate Images." In *Research in Micropolitics: Rethinking Rationality,* vol. 5, edited by Michael X. Delli Carpini, Leonie Huddy, and Robert Y. Shapiro, 97–123. Greenwich, CT: JAI, 1996.

Funk, Carolyn L. "Implications of Political Expertise in Candidate Trait Evaluations." *Political Research Quarterly* 50 (1997): 675–697.

Funk, Carolyn L. "Bringing the Candidate into Models of Candidate Evaluation." *Journal of Politics* 61 (1999): 700–720.

Gant, Michael M. "Citizens' Evaluations of 1980 Presidential Candidates: Influence of Campaign Strategies." *American Politics Quarterly* 11 (1983): 327–348.

Glasgow, Garrett, and R. Michael Alvarez. "Uncertainty and Candidate Personality Traits." *American Politics Quarterly* 28 (2000): 26–49.

Glass, David P. "Evaluating Presidential Candidates: Who Focuses on Their Personal Attributes?" *Public Opinion Quarterly* 49 (1985): 517–534.

Goodwin, Doris Kearns. *No Ordinary Time.* New York: Simon & Schuster, 1994.

Goren, Paul. "Character Weakness, Partisan Bias, and Presidential Evaluation." *American Journal of Political Science* 46 (2002): 627–641.

Goren, Paul. "Character Weakness, Partisan Bias, and Presidential Evaluation: Modifications and Extensions." *Political Behavior* 29 (2007): 305–326.

Graber, Doris A.. "Seeing is Remembering: How Visuals Contribute to Learning from Television News." *Journal of Communication* 40 (1990): 134–155.

Graber, Doris A. *Processing Politics: Learning from Television in the Internet Age.* Chicago: University of Chicago Press, 2001.

Green, Donald, Bradley Palmquist, and Eric Schickler, *Partisan Hearts and Minds.* New Haven, CT: Yale University Press, 2002.

Greene, Steven. "The Role of Character Assessments in Presidential Approval." *American Politics Research* 29 (2001): 196–210.

Hart, Roderick P. *Seducing America.* Thousand Oaks, CA: Sage Publications, 1999.

Hayes, Danny. "Candidate Qualities through a Partisan Lens: A Theory of Trait Ownership." *American Journal of Political Science* 49 (2005): 908–923.

Hayes, Danny. "Has Television Personalized Voting Behavior?" *Political Behavior* 31 (2009): 231–260.

Hayes, Danny. "The News Anew? Political Coverage in a Transformed Media Age." In *New Directions in Media and Politics,* edited by Travis N. Ridout, 193–209. New York: Routledge, 2013.

Hellweg, Susan A. "Campaigns and Candidate Images in American Presidential Elections." In *Candidate Images in Presidential Elections,* edited by Kenneth L. Hacker, 1–17. Westport, CT: Praeger, 1995.

Hellweg, Susan A., Michael Pfau, and Steven R. Brydon. *Televised Presidential Debates.* New York: Praeger, 1992.

Hershey, Marjorie Randon. "The Campaign and the Media." In *The Election of 1988,* edited by Gerald M. Pomper, 73–102. Chatham, NJ: Chatham House Publishers, 1989.

Hershey, Marjorie Randon. "The Campaign and the Media." In *The Election of 2000,* edited by Gerald M. Pomper, 46–72. Washington, DC: CQ Press, 2001.

Hetherington, Marc J. "The Election: How the Campaign Mattered." In *The Elections of 2012,* edited by Michael Nelson, 47–72. Thousand Oaks, CA: CQ Press, 2013.

Hibbs, Douglas A., Jr. *The American Political Economy: Macroeconomics and Electoral Politics.* Cambridge, MA: Harvard University Press, 1987.

Hillygus, D. Sunshine, and Todd G. Shields. *The Persuadable Voter.* Princeton, NJ: Princeton University Press, 2008.

Holian, David B., and Charles Prysby. "Determinants of Voter Perceptions of Candidate Personal Traits, 1992–2004." Paper presented at the annual meeting of the Midwest Political Science Association, Chicago, IL, April 3–5, 2008.

Holian, David B., and Charles Prysby. "Character First: Rethinking John McCain's 2008 Campaign Strategy." *American Review of Politics* 32 (2012): 318–342.

Iyengar, Shanto. *Is Anyone Responsible? How Television Frames Political Issues.* Chicago: University of Chicago Press, 1991.

Jackson, John E. "Issues, Party Choices, and Presidential Votes," *American Journal of Political Science* 19 (1975): 161–185.

Jacobs, Lawrence R., and Robert Y. Shapiro. "Issues, Candidate Image, and Priming: The Use of Private Polls in Kennedy's 1960 Presidential Campaign." *American Political Science Review* 88 (1994): 527–540.

Jacobson, Gary C. *A Uniter, Not a Divider: George W. Bush and the American People.* New York: Pearson Longman, 2007.

Just, Marion R. "Candidate Strategies and the Media Campaign." In *The Election of 1996,* edited by Gerald M. Pomper, 77–106. Chatham, NJ: Chatham House Publishers, 1997.

Kaid, Lynda Lee, and Mike Chanslor. "Changing Candidate Images: The Effects of Political Advertising." In *Candidate Images in Presidential Elections,* edited by Kenneth L. Hacker, 83–97. Westport, CT: Praeger, 1995.

Kearns, Doris. *Lyndon Johnson and the American Dream.* New York: Harper & Row, 1976.

Keeter, Scott. "The Illusion of Intimacy: Television and the Role of Candidate Personal Qualities in Voter Choice." *Public Opinion Quarterly* 51 (1987): 344–358.

Kenney, Patrick J., and Tom W. Rice. "Presidential Prenomination Preferences and Candidate Evaluations." *American Political Science Review* 82 (1988): 1309–1319.

Kenski, Kate, Bruce W. Hardy, and Kathleen Hall Jamieson. *The Obama Victory: How Media, Money, and Message Shaped the 2008 Election.* Oxford: Oxford University Press, 2010.

Kiewiet, D. Roderick. *Macroeconomics and Micropolitics: The Electoral Effects of Economic Issues.* Chicago: University of Chicago Press, 1983.

Kilburn, H. Whitt. "Does the Candidate Really Matter?" *American Politics Research* 33 (2005): 335–356.

Kinder, Donald R. "Presidential Character Revisited." In *Political Cognition,* edited by Richard R. Lau and David O. Sears, 233–255. Hillsdale, NJ: Lawrence Erlbaum, 1986.

Kinder, Donald R., Mark D. Peters, Robert P. Abelson, and Susan T. Fiske. "Presidential Prototypes." *Political Behavior* 2 (1980): 315–337.

King, Gary. *Unifying Political Methodology.* Cambridge: Cambridge University Press, 1989.

Knoke, David, and George W. Bohrnstedt, *Statistics for Social Data Analysis,* 3rd edition. Itasca, IL: F. E. Peacock, 1994.

Knuckey, Jonathan. "Racial Resentment and Vote Choice in the 2008 U.S. Presidential Election." *Politics & Policy* 39 (2011): 559–582.

Lang, Kurt, and Gladys Engel Lang. *Television and Politics.* New Brunswick, NJ: Transaction Publishers, 2002.

Lau, Richard R. "Political Schemata, Candidate Evaluations, and Voting Behavior," In *Political Cognition,* edited by Richard R. Lau and David O. Sears, 95–126. Hillsdale, NJ: Lawrence Erlbaum, 1986.

Lewis-Beck, Michael S., William G. Jacoby, Helmut Norpoth, and Herbert F. Weisberg. *The American Voter Revisited.* Ann Arbor: University of Michigan Press, 2008.

Lewis-Beck, Michael S., Charles Tien, and Richard Nadeau. "Obama's Missed Landslide: A Racial Cost?" *PS: Political Science and Politics* 43 (2010): 69–76.

Lodge, Milton, Kathleen M. McGraw, and Patrick Stroh. "An Impression-driven Model of Candidate Evaluation." *American Political Science Review* 83 (1989): 399–419.

Lodge, Milton, and Patrick Stroh. "Inside the Mental Voting Booth: An Impression-Driven Process Model of Candidate Evaluation." In *Explorations in Political Psychology,* edited by Shanto Iyengar and William J. McGuire, 225–263. Durham: Duke University Press, 1993.

MacKuen, Michael B., Robert S. Erikson, and James A. Stimson. "Peasants or Bankers? The American Electorate and the U.S. Economy." *American Political Science Review* 86 (1992): 597–611.

Manjoo, Farhad. *True Enough: Learning to Live in a Post-Fact Society.* Hoboken, NJ: John Wiley and Sons, 2008.

Maraniss, David. *First in His Class: A Biography of Bill Clinton.* New York: Simon & -Schuster, 1996.

Markus, Gregory B. "Political Attitudes during an Election Year." *American Political Science Review* 76 (1982): 538–560.

Markus, Gregory B., and Philip E. Converse. "A Dynamic Simultaneous Equation Model of Electoral Choice." *American Political Science Review* 73 (1979): 1055–1070.

McAllister, Ian. "The Personalization of Politics." In *The Oxford Handbook of Political Behavior,* edited by Russell J. Dalton and Hans-Dieter Klingemann, 571–588. Oxford: Oxford University Press, 2007.

McCann, James A. "Changing Electoral Contexts and Changing Candidate Images During the 1984 Presidential Campaign." *American Politics Quarterly* 18 (1990): 123–140.

McCombs, Max, R. Lance Holbert, Spiro Kiousis, and Wayne Wanta. *The News and Public Opinion: Media Effects on Civic Life.* Cambridge, UK: Polity Press, 2011.

McGraw, Kathleen M., Mark Fischle, Karen Stenner, and Milton Lodge. "What's in a Word? Bias in Trait Descriptions of Political Leaders." *Political Behavior* 18 (1996): 263–287.

McWilliams, Wilson Carey. "The Meaning of the Election." In *The Election of 2000,* edited by Gerald M. Pomper, 177–201. Chatham, NJ: Chatham House Publishers, 2001.

McWilliams, Wilson Carey. "The Meaning of the Election: Ownership and Citizenship in American Life." In *The Elections of 2004,* edited by Michael Nelson, 187–213. Washington, DC: CQ Press, 2005.

Merrill, Samuel III, and Bernard Grofman, *A Unified Theory of Voting.* Cambridge: Cambridge University Press, 1999.

Meyers, Lawrence S., Glenn Gamst, and A. J. Guarino, *Applied Multivariate Research.* Thousand Oaks, CA: Sage Publications, 2006.

Miller, Arthur H., Martin P. Wattenberg, and Oksana Malanchuk. "Schematic Assessments of Presidential Candidates." *American Political Science Review* 80 (1986): 521–540.

Miller, Warren E., and J. Merrill Shanks. *The New American Voter.* Cambridge: Harvard University Press, 1996.

Mondak, Jeffery J. *Nothing to Read: Newspapers and Elections in a Social Experiment.* Ann Arbor: University of Michigan Press, 1995.

Mutz, Diana C. "Effects of 'In-Your-Face' Television Discourse on Perceptions of a Legitimate Opposition." *American Political Science Review* 101 (2007): 621–635.

Nelson, Michael. "The Election: Turbulence and Tranquility in Contemporary American Politics." In *The Elections of 1996,* edited by Michael Nelson, 1–13. Washington, DC: CQ Press, 1997.

Nelson, Michael. "The Election: Ordinary Politics, Extraordinary Outcome." In *The Elections of 2000,* edited by Michael Nelson, 55–92. Washington, DC: CQ Press, 2001.

Nelson, Michael. "The Psychological Presidency." In *The Presidency and the Political System,* 10th ed., edited by Michael Nelson, 167–190. Washington, DC: CQ Press, 2014.

Neumann, W. Russell, Marion R. Just, and Ann R. Crigler. *Common Knowledge: News and the Construction of Political Meaning.* Chicago: University of Chicago Press, 1992.

Neustadt, Richard E. *Presidential Power and the Modern Presidents: The Politics of Leadership from Roosevelt to Reagan.* New York: Free Press, 1991.

Nimmo, Dan, and Robert L. Savage. *Candidates and Their Images.* Pacific Palisades, CA: Goodyear, 1976.

Orren, Gary R. "The Nomination Process: The Vicissitudes of Candidate Selection." In *The Elections of 1984,* edited by Michael Nelson, 27–82. Washington, DC: CQ Press, 1985.

Owen, Diana. "The Campaign and the Media." In *The American Elections of 2012,* edited by Janet M. Box-Steffensmeier and Steven E. Schier, 21–47. New York: Routledge, 2013.

Page, Benjamin I., and Richard A. Brody. "Policy Voting and the Electoral Process: The Vietnam War Issue." *American Political Science Review* 66 (1972): 979–995.

Page, Benjamin I., and Calvin C. Jones. "Reciprocal Effects of Policy Preferences, Party Loyalties, and the Vote." *American Political Science Review* 73 (1979): 1071–1089.

Patterson, Thomas E. *Out of Order.* New York: Alfred A. Knopf, 1993.

Petrocik, John R. "Issue Ownership in Presidential Elections, with a 1980 Case Study." *American Journal of Political Science* 40 (1996): 825–850.

Pfau, Michael, Jaeho Cho, and Kirsten Chong. "Communication Forms in U.S. Presidential Campaigns: Influences on Candidate Perceptions and the Democratic Process." *Harvard International Journal of Press/Politics* 6 (2001): 88–105.

Pierce, Patrick A. "Political Sophistication and the Use of Candidate Traits in Candidate Evaluation." *Political Psychology* 14 (1993): 21–35.

Piston, Spencer. "How Explicit Racial Prejudice Hurt Obama in the 2008 Election." *Political Behavior* 32 (2010): 431–451.

Plotkin, Henry A. "Issues in the Campaign." In *The Election of 1984,* edited by Gerald M. Pomper, 35–59. Chatham, NJ: Chatham House Publishers, 1985.

Pomper, Gerald M. "The Presidential Election: The Ills of American Politics After 9/11." In *The Elections of 2004,* edited by Michael Nelson, 42–68. Washington, DC: CQ Press, 2005.

Pomper, Gerald M. "The Presidential Election." In *The Elections of 2008,* edited by Michael Nelson, 45–73. Washington, DC: CQ Press, 2010.

Popkin, Samuel L. *The Reasoning Voter: Communication and Persuasion in Presidential Campaigns.* Chicago: University of Chicago Press, 1991.

Popkin, Samuel L. *What It Takes to Win—And Hold—the White House.* Oxford: Oxford University Press, 2012.

Price, Vincent, and John Zaller. "Who Gets The News? Alternative Measures of News Reception and Their Implications for Research." *Public Opinion Quarterly* 57 (1993): 133–164.

Prysby, Charles. "Perceptions of Candidate Character Traits and the Presidential Vote in 2004." *PS: Political Science and Politics* 41 (2008): 115–122.

Prysby, Charles. "Explaining the Presidential Vote" In *Winning the Presidency 2012,* edited by William J. Crotty, 116–125. Boulder, CO: Paradigm Publishers, 2013.

Prysby, Charles, and David B. Holian. "Perceptions of Candidate Personal Traits and Voting in Presidential Elections, 1996–2004." Paper presented at the annual meeting of the American Political Science Association, Chicago, IL, August 29 to September 2, 2007.

Prysby, Charles, and David B. Holian. "Studying Voter Perceptions of the Character Traits of Presidential Candidates: Methodological Questions and Problems." Paper presented at the annual meeting of the Southern Political Science Association, New Orleans, LA, January 5–8, 2011.

Prysby, Charles, and David B. Holian. "Candidate Character Traits in the 2012 Presidential Election." Paper presented at the annual meeting of the American Political Science Association, Chicago, August 29-September 1, 2013.

Prysby, Charles, and Carmine Scavo. "Who Hates Hillary? Public Opinion Toward the First Lady." *Politics and Policy* 29 (2001): 521–544.

Quirk, Paul J. "The Election." In *The Elections of 1988,* edited by Michael Nelson, 63–92. Washington, DC: CQ Press, 1989.

Quirk, Paul J., and Jon K. Dalager. "The 1992 Presidential Election: A 'New Democrat' and a New Kind of Presidential Campaign." In *The Elections of 1992,* edited by Michael Nelson, 57–88. Washington, DC: CQ Press, 1993.

Quirk, Paul J., and Sean C. Matheson. "The Election and the Prospects for Leadership." In *The Elections of 2000,* edited by Michael Nelson, 161–184. Washington, DC: CQ Press, 2001.

Rahn, Wendy, John H. Aldrich, Eugene Borgida, and John L. Sullivan. "A Social-Cognitive Model of Candidate Appraisal." In *Information and Democratic Processes,* edited by John A. Ferejohn and James H. Kuklinski, 136–159. Urbana: University of Illinois Press, 1990.

Rahn, Wendy M., Jon A. Krosnick, and Marijke A. Breuning. "Rationalization and Derivation Processes in Survey Studies of Political Character Evaluation." *American Journal of Political Science* 38 (1994): 582–600.

Rapoport, Ronald B., Kelly L. Metcalf, and Jon A. Hartman. "Candidate Traits and Voter Inferences: An Experimental Study." *Journal of Politics* 51 (1989): 917–932.

Rapaport, Ronald B., and Walter J. Stone. *Three's A Crowd: The Dynamics of Third Parties, Ross Perot, and Republican Resurgence.* Ann Arbor: University of Michigan Press, 2005.

Robinson, John P., and Dennis K. Davis. "Television News and the Informed Public: An Information-Processing Approach." *Journal of Communication,* 40 (1990): 106–119.

Rosenberg, Shawn W., Lisa Bohan, Patrick McCafferty, and Kevin Harris. "The Image and the Vote: The Effect of Candidate Presentation on Voter Preference." *American Journal of Political Science* 30 (1986): 108–127.

Rudalevige, Andrew. *The New Imperial Presidency.* Ann Arbor, MI: The University of Michigan Press, 2006.

Schlesinger, Arthur, M. *The Imperial Presidency.* Boston: Houghton Mifflin, 1973.

Stanley, Harold W. "The Nominations: Republican Doldrums, Democratic Revival." In *The Elections of 1996*, edited by Michael Nelson, 14–43. Washington, DC: CQ Press, 1997.

Stroud, Natalie Jomini. *Niche News: The Politics of News Choice.* Oxford: Oxford University Press, 2011.

Sullivan, John L., John H. Aldrich, Eugene Borgida, and Wendy M. Rahn. "Candidate Appraisal and Human Nature: Man and Superman in the 1984 Election." *Political Psychology* 11 (1990): 459–484.

Sunstein, Cass R. *Republic.com 2.0.* Princeton, NJ: Princeton University Press, 2007.

Sunstein, Cass R. *Going to Extremes: How Like Minds Unite and Divide.* Oxford: Oxford University Press, 2009.

Tseng, Margaret. "The Clinton Effect: How a Lame-Duck President Impacted His Vice President's Election Prospects." In *The Election of the Century*, edited by Stephen J. Wayne and Clyde Wilcox, 200–216. Armonk, NY: M. E. Sharpe, 2002.

Tufte, Edward R. *Political Control of the Economy.* Princton, NJ: Princeton University Press, 1978.

Tulis, Jeffrey K. *The Rhetorical Presidency.* Princeton, NJ: Princeton University Press, 1987.

Wattenberg, Martin P. *The Rise of Candidate-Centered Politics.* Cambridge, MA: Harvard University Press, 1991.

Weaver, David, and Dan Drew. "Voter Learning and Interest in the 2000 Presidential Election: Did the Media Matter?" *Journalism and Mass Communication Quarterly*, 78 (2001): 787–798.

West, Darrell M. *Air Wars,* 5th edition. Washington, DC: CQ Press, 2010.

Wooldridge, Jerry M. *Introductory Econometrics: A Modern Approach.* Cincinnati, OH: South-Western College Publishing, 2000.

Zaller, John. *The Nature and Origins of Mass Opinion.* Cambridge: Cambridge University Press, 1992.

Index

Page numbers followed by *f* indicate figures by n indicate notes and by *t* indicate tables

about governmental affairs 12,
26, 27; leadership of 25, 73, 74,
76, 106, 107, 193; and McCain,
John 198–9; measuring perceptions of traits 31–41; military
service of 78; misstatements
by 75; NASCAR race 30;
September 11 terrorist attacks
15; warmth, likability, and a
common touch 30, 58, 144, 197;
see also presidential elections of
2000 and 2004

Cain, Herman, lack of experience 26
campaign coverage sources, media
consumption 169, 186
candidate character trait conclusions
192–202; candidate character
trait perceptions are affected by
political attitudes 17, 198–9;
candidate character trait perceptions vary across elections
197–98; candidate character
traits matter to voters 16,
194–6; implications for future
research 200–2; media consumption may affect how voters use
character traits 17, 199–200;
voters assess the character of
presidential candidates 192–4
Carter, Jimmy: and Anderson, John
85n10; competence of 27; debate
with Reagan 10; defeated as
incumbent 163; handling of the
presidency 121n3, 129; integrity
of 28, 62, 63; leadership of 24,
61, 62, 85n10, 128; *see also*
presidential election of 1980
Castellanos, Alex 19n32
causal direction, character trait perceptions as voter rationalizations
111
CBS News/New York Times polls
85n10
character trait perceptions as voter
rationalizations 110–17; candidate behavior 112; causal direction 111; media 110, 112; models
of vote rationalization 113–14,
113*f*, 116, 117; partisan bias
116–17; perceptions vary over
time 111, 112; policy issues 111,
118, 124n25; political attitudes
110–11; presidential campaigns

110, 112; regression analysis of
candidate trait perceptions and
presidential vote 114–16, 115*t*;
retrospective evaluations of
performance 111; voters are
encouraged to rely on character
traits 12–15, 110; voters find
it easy to use character traits
10–12, 110; *see also* impact of
character trait perceptions on
the vote
character traits and presidential elections *see* presidential elections
character traits defined 22
Cheney, Richard 78; competence of 26
Clinton, Bill 86n33; Arkansas days 70;
avoiding the draft 71; bridge
metaphor 71, 87n46; competence of 27, 52, 71, 72; empathy
of 29, 66, 69, 70, 71, 77, 82,
107, 193, 198; impeachment
by the House 72, 73; integrity
of 12, 28, 52, 57, 59, 60, 63,
67, 68, 71, 72, 130, 193, 194;
leadership of 25, 58, 59, 68, 69,
70, 71, 109, 123n22, 130, 147;
measuring perceptions of traits
31–41; remembered in personal
terms 14; saxophone playing 30;
warmth, likability, and a common touch 30; *see also* presidential elections of 1992 and 1996
Clinton, Hillary 72, 79
Colbert, Stephen 19n32
competence 25–7, 60, 83, 193; importance of 121; *see also* names of
presidential candidates
conceptualizing character traits 22–31,
193; authenticity 30–1; character
traits defined 22; competence
25–7, 60, 83; Conover, Pamela
23; elitism 30, 51n23; empathy
29, 83, 91; Funk, Carolyn 23;
integrity 28, 83; Kinder, Donald,
1986 study 22–3; leadership
24–5, 83, 91; long list of traits
22; Markus, Gregory 23; mean
trait scores for presidential candidates (1980–2012) 151–2, 151*f*;
mean trait scores for Republican
candidates (1980–2012) 152–3,
153*f*; negative list of traits 232;
physical or demographic characteristics 22; warmth, likability,

For Product Safety Concerns and Information please contact our EU
representative GPSR@taylorandfrancis.com
Taylor & Francis Verlag GmbH, Kaufingerstraße 24, 80331 München, Germany

9 7 8 1 1 3 8 2 8 6 1 7 7